Perspectives in European History

No. 8
TORYISM AND THE PEOPLE 1832-1846

D1326824

TORYISM
AND THE PEOPLE
1832 - 1846

by

R. L. HILL

With a Foreword by

KEITH FEILING

PORCUPINE PRESS

Philadelphia 1975

First edition 1929
(London: Constable & Co., Ltd., 1929)

Reprinted 1975 by
PORCUPINE PRESS, INC.
Philadelphia, Pennsylvania 19107
By arrangement with Constable & Co., Ltd.

Library of Congress Cataloging in Publication Data

```
Hill, Richard Leslie.
   Toryism and the people, 1832-1846.

   (Perspectives in European history ; no. 8)
   Reprint of the 1929 ed. published by Constable,
London.
   Bibliography: p.
   Includes index.
   1.  Tories, English.  2.  Conservative Party
(GT. Brit.)  3.  Labor and laboring classes--Great
Britain.  I.  Title.
JN1129.T7H5  1975     322'.2'0941     75-25724
ISBN 0-87991-614-1
```

Manufactured in the United States of America

FOREWORD

THE present study, like a high proportion of all recent historical work in this country, was undertaken with the encouragement of the late Professor Henry Carless Davis. It was his conviction, often advanced as one motive for the abrupt change in his own studies from medieval to modern, that the current version of early nineteenth-century British history was in some grave respects misleading, and that ignorance of our immediate past was a serious present evil. His Ford lectures, on the Whigs and Peelites, was the one contribution which he himself was able to make before his premature death, but this, taken with his share in inspiring Mr. Aspinall's admirable study of Lord Brougham and Mr. Hill's work, show that Party was one angle from which he would have wished such a historical revision to proceed.

To prove the continuity of forces that enlist passionate support over generations is a natural piety, and the intellectual genealogy of Toryism has been dissected of late with as much ardour and diversity as that of Communism or the English Church. But two gaps in this postulated continuity always catch the eye : the one between the Harley-Bolingbroke *débâcle* of 1714 and the younger Pitt, which Professor Trevelyan has done something to fill—the other, that hiatus between Pittite Toryism, attenuated as it became with the Eldons and Crokers, and Disraeli's

v

Tory democracy. It is at this latter point that Mr. Hill's work suggests clues of considerable value.

One of these, no doubt, only elaborates a constant position of Canning and Disraeli, that the structure of Great Britain is 'territorial.' There is one Toryism of Yorkshire, another of Essex, and not the same Toryism ; a party is compounded of many local *foci*, each instinct with inherited prejudices or, it may be, with disease peculiar to itself. There is plenty of room, and not in regard to party only, for historical studies upon the public opinion of East Anglia, or Lancashire, or any other of these persistent units, from the Reformation onwards.

A second, connected with the first but less tangible and more slippery, is the doctrine here expounded that Toryism, in contrast to nineteenth-century Radical belief in the ballot-box majority, has always dealt with 'interests.' The very word has a long party history. Originally denoting, in seventeenth-century correspondence, the personal or semi-feudal following of a man or a family, it has taken to itself, as the common prefixes 'vested,' 'sinister,' or 'reactionary' suggest, a connotation more dubious or deprecatory. 'An Oxford man who had gone into the Liberal party because the Tory party was under *influences*,'—this was the impression sketched of Gladstone in old age by a Liberal Unionist of sure judgment.

But, waiving all epithets and platform associations, there is here a conception worthy of more serious treatment. The subdivision of which Burke spoke, the great corporations of mercantile companies, colleges, and learned bodies, the corporation sole of parsonage or crown, the 'interest' of Nabobs or planters—on

FOREWORD

the support of this system of group-relations the older
Toryism as a party, and much of its philosophy, was
founded.

More vital, or at least more immediate, doubtless, is
the central theme of this book, which depicts that close
connection between one section of that we call ' Toryism '
and something we may call ' the people.' It has been
clothed in many living forms, and an imaginative anatomy
has invented others ; there are threads, spiritual or incor-
porate, to be drawn from Strafford's benevolent Caesarism,
from Bolingbroke's anti-Parliamentary conception of a
patriot monarchy, from Pitt's sentimental economics,
Young England, or Catholic revival, or from the curious,
yet not accidental, temporary partnerships between Chartists and Tories. That this ancient, but elusive, connection is a historical fact, we cannot doubt ; it is less
certain that it is compatible with a capitalist and an
individualist-Protestant predominance.

Mr. Hill's widely-derived mass of evidence suggests,
to those interested in party origins, countless questions
for further pursuit ; there is, for instance, the whole
history of political clubs, which run back at least to the
duel between Danby and ' Achitophel.' I confine myself to two, one a special demurrer, the other a general
caveat, which I believe might stand as a notice-board for
all those who, like Mr. Winkle's sagacious dog, trespass
on a ground studded with gins and snares. The permanent influence of the Lake poets (p. 18) ought, some
of us will feel, to be put appreciably higher. To be a
' Laker ' did not necessarily, after all, involve swallowing
a mere watery opinion, and long before Disraeli's day
Coleridge and Southey outlined not only a transcendental

philosophy, but a specific political programme, for the victims of eighteenth-century revolutions.

And, more generally, the study of party, which leads one in the first instance to look to the past for the fixed origins of present-day ideals, leads with experience to one safeguarding formula : that the parties of the Right, or Conservatism, are themselves fluid, because they are perpetually receiving the second generation of the Left. This process, long continued, brings results, surprising or uncomfortable or reassuring, according to the point of view ; there is State Socialism in Strafford, ' little-Englanderism ' in Bolingbroke, and Whiggism in Peel. ' The wisdom of our fathers,' much applauded by Eldon, can be used to point a Radical moral, and the orthodox churches of party are commonly endowed with the spiritual goods of heretics or converts. The many types whom Mr. Hill discovers under the name of ' Tory ' seem to suggest that we should not mistake diversity for lack of faith, or substitute labels for a texture of mind.

KEITH FEILING.

PREFACE

MY purpose in this book is to examine the points of contact between the Tory party and the working classes during the fourteen years which separate the passing of the First Reform Act and the *débâcle* of 1846.

The history of the Tory party during this period has not hitherto received very enthusiastic attention. From Kebbel's *History of Toryism*, published in 1886, to Miss Ramsay's *Sir Robert Peel*, published last year, interest has centred chiefly on the political development of the party. There has been no attempt to produce a comprehensive study of nineteenth-century Toryism in its relation to the England of the day. Until the appearance of the highly provocative works of the Webbs and the Hammonds, surrounded by a host of attendant satellite monographs, nobody seemed to think it worth his while to disinter the mouldy pages of Alison or bring back Eldon from the dead.

Lately, however, the voluminous scholarship devoted to social and economic movements of the Left Wing— the rise of Socialism, the Trade Union movement— has provoked a similar interest in the activities of the Die-hard Right. It is significant that those peculiar prejudices of reactionary Toryism, which the following generation believed to be discredited, are being re-examined with a sympathy which perhaps Spencer Walpole, and certainly Lord Morley, would have regarded as ridiculous. Modern political fact, if not modern political thought, shows a steady tendency to follow principles rejected for good and all by the band of confident young men who marched behind the standards of Gladstone, Bright and Mill. From being one of the most neglected periods of modern history the age of Grey and Peel has come to be invested with a new interest and a glamour almost incredible.

An explanation is simple. The world which rejected Toryism as an obsolete relic of barbarous times is itself passing rapidly away. It is one of the caprices of history that the infant generation which took its stand upon Progress, Reform and the March of Intellect is being supplanted by a still more restive child with a genius for smashing things. A century ago disconsolate Tories of the old school were asking themselves whither the March of Intellect was leading us. We are asking the same question to-day.

In drafting the plan of this study I have abandoned all attempt to make a chronological survey. For reasons which the following pages will, I hope, justify, I have rarely overstepped the boundary set by the events of 1846, for it was from that year that the old Country Party ceased to be counted among the active political forces of the time.

Since the terms 'Tory' and 'Tory party' are not fixed or constant political quantities, the introductory chapter is concerned with definitions. My first object is to define the position of the Tory party in relation to those great forces which, during this period, lay behind the public action of our people. My further object is to examine the ancestry of Tory social ideas. The succeeding chapters extend the inquiry to the attitude of the Tory party, in and out of Parliament, to the principal labour questions as they arise.

The bitterest of the struggles between Tory prejudice and Conservative enlightenment was waged within the ranks of the Parliamentary Conservative party. Parliamentary politics cannot, therefore, be wholly neglected. Sir Robert Peel and the official leaders were dealing with an articulate Conservatism, a concrete political entity. Their work consisted in keeping the party together. The instrument by which they kept in touch with the labouring classes was the party machine. Peel developed this machine to an extent previously unknown. He gave unceasing attention to the organization of the party. Hence the second chapter has for its purpose an estimate of the importance of the party machine in determining the relations between the Parliamentary Conservative party and the working classes, and the degree to which Tory social ideas were reflected in Parliament, at the Conservative party headquarters, and in the political machinery which had by this time been set up in the constituencies.

The sequence of the remaining chapters is determined by considerations of utility. I have divided the principal working-class questions into three categories : political, associative (for want of a better English equivalent), and social. Under the heading of political aspirations I have treated those movements among the masses which had for their object reforms in the structure of Parliamentary and local government. Under the still broader heading, association of labour, I have traced the incidence of

Tory opinion and the principal types of organized groups of working men whether for industrial, for provident, or for educational purposes. My excuse for including in the second category a study of Toryism and popular education is not that Tory scholastic principles closely connected popular education with popular discontent—a proposition of undoubted truth—but that the Mechanics' Institute represented a distinctive type of working-class association. In the third category I have examined the Tory element in the various phases of active social revolt. I have reserved for the last chapter a review of the social consequences of the defeat and disintegration of the Tory party in its own stronghold upon the land.

CONTENTS

ERRATA

P. 28, note 1, for ' 1828,' read ' 1838.'

P. 183, line 15, for 'political economy,' read 'Political Economy.'

P. 227, line 21, for ' unintelligible to them,' read ' unintelligible to Tories.'

P. 237, note 1, delete ' *ibid.*,' and read ' Alison (A.), *History of Europe*, vol. vi. p. 323.'

TORYISM AND THE PEOPLE

1832–1846

CHAPTER I

INTRODUCTION TO THE STUDY OF
TORY LABOUR IDEAS, 1832-1846

THERE are certain difficulties in defining the terms ' Tory '
and ' Tory party,' which are not made easier by their
connection with the rough-and-tumble of party conflict.
Politicians of the early nineteenth century allowed themselves a generous latitude in their choice of abusive
expressions whenever there happened to be cause worth
opposing. Political audiences, then as now, prefer to
be roused, not educated, and politicians are always ready
to oblige.

One of the most diverting, and perhaps the most
fruitless, of practices consisted of classifying Englishmen in all-inclusive divisions, Whig and Tory, or Liberal
and Conservative, and of inventing rules-of-thumb whereby the classification in all cases became infallible.
Grotesque caricatures of the Old Tory who opposed the
Reform Bill and stood by the Corn Laws were accepted
as faithful portraits by whole generations of Victorians.
During the middle nineteenth century, when social and

political ideas hostile or indifferent to Toryism were in the ascendant, it was a common practice to caricature the typical Tory as a kind-hearted though grossly prejudiced gentleman, and the Tory party as the embodiment of obsolete policies interesting only to the historian. 'One can hardly picture to oneself the Tory otherwise than as a pattern country gentleman,' wrote J. M. Ludlow, 'who comes but little in contact with the speculations or the vices of towns, and is thus much less of a thinker than of an honest, hearty, natural sensualist.' 'The Conservative,' he concluded, 'has not the enthusiasm, the hearty, life-long self-delusions, the passionate political predilections of the old Tory.'[1]

The Tory party generally came in for less complimentary definitions from a generation educated in the Liberal atmosphere of Ludlow's day. Broken beyond all repair in the turmoil of 1846, the old Country Party survived in the recollections of the victors only as a living protest against a succession of new ideas, a die-hard party of men whose crotchets ceased to have serious import in the world of practical politics. To-day we are far removed from the point of view of those optimists of Progress and Reform who so confidently stigmatized as antiquarian all those whose views did not coincide with their own. At the present time, when the doctrines of individualism have lost their influence alike over the intellect and the imagination, it is less difficult to estimate the relative position of Tory and Liberal social ideas than in the days of unquestioned Liberal supremacy.

Unfortunately, in spite of modern devotion to scientific method, the passion for simplifying history seems as

[1] *Politics for the People*, No. 7, June 10, 1848.

persistent as ever. Groups and classes during the period covered by this study have been invested with a highly-developed sense of corporate personality which in fact they never possessed. The laborious and complex manifestations by which these groups and classes sought expression have been interpreted as the spontaneous workings of the group-mind endowed with a convenient if unhistoric consciousness of its service in the cause of making modern history easy to understand.

The simple requirements of such an interpretation offer to the investigator of the period intellectual temptations well-nigh irresistible. Few political writers contemporary with the age of Reform can escape the suspicion of guilt. And it must be frankly admitted that the worst offenders appear among the Tory ranks. Some of the most hardened Tories not infrequently denied the name ; others, Radicals by upbringing and temperament, proclaimed their Toryism before astonished audiences. But citation from a list of public men, most of them profoundly disbelieving in set policies and formal political catchwords, does not help to clear away the tangled undergrowth of definitions. All those who invoked the great name of Mr. Pitt were not Tories, neither were all Whigs who reverenced Chatham or followed Grey. Disraeli, alone among Tory leaders, attempted a comprehensive definition, and the result was a brilliant idealization, splendid but not historical. He did not of course originate the ' fine old Tory squire ' ; Sir Roger de Coverley preceded Disraeli by a century. The model Tory gentleman was not so much a legend exclusive to the Tory party as a national institution, the common property of all.

3

TORYISM AND THE PEOPLE

Political necessity influenced the use of the term. M. T. Sadler, not too suffused with Evangelical quietism to lose his instinct for honest party advantage, thought fit, during his Huddersfield speeches of 1833, to say as little as possible about his political affinities. 'With respect to myself,' he bawled at some Whig interrupter, 'I am not a Whig, it is true ; but, in the sense in which it is represented to you, neither am I, nor ever was I, a Tory.' Most assuredly, he repeated, he was not a Whig, 'God forbid ! '[1] Richard Oastler, a master of political invective, greeted as Tories all who were not 'snod-faced Dissenters,' all who hated oppression and the March of Intellect and who loved the young Queen. Ruskin called himself a Tory, because he saw his beloved Lake District pitted with ugly railway stations, and he hated ugliness in all its forms.

In Disraeli's idealization of political history lies a source of much confusion. Disraeli depicted the historic Tory party as the lifelong enemy of the Whig oligarchs, who considered that their title-deeds, dated from 1688, gave them a right to perpetual tenure of office. Toryism in Disraeli's eyes was the great popular party deriving its strength from a union of Crown and People. And when the old social order was dissolving before his gaze, he held fast to the view that English society was a social pyramid, a hierarchy of classes and groups and interests, and refused to recognize in principle the right of any one section of society to preponderate. One thing Disraeli did not do : he never admitted the sovereignty of the people at large—an admission which he would have thought preposterous. Even the light-hearted mysticism

[1] *Leeds Intelligencer*, December 19, 1833.

of Young England stopped short of the humourless political metaphysics of Mill.

When Young England preached Disraeli's principles, they were accused of propagating Socialist doctrines. Cobden spoke almost with sympathy of the trouble to which Peel and Graham were put by ' the Socialist doctrines of the fools behind them.' [1] It was said that Toryism, beaten in Parliament, was reaching in desperation towards the abettors of social revolution. Young England, to the scandal of Tories no less than of Whigs, was rumoured to be falling under the influence of Newman and the Tractarians. 'What would be the practical results,' wrote George Cornwall Lewis apprehensively, ' of that compound which has been formed out of the doctrines of the Catholic Church of the middle ages, and the principles of the modern Communists ' he scarcely dared envisage. [2]

In a study of the relation of the Tory party to the labouring classes during the years 1832-46 this criticism is worthy of notice. It implied the existence of a serious belief among intelligent leaders of the Liberal side that a Tory-Radical union was a possibility to be considered. That such an alliance did not become a serious political problem detracts nothing from the significance of the supposition. Many of the most authoritative Liberal politicians were genuinely exercised to discover the precise motives which brought Tory and Radical into unanimity on several of the leading questions of the day. Perturbed by their failure to reconcile two points of view, both so different from their own, they took refuge

[1] Morley (J.), *The Life of Richard Cobden* (1881), vol. i. p. 302.
[2] *Edinburgh Review*, No. 167, 1846.

in the use of vague generalizations, 'Tory Socialism' and 'Tory Chartism,' to indicate the union which they abhorred. 'Oh, shades of Pitt, Castlereagh, Liverpool!' wrote one in high indignation, 'are these the men who inherit the blue mantle of Toryism?'[1]

The progress of events after 1846 appeared to outstrip the speculations of the most progressive of contemporaries, and by the last quarter of the century the foremost in praise of what was known by the high-sounding name of Representative Parliamentary Democracy were those whose political ancestors, appalled by the ruin of 1832, seriously meditated withdrawing altogether from Parliament as an assembly unfit for English gentlemen. The younger generation accepted almost without question the political excellence of representative institutions and an equal franchise. A world which had scarcely recovered from the shock of seeing a Conservative Prime Minister pass the Reform Bill of 1867 was provided with the further astonishing spectacle of a Conservative politician preaching to the miners of Lancashire the faith of Tory Democracy. Toryism had a long way to travel from Lord John Manners to Lord Randolph Churchill, but it travelled with amazing speed.

In seeking a definition of the term 'Tory party' care must be taken to avoid confusing party with class. The futility of such confusion is easily apparent when an attempt is made to view as a whole the diversity of groups and interests sheltering under the all-inclusive title, Tory party. It cannot properly be said of a party which contained leaders so different as Wellington, Peel, Sadler, Ashley, Oastler, and Walter, all of whom answered in

[1] *Sheffield Independent*, February 7, 1835.

varying degrees of alacrity to the name of Tory, that it was the corporate expression of an exclusive class. Even the Landed Interest was at no time sufficiently unanimous on public questions to commit its fortunes into the hands of one political party. Any restricted definition of the term, which limited its applicability to the majority of the Lords and to the Right Wing of the Conservative party in the Commons, would ignore the vast reservoir of Toryism of which the Parliamentary party was as a ripple upon the surface. To confine the term within the walls of Parliament would be a concession to party controversy unjustified by the facts of the time. If Oastler and Walter were not according to this narrow interpretation Tories at all, neither in the same sense were Wellington and Peel.

And if the Tory party was composed of such diverse elements as to forfeit all claim to be a party of class exclusiveness, it can be shown that Toryism overstepped the limits of the Tory party. The Conservatism of Peel and Graham, far from being the direct heir to the older Toryism, had all too little in common with it. On the other hand, a great body of Tory opinion never found adequate representation in the Parliamentary Conservative party. Parliamentary Conservatism was drawn from a strand of political opinion almost directly at variance with the Toryism of the Country Party, Disraeli's Olympians of 1846.

Despite the fact that the label ' Tory ' had become an object of abuse by one party and of idealization by the other, Toryism represented a profound political and social conviction in a great mass of the people.

Restriction of the term to the Parliamentary party is

7

therefore vain, and a satisfying definition is to be found only after the whole area of Tory activity is taken into consideration. It is rather in the thought and action of the individuals and groups comprising the whole party that the true meaning of the term 'Tory' becomes intelligible.

In this sense and without apology is the term used in the following chapters. There were certain principles and opinions common to the national group with which this study is concerned; 'Tory' is the one word suitable for describing them. What is called the Tory party is the public body, whether in Parliament or outside, in which these principles and opinions found readiest expression.

Class selfishness and political greed are not the only motives which lead a party to refuse concessions to the political and economic demands of a new age. There can be no more barren interpretation of history than to imagine that public activity in all its phases can be confined within the narrow limits of Right, Left and Centre, and to imagine that each separate 'Wing' represents an unchangeable, stereotyped point of view. The Centre does not always contain the moderate elements of political action, the Left is not invariably revolutionary or even progressive, reaction and conservatism are not the immutable attributes of the Right. Those who expect to find among the party struggles of the time a constant 'Tory attitude' towards this or that question will be disappointed. A uniform line of conduct, applied to a given number of individuals working together for a given period, is an intellectual concept which has little place in reality. The Tory attitude to labour questions implies, therefore, a movable and relative point of view.

THE STUDY OF TORY LABOUR IDEAS

For two reasons this is so : firSt, that the Tory social attitude was the result of composite, and often self-contradictory, motives; secondly, that the ties which bound Tories together in Parliament, in Quarter Sessions, and on the huStings were not a compound of nicely-calculated policies and compromise, but something much less tangible and less rational.

In any inquiry into the parentage of those principles which dominated the active social policy of the Tory party in Parliament, and the social opinions of Tories in the provinces, due regard muSt be paid to the influence of these intangible bonds of union. There was the influence of tradition, a mighty welding-force of political parties. IdealiSts fondly reached back to the remote paSt, some to the days of Harley and St. John, some to Tudor times, when it was imagined that the relation of maSter and man was based upon principles of natural juStice, when there exiSted a juSt balance between rights and duties, and when nobody was oppressed. In this spirit Cobbett drew the attention of labourers in the Vale of Pewsey to the excellent syStem by which the farmer used to board his men under his own roof in happier times, before the National Debt, expensive wars and Stock-jobbers were thought of. Disraeli, captivated by the glamour of a Crown which once possessed power, deplored the havoc wrought upon the social syStem by the Venetian Oligarchs of the Whig Revolution. John Walter of the *Times* addressed the rough weavers of Nottingham telling them of that good queen who provided English working men with an equitable Poor Law of which the Whigs were about to deprive them.

9

Believers in the Golden Age were as numerous as the Utopians, and their faith was perhaps the sounder. Better find in the past a Golden Age which they supposed their fathers to have experienced, than a future Utopia which did violence to their imaginations. Toryism, even under Disraeli's magic spell, was never Utopian.

A study of the meeting-points of Toryism and Labour during the period from 1832 to 1846 necessarily leads the inquirer far from the beaten track of London politics. For Toryism was in its essence a Country Party point of view. It was a habit of thought originating in the daily life and work of country people. Even as late as the period of disintegration which accompanied the repeal of the Corn Laws, Toryism, in spite of the ever-growing importance of industrial politics, remained to the last the attitude of rural Englishmen.

Since Toryism was the faith of men bred among country associations, Tory labour ideas found their origin in the soil. In Parliament Tory members repeatedly approached questions involving the working classes from the restricted, if not ungenerous, point of view of country gentlemen. The social conceptions of ' rank and station' and ' deference to one's betters,' no less than the political conception of government by vested interest, are primarily feudal, almost patriarchal in their antiquity.

It is clear beyond all doubt whatever that a political and social faith such as this could not possibly acquiesce in all the consequences of the revolution which converted England from a predominantly agrarian to a predominantly industrial state. Toryism as a working political faith could not permanently co-exist alongside the accomplished facts of the Industrial Revolution. In their rooted distrust of social movement—a prejudice governing their attitude towards the labouring classes—Tories personified a continual protest against the supersession of a rural England which they knew, by an industrialized England which they knew not.

The feeling of intense suspicion with which provincial Tories regarded the new industrial supremacy was shared by many who were its victims. Under the cover of a common hostility to organic changes in the structure of society developed that curious phenomenon Tory-Radicalism, the union of Right and Left in resistance to the transformation which revolutionized the social life of England during the preceding fifty years.

Statesmen who lived among the realities of party strife and whose concern was with the hard facts of estimates, revenue and taxation had little leisure to meditate upon the changes which were overtaking them. Not altogether unreasonably the leaders of Parliamentary parties scoffed at the turgid, reactionary spirit manifested in the multitudes of their followers. The scorn with which Pitt and Peel, each in his day the exponent of what may be called Progressive Conservatism, dismissed the most treasured prejudices of their supporters arose from their consciousness of superiority to the backwoodsmen whom they led. Progressive Conservatives joined with Canning and Huskisson in accepting the commercial implications of the Industrial Revolution as an act of destiny. They were troubled by no misgivings about it ; they asked no questions. Their duty lay with the business of the moment. With their guidance or without, England had become the greatest industrial and commercial power in

the world. Naively they never doubted that the change
was for the better.

The influence exerted upon Tory labour legislation by
the more progressive members of the party was considerable from the first. It cannot be denied that the policy
of the younger Pitt, combined with the necessities of the
French War, seriously affected the character of the Tory
party, and indirectly, the quality of Tory statesmanship.
Pitt brought in new men to serve the State, and these
new men came with new ideas. They were clever young
statesmen whom the Minister delighted to honour,
intellectuals and students of the new Political Economy.
These infused a new spirit into the Tory party and prepared the way for the transference of the base of political
power which characterized Peel's ' Great Conservative
Party.' They represented, in Cobbett's language, the
' mere buyers and sellers,' the capitalistic element which
was henceforward to dominate public life. Disraeli
with his tongue in his cheek spoke of the ' plebeian
aristocracy of Mr. Pitt.'

By the older school of Tories the addition of elements
typified by Canning and Huskisson was regarded with
mixed feelings. They distrusted the high intellectual tone
in which the new men were accustomed to express their
opinions ; they detested their views on the subject of
Political Economy. They feared the Catholic leanings
of the younger school. Lord Talbot, commenting upon
the drift of Canning's politics in 1827, and upon the confusion in the Tory party, wrote to Gregory—' The political changes are to me quite appalling. I feel as if some sad
calamity had befallen me, having for so many years supported, and with all my heart, the Government, I cannot

conceive how and why I find myself opposed to it.' [1]
And when a strange destiny struck Canning down, there
were Tories who saw in the event a portent from Heaven.
' I last night heard to my great surprise and concern of
Mr. Canning's death. The only remark I shall permit
myself is, that the ways of Providence are awful and
mysterious.' [2] Tories who believed in portents were to
have their faith confirmed with horrid suddenness by the
tragic death of Huskisson.

When the favourite doctrines of the Progressives were
merged in the principles of the Anti-Corn Law League,
the resentment which Tories bore to the memory of
the school of Huskisson lived again. Oastler, now a
prisoner in the Fleet, continually warned his hearers what
they might expect from Peel and the enlightened Conservative Ministry. Tories must now stand fast for social
righteousness or for Political Economy, for the common
people or for the moneyed interest. The old ' King '
valiantly supports his teaching by appeals ' to the written
words of the acknowledged masters of each school—
St. Paul and Mr. Huskisson.' [3]

Although the doctrine of *laissez-faire* has never, at any
period, been accepted in all its consequences—not even
by Bentham, certainly not by Brougham—Parliamentary
Political Economists showed no hesitation in applying the
doctrine to questions involving the welfare of the working
classes. Liberal Intellectuals spurned both the demagogy
of Chartist labour leaders and the servile paternalism of

[1] Talbot to Gregory, July 4, 1827 (*Mr. Gregory's Letter-Box, 1813-
1830* (1898), p. 296).
[2] *Ibid.*, August 10, 1827, p. 299.
[3] Fleet Papers, vol. ii., No. 11, February 1842.

the Tories. The doctrine of the freedom of labour, the theory that the labourer not only ought to be free in all sound economy, but must be free for his own moral good, was accepted as a self-evident, dogmatic truth. They held that the principle of competition, distrusted by Tories and detested by extremer Radicals, should alone determine the condition of the labouring classes. ' Industrial freedom,' proclaimed the Anti-Corn Law League, ' has become the question of the day.' [1]

The conception of the freedom of labour followed logically from the application of the doctrine of *laissez-faire* to the relations of master and man. Parliamentary Conservative leaders consciously or unconsciously embodied the conception in their labour legislation. The presence of progressive elements within the party did much to deprive that legislation of its true Tory character and to render its whole attitude to labour questions a hybrid of incongruous strains. The fatal ability of the Progressives to imbibe new ideas tended to divorce them from the affections of the working classes and, in the end, took pride of place in destroying the party.

From other sources the Tory party received inspiration which gave to its social views life and vigour. Although Tory loyalty to the House of Stuart was insufficient to rouse the English countryside in 1745, the indirect influence of Jacobitism was long felt in the party. John Wesley noticed that Jacobite sentiment was very much alive in the country districts during the period of his missionary journeys. For every clergyman who denounced Wesley as a Jacobite there was another who

[1] Report of the Statistical Committee appointed by the Anti-Corn Law League (1842).

detested him because he was for the Hanoverian Succession. ' The warmest opposers,' he wrote of his persecutors, ' are the Jacobites, who do not love us, because we love King George.' [1] Catholic and Jacobite influence in the provinces survived to the days of the Great Conservative Party, and on the eve of the General Election of 1837 a Tory magnate notes with satisfaction that the great Catholic influence of the North was being placed in the Conservative scale.[2] Daniel O'Connell, though his political career was bound up with the fortunes of the Liberal party, used to say of himself that he was a Tory at heart. The biographers of Dr. Lingard, in the course of their survey of contemporary English Catholicism, explain the Irish hostility to the Conservative leaders in the circumstance that Romanists had been driven into the arms of the Whigs by the determined refusal of the Tories to grant them political emancipation ; but that, on most of the other political and social questions, their attitude inclined to Conservatism.[3]

It should be realized that the generation from which the Tory remnant of 1832 was sprung was not accredited with feelings expressive of the most lively loyalty to the Hanoverian cause. All Tories were not carried off their feet by the glamour of a youthful monarch educated in the doctrines of the *Patriot King*. Some years before the accession of George III. the Court Party had every reason for suspecting that the association of ' Independent

---

[1] *The Journal of the Rev. John Wesley, A.M.*, ed. London (1909), vol. iii. p. 130, and vol. iv. p. 108.
[2] Lord F. Egerton to Peel, August 6, 1837 (Addit. MSS. 40,424).
[3] Haile (M.) and Bonney (E.), *Life and Letters of John Lingard, 1771-1851* (1911), p. 291.

Electors of Westminster ' was actively engaged in Jacobite propaganda.[1] The Jacobite, Lord Lovat, was known to be held in high honour by the Tories of the time. Gibbon thought that the Fellows of Oxford in his day were anything but Hanoverian in their hearts.

From a lingering Jacobite sentiment Young England drew freely. The social outlook which Disraeli created for the chief characters of *Sybil* was not the outlook of the Protestant Church-and-King party with which the author was associated. The social atmosphere of *Sybil*, the very vocabulary of labour unrest in which Disraeli describes the menace of the Two Cities, is reminiscent rather of Lacordaire and the Democratic Ultramontanes in France than of the Tory social reformers in England. If the social doctrines of Young England were not pure Popery, as Quarterly Reviewers suspected, they were at least sufficiently infused with the spirit of Gallicanism to allow Disraeli and Manners, while rejecting the Pope, to embody to the full the principles of a Catholic social policy.

Young England held the English Catholics in great respect, and we find one of their number making urgent appeal to ' the Howards and the Eyres, the de Cliffords and the Townleys, the Throckmortons and the Vavasours, the Constables and the Jerninghams ' to throw in their lot with the Young Tory cause, and prevent the estrangement of the aristocracy from the labouring classes, which would surely follow the triumph of Atheists, Dissenters

[1] Grego (J.), *A History of Parliamentary Elections and Electioneering in the Old Days* (1868). (An inadequate work, of use only for its quotations.)

and Levellers.[1] Small wonder that the orthodox Protestant Toryism of the *Quarterly Review* rebelled against these innovations, and Protestant pulpits rang with fulminations against the evil influence of Puseyism, which was corrupting the youth of England. Even the *Spectator*, in its graceful defence of Young England's eccentricities, confessed that, for all the sympathy of these young reformers for the working classes, ' it was not of Tory or High Church principles the party was enamoured, but of their own ideas of what High Church and Toryism ought to be.' [2]

If we limit our inquiry solely to the politics of Young England, we shall find overwhelming evidence of Jacobite inspiration. Young Englanders were avowedly Young Stuarts in their views on Monarchy. But if we go further afield and resort to the Jacobite fountain-head for the source of Tory social ideas we must expect to find the stream half dry. Disraeli's transcendent imagination conceived of Tory tradition as a mystic bridge spanning the chasm which divided the Jacobitism of 1745 from the romantic world of Coleridge, Wordsworth and himself. Here Disraeli stopped.

This is as far as we too can safely go. A yard further and we are floundering among slippery unrealities in which the Lake Poets become the prolific fathers of almost every movement under the sun—the New Conservatism, Tory Democracy, the Factory Reform Movement, Christian Socialism.

---

[1] Anglo Catholicus (Lord John Manners ?), *What are the English Roman Catholics to do?* The Question considered in a Letter to Lord Edward Howard (1841).

[2] *Spectator*, July 15, 1843.

The contribution of Romanticism and of Young England to the stock of Tory social ideas was not of this kind. Whatever influence either movement wielded over the national imagination neither had power to alter the social principles of the Tory party. The literary men—the Scotts, the Coleridges, the Southeys, the Wordsworths—effected nothing to influence the Tory attitude towards Chartism, Trade Unions and the Corn Laws. These were practical matters in which literary inspiration counted for nothing. The literary men aimed higher. The Tory was a Romantic only in so far as his prejudices and ideals were moulded in natural instinct and not in the conscious promptings of an intellectual system.

So with Young England. The influence of half a dozen youths was too subtle to have immediate tangible effect upon the character of our political life. The strength of Young Englanders lay in the largeness of their vision, not in their ability to make laws. 'The error of these men is that they carry the conception of poetry into the unsuitable atmosphere of public life.'[1]

This adversary's verdict is either profoundly wise or egregiously silly. In the chill year of 1849, when Young England was already dead, it took a courageous Edinburgh Reviewer to concede the tribute of a hidden compliment.

Although the Reform Act of 1832 broadened the basis of the franchise, it did nothing to increase the Parliamentary representation of minorities. It is doubtful whether even the majority of the people, the non-electors, were as well represented after 1832 as they were before. Throughout the fourteen years which followed the pass-

[1] Greg (W. P.) in *Edinburgh Review*, No. 182, October 1849, p. 501.

ing of the Act there was a large body of Tory opinion which was but inadequately represented in the Conservative party, and often denied a hearing in Parliament. The hold which the doctrines of Liberal Reform had obtained over the intellectual classes was irresistible, yet the feeling of contentment which was afterwards to develop into mid-Victorian complacency was alive only in those who benefited by the changes which were taking place in commerce and industry. The working classes were not well enough off to have reason for thanking the nation for their condition or to receive with enthusiasm the assurance that all was going well. There were vast masses of industrial and rural labourers into whose homes the new optimism never penetrated, and wide areas over which the enlightenment of the Political Economists spread in vain.

It is as well to take special precaution in referring to the character of the factory and mining populations of the time. Because they had become proletarian in the economic sense, they were not yet entirely proletarian in mind. By far the great majority of them had not been transported to the manufacturing areas to feed the growing appetite of industry. This was their native soil; they had, most of them, lived upon it for generations, and even when the face of the land was transformed before their eyes, they clung to the memories of the plough. Hunger made Manchester spinners and Huddersfield weavers turn retrospective.

The restless masses sought leaders of their own making. There were exceptions ; such was Feargus O'Connor who thrust himself upon them, and they accepted him. There was Lovett, one of themselves, whom they virtually rejected. Lovett's leanings were towards Reform and Self-Improvement. His methods were ' meliorist ' ; he was suspected by the northern operatives of being a bourgeois in disguise. O'Connor on the other hand preached to the masses what the masses wanted to hear. His Tory-Radicalism gave to their sordid struggles for bread something of the glamour of a Holy War.

The hold which these leaders obtained over the affection of the working classes was amazing, and Tory-Radicalism became a giant power among the people. But because it had no representation in Parliament it was politically blind, and its social strength was dissipated.

Tory-Radicalism is best studied in the lives and utterances of its more coherent exponents. These taught no rigid and uniform doctrine ; but a common faith united them. Sadler was a Tory and a Wesleyan, the son of religious piety and stern morality. Oastler, educated among Tory-Wesleyan surroundings, became a hot and strong Church-and-King man, a preacher of loyalty to Throne and Altar. Bull, the parson of Brierley, was a Tory in social teaching and an Evangelical in theology. Stephens, who dwelt on the Radical side of the Tory-Radical frontier, never ceased to proclaim the Tory sentiments which filled him.

A proper understanding of the part played by Michael Sadler in educating the Tory party in its duty towards the working classes cannot be attained without some knowledge of a curious and powerful ingredient of pre-Reform Toryism, of which Sadler was a representative—the Tory-Wesleyan connection.

Before the Reform Act had worked havoc upon the constitution of the old Tory party, the Parliamentary influence of the Tory-Wesleyan connection was considerable. Joseph Butterworth, as active a Tory as he was a Methodist, and George Thomson, one of a group of Methodists who on social grounds opposed the Abolition of Slavery,[1] were Sadler's personal friends. The connection virtually ceased in 1832, when the Wesleyans, hitherto a conservatively-minded body, possessed of an astonishingly high aggregate property qualification, were swamped by the hosts of dissenting sects who voted Liberal. Even after 1832, when Methodism began its swing towards the Left, Toryism died hard among the older school of leaders. Wesleyan Conferences were told of ministers in the North who introduced Church and State petitions into their chapels in opposition to petitions from the Radicals.[2] Lord John Russell attributed his defeat at Bedford to Wesleyan influence.[3] During the examination of J. R. Stephens before the Conference of 1834, the veteran Jabez Bunting asserted that every minister had a right to his own political opinions. ' Some say that a strong arm must be laid on the Tory side. They tried to catch me in order to fry me, but they failed. I wish (turning sympathetically to Stephens) they had not caught one on the Liberal side.' [4]

Sadler was from first to last a Wesleyan, and he bore in his person all the qualities, good and bad, of militant piety. His appeal, whether in Parliamentary elections or on the Tory Reformers' platform, was made primarily to the Wesleyans and Nonconformists who understood him best. Throughout his Factory Reform campaign of

---

[1] Gregory (B.), *Side Lights on the Conflicts of Methodism* (1898), p. 94.
[2] *Ibid.*, p. 147.   [3] *Ibid.*, p. 147, and *D.N.B.*
[4] *Ibid.*, p. 164.

1831-32 his name was the object of godly praise from a thousand chapels where factory meetings began with political resolutions and ended with Doxology and prayer.[1]

But Sadler was no mere guileless idealist, hopelessly out of touch with the realities of the hour. Sadler had a shrewd eye for tactical advantages both on the hustings and in Parliamentary Committee. In his native Yorkshire he knew his audience and could be trusted to resort to a stand-up oratorical tussle whenever required. A hostile journalist present at a Nomination Day fracas in Cloth Hall Yard during the Leeds Election fight of December 1832, reported that Mr. Sadler was supported by a bodyguard of hooligans of the worst type. A tradesman in Parkgate, who happened to have got forced among the Blues, observed that a number of them were armed with bludgeons. Anyway, when speech-making was over fifteen persons were taken to the Infirmary.[2]

In this election Sadler acted wisely. He fought the election (as he chose to fight it) on the issue, not of Parliamentary, but of Factory Reform. He approached the ' electors and non-electors,' not as Sadler the Tory— for that would have been unsafe—but as Sadler the Humanitarian, the friend of the factory operatives.[3] In the course of the election, while Macaulay from a window of Stansfield's warehouse ' made a long speech on things in general,' [4] Sadler, from a neighbouring window, was

[1] Northern Newspapers, 1831-33, *passim*.
[2] *Halifax and Huddersfield Express*, December 15, 1832.
[3] *Leeds Intelligencer*, December 14, 1832.
[4] See notice ' To the Electors and Non-Electors of the Borough of Leeds, especially the Wesleyan Methodists and Dissenters,' in which the Sadler party impugn Macaulay's theological orthodoxy. (*Leeds*

shouting to the crowd below, appealing for the Non-conformist vote. That Sadler lost the election was not the fault of the non-electors nor from want of trying.

A comparison between the personalities of Sadler and Oastler is needless, for they were demonstrably complete opposites. Of the two Oastler was perhaps the truer Tory. Though half Wesleyan in ancestry, he had none of Sadler's somewhat heavy piety, but was a more generous character, more Dantonesque, and less exercised by conventionality and the problems of the Future Life.

Oastler was a thoroughgoing Church-and-King man. He was ever for the Establishment. ' Show me a reason why I, as the head of my family, should not support an altar in my house, and I will show you a reason why the Government of this country should not establish a national altar.' [1]

Unlike Sadler, Oastler had no love for Yorkshire Non-conformity. Sadler died before the control of Dissent in the northern industrial districts fell into the hands of the manufacturing classes ; Oastler lived to see the gradual ousting of the old Tory element from the chapels. War had for some time been declared between himself and the elder Baines of the *Leeds Mercury*.[2] To Edward Baines' Parliamentary attitude towards the Ten Hours Bill Oastler took violent exception. Baines and his clique are demolished in two pamphlets in which Oastler

Intelligencer, December 13, 1832.) Direct Tory appeals to the political interests of Nonconformity are rare after 1832.

[1] Speech of Richard Oastler, Esq., at the Anniversary Dinner of the Huddersfield Loyal and Constitutional Association. April 20, 1838. Handbill.

[2] In private life the two men seem to have been friends. (Alfred, *History of the Factory Movement, 1807-1847* (1857), vol. i. p. 93.)

pokes fun at the local Member for openly boasting that he broke the Factory Regulation Act and at the same time took a prominent part in chapel life, 'helping another old schoolfellow of mine, the Revd. John Smith, to hand about the " Elements." ' [1]

Oastler hit out right and left against those he termed the oppressors of the factory children. A correspondent in a local newspaper suggested that ' the direct and visible object of the inventor and mover of the Factory Bill was to run his bill against Parliamentary reform, slave emancipation,' and the like. 'I'll be bound for it,' retorted Oastler, springing at the neck of this intruder, ' he is a genuine Liberal of the Nineteenth Century—a man who *professes* to feel for sufferings he never witnessed, a trumpet-tongued declaimer against abuses by which he has never profited.' [2] Eight years later, to another critic of Factory Reform he replied, ' You have not dwelt in a manufacturing district, you have not spent much time in factories, mayhap you have never been in one. I have dwelt in the midst of the ravages of the Factory system, I have witnessed its destruction of the human frame, its dreadful havoc on the moral faculties, its smothering and withering of all domestic ties, its ruinous effect on the religious principles both of its victims and of its priests.' [3]

Oastler was the child of local influences, and nowhere perhaps but in the West Riding and Wales was this rugged family of orator-prophets bred in such numbers. Excited mobs of hungry working men would gather round him

---

[1] *The Huddersfield Dissenters stark staring mad!!!!* (1835). *Yorkshire Slavery. The ' Devil-to-do ' among the Dissenters in Huddersfield* (1835).
[2] *Bolton Chronicle,* May 1833.
[3] Fleet Papers, vol. 21, May 1841.

in Huddersfield or Leeds, and he would appear among them dishevelled and waving a silk hat battered by Whig opponents. ' This is Whig liberty, my friends ! ' he would cry; 'Look also at my coat—rent from bottom to top by Whig patriots,'[1] and, after a speech of fierce eloquence, he would assure them that their wrongs would be avenged, that God had not gone to sleep.

In Oastler's day there still existed a powerful local Toryism, largely unaffected by the course of Parliamentary politics, and differing from county to county. West Riding Toryism was distinct from Birmingham or Liverpool Toryism, and though the centralizing influence of Peel's party organization tended to obliterate these local distinctions, they persisted until long after 1832.[2]

Oastler was not unknown in London. He spoke there at Factory Reform meetings, and it was he who met John Walter in 1841 and handed him a requisition, ' signed by the influential electors of the Tory and Chartist parties ' of Manchester, requesting him to become their candidate.[3] Both in London and in his native Yorkshire he was beloved by the people. ' He is an odd fellow,' was Place's opinion of him, ' but so is every man who thinks for himself—you are odd, and so people say I am. Oastler calls himself a Tory, and in some matters he and I differ very widely, but he does much to serve the working

---

[1] *Damnation ! Eternal Damnation to the Fiend-Begotten,* '*Coarser Food*,' *New Poor Law* (1837).

[2] Yorkshire Conservatives, for example, exhibited a remarkable unanimity on the issues of Factory Reform, the New Poor Law, and the Introduction of Rural Police. A proposal to introduce the New Police was barely passed at a West Riding Adjourned Sessions ; Edmund Denison, Colonel Tempest and an influential county following led the opposition. (*Leeds Intelligencer*, April 17, 1841.)

[3] Alfred, *op. cit.*, vol. ii. p. 166.

people in the way he thinks best, and we have a sort of bargain between us, that we will contrive to disagree without quarrelling.' [1]

Bull, after his fashion, was also a Church-and-King man. Like so many of the better Low-Church Clergy of the time, he reinforced his spiritual teaching with sound material advice and admonition. No one among the Factory ' Saints ' was less of a Quietist. He appears to have been one of the few northern Clergy who understood, and were understood by, coal miners. His frequent sermons for their benefit show us that he loved them. If he made a sermon an occasion for a mild scolding he scolds without false dissimulation. ' *An idle man,*' Bull preaches, '*is the devil's man.*' Apply yourselves diligently to your calling . . . be not like some who *work hard* a few days, and *drink hard* the rest. . . . Three things then let me recommend—Religion as *the root*, and Industry and Patriotism as *the branches*. [2]

He had little time for those frivolous dilettanti who supposed the working people to be as a whole profligate. He had a firm belief, however, that loose morals and consequent bad workmanship had been partly responsible for supplanting the handlooms by machinery. [3] He scolds his flock for the crime of undercutting one another in wages through the envy which one man bears for another's skill and remuneration. ' There are frequent instances in which the working men, by receiving and oppressing each other, have effected a ruinous reduction

[1] Place to M. H. Sadler of Leeds. October 1835. (Place Coll., vol. 52.)

[2] Bull (G. S.), *The Gospel of Christ recommended to Coal Miners* (1834).

[3] Bull (G. S.), *The Oppressors of the Poor ; and the Poor their own Oppressors* (1839), p. 13.

in the wages of a whole class of labourers, and that where necessity could not be pleaded as an excuse.'[1]

The workers were not always to blame. Parson Bull insisted that mine managers and undertakers should watch carefully against waste of human life. To avoid carelessness, which causes most accidents in the pits, should be the aim of employers of labour. In view of possible explosions passages must be kept clear and miners must beware of loose stones and rickety shafts. Above all, for God's sake let the men refrain from foul language in the mines.

Place once said of Stephens that he ' professed himself a Tory, but acted the part of a democrat.'[2] Holyoake, who knew Stephens intimately, described him as politically a Conservative,[3] yet this Conservative was expelled from the Wesleyan body for holding Radical views on the connection of Church and State. A more doubtful authority somewhat petulantly relates that Stephen's political opinions were for long a matter of uncertainty ; ' he was not prone to be explicit, and preferred in politics to enjoy the advantages, and bear with the disadvantages, of mystery.'[4]

It is unnecessary for the purposes of this chapter to inquire further into the particular political allegiance which Stephens professed. His speeches are the only reliable guide to his political views, and politics did not excessively concern him.

In common with his fellow Tory-Radicals, Stephens

[1] *Ibid.*, p. 15.
[2] Art., Stephens (J. R.) in *D.N.B.*
[3] Holyoake (G. J.), *Life of Joseph Rayner Stephens* (1881), p. 11.
[4] Alfred, vol. ii. p. 103.

looked upon the highly-industrialized, highly-capitalized society which surrounded him as fundamentally unstable. With Cobbett, Oastler and Disraeli he blamed the Whigs, who were supposed to personify the hated ' spirit of the age ' which ignored the social condition of the masses. ' I am so far a Conservative ' (he spoke of his social outlook) ' that I do not wish to see the old English institutions destroyed.' ' I am so far a Conservative,' he told the working classes of Manchester in 1838, ' that I will exert myself to the utmost of my power, and I will call upon the people to back me, to prevent the destruction of those institutions which the Radicals never asked to be destroyed, but which it is now proved the Whigs wish to destroy.' [1] Thomas Attwood had said as much in his election address the year before when he crowned a condemnation of the Whigs with a defence of aristocracy.[2]

Stephens combined in his person the romantic Tory and the fiery Radical. He was received with wild enthusiasm at the Chartist Convention of 1839. Yet he was markedly hostile to almost all the political ideals of Chartism. He opposed both the threat of physical force and the proposal for a National Holiday. Though in his religion he was liberal enough, he was hotly opposed to the Chartist Democratic chapels.[3] He was quick to perceive the gulf that lay between Tory Chartism and the doubtful religious experiments of the ' people's parsons.'

It may be argued that the Toryism of Oastler and

---

[1] *Northern Star*, June 9, 1828. Quoted in Holyoake, p. 106.
[2] Wakefield (C. M.), *The Life of Thomas Attwood* (1885), p. 308.
[3] Sermon at Hebden Bridge, August 18, 1849. Quoted in Holyoake, p. 131.

Stephens and the masses whom they inspired was completely divorced from the Parliamentary Tory party, and that the use of the term ' Tory ' to apply to both is a confusion of words.

From the political point of view the criticism must be held valid. Politically the Tory party would never have admitted the least party connection with these northern firebrands. Had the Tory remnant of 1832 identified itself actively with those who were shortly to become the leaders of the Yorkshire and Lancashire masses, the subsequent history of the Conservative party might have been far different from what it was. Such a union was never likely to take place.

From the social point of view, however, the criticism does not hold. There was everything in common between the two groups in their outlook upon the great labour questions of the day. What differences there were were differences of expression. Both were permeated with the same basic social ideas.

In essence rather an instinct than a rational set of principles, Toryism still possessed a powerful hold over all those classes who were not brought directly into touch with the new intellectualism of Bentham's disciples. The same social prejudices are found to dominate the thought of Birmingham Political Unionists, Tory Chartists and Tory Peers. Here the inherent Toryism of the masses is seen in the hero-worship of ' good old ' Lord Eldon, who received almost divine honours from the Anti-Poor Law mobs of 1838. Here Toryism appears under the shadow of an anti-capitalist movement, there as a protest against the credit system. Here centralization is opposed, there the New Police. Everywhere under innumerable disguises reappears the many-headed hydra which the enlightened believed they had scotched in 1832.

In point of theory alone there was little to choose between the Ultra-Tories of Peel's Right Wing and the older Radicals ' in all matters pertaining to the arrangements of a state.' It was not chance that made Lord Eldon and Lord Western devotees of Thomas Attwood's financial views or drove Cookesley of Eton and the Dissenting Stephens along the road to Poor Law opposition. Political opponents recognized the fact of this curious ubiquity of Tory sentiment, and not unnaturally suspected it. Ebenezer Elliott, the future propagandist of the Anti-Corn Law League, championed newsrooms and political knowledge as the best antidote to Tory Slavery. 'Be not deluded,' cried this worthy verse-maker, ' by the Owens, the Oastlers, the Bulls and the Sadlers, these dupes of the enemy.' [1] Sadler would scarcely have felt at ease with Owen as his bedfellow, but the analogy, for a partisan, was not unjustly drawn.

The changes which came over English society during the half-century preceding the Reform Act of 1832 had thrown existing social ideas into utter confusion. From the wreckage emerged two great bodies of social opinion. Those who were able to deduce a code of rational economic and social laws from the havoc which had taken place were the orthodox Political Economists and the educated Liberals of thought and action. Those to whom the changes signified nothing less than the herald of national ruin, and who were unable to recognize in the chaos any rational design beyond the wrath of Heaven,

---

[1] Holyoake (G. J.), *History of Co-operation* (1906), vol. i. p. 141.

formed the ranks of the Ultra-Tories and the extreme Radicals. Hostility to social change inspired both.

The Industrial Revolution left in its train a great body of people who saw only its evil side. The Tory whose little world of rank and station was being overturned in the march of progress, and the Radical whom the march of progress had rendered desperately hungry, together looked to the past, to a half-legendary paradise when there was no machinery, no Political Economy, no Huskisson and no Ure. This ill-defined but powerful sentiment, half resentful, half bewildered, transcended class and party. Expressed in social terms, it provided the motive power of Tory labour ideas.

CHAPTER II

CONSERVATIVE PARTY ORGANIZATION AND THE WORKING CLASSES

CONTACT between the Tory party and the working classes was maintained in two separate spheres of political activity. There was the contact maintained through the medium of public and party institutions, and that which was achieved through the private relationship of landlord to labourer, employer to employed, man to man.

It is with the first, the relation of the Conservative party to the working classes, that I am here concerned. In the course of the last chapter I attempted a general survey of the various strands of thought existing within the Tory party ; in this I propose to investigate the extent to which Tory social principles found expression through the agency of the Conservative party machine. The aim of such investigation will be to discover the lengths to which the Parliamentary party was prepared to go in allying itself with labouring people in the furtherance of its policy, and to estimate how far Conservative leaders were willing to meet the aspirations of non-electors to a share in the fortunes of the party. The chapter concludes by a study of Peel's relations with the Tory group in the furtherance of his party projects.

The object of pursuing inquiry along these lines will readily be understood. The history of the connection

32

between the Conservative party organization and the working classes during these years is part and parcel of a larger question which has agitated political life for over a century : in effect, the ability of the Right Wing to capture and retain the support and affection of the masses.

The Reform Act of 1832 wrought organic changes in the mechanism of English political parties. Not that the result of the changes was superficially apparent or that the mere Act made the difference. Those who look for marked alterations in the character of the legislation or in the personnel of the House of Commons look in vain.[1]

What changes there were—and their enormous importance is not disputed—came from outside. A mighty force was at work which was destined to make havoc of all preconceived notions of the rôle of party politics in the constituencies. The significance of the Reform Bill was that it symbolized the first triumph of an electoral theory.

Although party organization is by no means the monopoly of democratic peoples, there will be found to exist an interesting relation between the extension of the franchise and the development of party organization. Each successive broadening of the base of the representation is accompanied by a corresponding expansion of the machinery by which political parties seek to discipline and control the vote. The intimate relation of one with the other is a sinister feature of recent political history. And if the history of the British franchise during the

---

[1] The Act left each party in secure control of its former interests. (Thomas (J. A.), ' The House of Commons, 1832-1867. A Functional Analysis.' *Economica*, No. 13, March 1925.)

course of the past century is one long tale of successive broadenings and extensions and adjustments, it is also true that the results of the organizing genius of Peel, Disraeli and Joseph Chamberlain show a parallel development. Peel countered the consequences of the Reform Act by the creation of a party machine in the constituencies, Disraeli placed at the service of his newly-enfranchised industrial workers of 1867 the benefits of a professionalized party headquarters in Bridge Street, Westminster, and what Disraeli left undone, Tory Democracy, the Primrose League and the Birmingham Caucus brought to a successful consummation. With each extension of the franchise a new race of Tadpoles and Tapers spring into exuberant life.

During the first ten years which followed the Reform Act investigation will be concerned mainly with the growing ascendancy of what are loosely called the middle classes, and with Peel's attempts to accommodate those classes by adjustments to the Conservative party machine. Everywhere the ideas of the new *bourgeoisie* were seen to predominate. Even the accepted vocabulary of party politics underwent a revolution. A political and social outlook compounded in part of complacent optimism, and in part of self-pride, began to be accepted by foreigners as the hall-mark of the English character. The party catchwords indicating the Church-and-King loyalty of the eighteenth century, the political tags of ' Lord George and the Protestant succession! ' and ' John Wilkes for ever ! ' now gave way to phrases better suited to the time. Respectability became not only the national catchword of the Englishman but a positive force in politics. In the election of 1832 the young Mr. Macaulay supported by the Respectability of Leeds, Parliamentary petitions ' numerously and respectably signed,' and deputations of ' respectable gentlemen of the middling classes ' herald the near approach of the Victorian Age.

Behind the triumphant political forces of 1832 were ranged those classes as yet largely inarticulate, though destined before long to become a power in politics. ' The working people,' Cobbett wrote in 1825, ' are not, then, a great interest ! They will be found to be one by and by.' [1] Within five years Cobbett's prophecy was realized, and, in the struggle waged round the Reform Bill, the working classes played an important part. Guided by the Radical orators of Birmingham and London the electoral power of the mob proved the decisive factor in the Reform campaign.

Unlike the existing instruments of party warfare which Parliamentary custom had sanctioned for the guidance of members—the party discipline and the system of whipping in—these new political institutions were wholly unconnected with the constitutional organs of government.[2] They sought, it is true, to influence Parliament, but their proper field of activity lay outside. At their best the weapon in their hands was peaceful persuasion ; at their worst their course of action followed fitfully along the ill-defined frontier between persuasion and intimidation.

The correspondence of Sir Robert Peel leaves the impression that the efficient organization of the Political

---

[1] *Rural Rides* (ed. 1853), p. 303.
[2] Lowell (A. L.), *The Government of England* (ed. 1912), vol. i. pp. 472 foll.

Unions had considerable influence upon his mind. It is certain that, when he undertook the construction of what contemporaries in admiration called the Great Conservative Party, he appreciated to the full the possibilities of capturing the favour of public opinion.

To be effective public opinion must be mobilized and regimented, and it is during the earlier years of the period between 1832 and 1846 that the extra-Parliamentary political association, with its strict party discipline, its propaganda and its campaigns, attains an importance hitherto unknown. Henceforward power lay with him who attracted the force of organized public opinion to his side.[1]

Until the years of Peel's thoroughgoing reconstruction of the old Tory party and its conversion from a battered remnant to a powerful political combine, there existed but the shadow of an organized party. Everything which at the present day is usually associated with the life of political groups was then lacking save in the most elementary form. The highly-centralized party headquarters,

[1] The development of the 'campaign' as a weapon of political warfare may be traced through the seventeenth and eighteenth centuries. But the character and scope of the campaign altered from time to time. Those early associations, having for their object the maintenance or abolition of Acts of Parliament or the defence of exalted persons, conducted somewhat crude campaigns to achieve their ends. Associations of the kind organized by Shaftesbury in 1680, avowedly for the maintenance of English liberties, or that which in 1708 rallied to the cry of 'Church in Danger,' marked a fresh development in party tactics. Even these were but primitive counterparts to the highly developed political societies which arose in the early nineteenth century. Not until the advent of the Catholic Association and the Birmingham Political Union was there anything approaching a full consciousness of the possibilities of campaigns and propaganda. Both organizations were in this respect totally eclipsed by the Anti-Corn Law League.

36

the myriad local associations diſtributed through every conſtituency, the ceaseless propaganda, the scientifically-directed political campaign, were non-exiſtent. And what is more, the old Tory party came near to perishing for want of them.

By this it is not, of course, to be inferred that before Peel's reorganization there was no Tory party machine or that the Tory party entered the Reform ſtruggle unarmed. There were the half-social, half-political London clubs—White's for High Society, Brooke's, much decayed since Fox's time, and Boodle's for Tory gentlemen up from the country.[1] In the conſtituencies there were the cuſtomary, and ſtill effective, weapons of patronage and local influence. The weakness of the Tory Remnant of 1833 lay in its ſtolid refusal to make use of those weapons of party warfare by which its enemies had lately triumphed. It was to the merit of Peel that he forced an unwilling party to wield arms which the day demanded.

Up to the time when Disraeli transferred his party hcadquarters to more suitable premises opposite the Houses of Parliament, the centre of gravity of the Conservative machine was in the Carlton Club. This Club was founded in 1831, in the height of the Reform controversy, by a group of party leaders led by the Herries and the Duke of Wellington.[2] Herries' biographer implies that the ſtormy wranglings which were the heritage from George Canning's day had made the

---

[1] Timbs (J.), *Club Life in London* (1866), vol. i. *passim.*

[2] Previously Tories were in the habit of meeting in premises in Charles Street, St. James's Square. (Herries (E.), *Memoir of the Public Life of the Right Hon. John Charles Herries* (1880), vol. i. p. 119.)

older meeting-place the scene of party recriminations. It was felt that the opening of the Carlton Club would tend to reunite the warring factions under one roof.

Within the new club grew up a party bureaucracy. But it was an amateur bureaucracy, and so it remained until long after the conclusion of the Peelite period.[1] Like most amateur bureaucracies the gentlemen of the Carlton suffered occasionally from an excess of zeal, and on occasion they exacted a degree of party obedience which must have disconcerted the tactical mind of the Master.[2]

Soon after 1833 the political world began to take notice of the Carlton ; within three years opponents and friends alike were referring to it as the headquarters of the party.[3] It dawned upon contemporaries that the Carlton was something more than a social amenity.

It was evident that the recent changes in the system of representation would entail corresponding changes in the mode of managing election campaigns and in the selection of candidates for constituencies not otherwise provided for. The registration early claimed the attention of the party headquarters, and from the General

---

[1] T. S. Duncombe in a playful thrust at the assiduity of Conservative agents in the constituencies told the House of Commons that the real influence lay in ' a little coterie at the Carlton Club, presided over by the Hon. and gallant Colonel [Forester] opposite.' (*Hansard*, cxxvii. 145, May 10, 1853.)

[2] ' Have you no influence with these madmen of the Carlton ? ' wrote Croker to Peel in July 1835, when the Club talked of punishing Pusey and Young for their desertion of the party in voting for the Government in a decision on the Irish Church and Tithes Bill. (Addit. MSS. 40,321.)

[3] Londonderry to Buckingham, March 9, 1836. (The Duke of Buckingham and Chandos, *Memoirs of the Courts and Cabinets of William IV. and Victoria* (1861), vol. i. p. 228.)

Election of 1835 onwards the Club provided the initiative for scrutinizing electoral rolls. Mysterious agents arriving apparently from the skies were found defending the Blue votes and objecting to the votes cast by the Yellows.[1] Whenever an election petition was being organized by the friends of a defeated Tory candidate, the sombre figure of Mr. Spofforth ' from London ' appeared with his legendary bags of gold.[2] The party club became the successor of the boroughmongers.

The local prestige acquired by a candidate for Parliament through his reputed connection with one of the great London political clubs is shown in the case of Disraeli's unlucky Taunton candidature in April 1835. The *Taunton Courier*, a Tory newspaper, having affirmed that Mr. Disraeli possessed the confidence of the Conservative Club, the *Morning Chronicle* replied that this was impossible, since he was still a member of the Westminster Club.

In spite, however, of the great influence which the Carlton Club undoubtedly possessed in the constituencies, its chief influence lay with the party in Parliament ; once the elections were over it left the constituencies to look after themselves.

The Carlton Club professed to be a party headquarters, no more. One thing it did not do. However harsh may have been the hold which the Club exercised over party discipline at Westminster, it did not arrogate to itself a domineering control over the constituencies. The net-

[1] Report on Bribery at Elections (1835, vol. viii.) ; Mins. of Evidence, Q. 1419, foll.
[2] Rae (W. F.), ' Political Clubs and Party Organization ' (in *Nineteenth Century*, vol. iii. No. 15, May 1878).

work of Conservative Associations which were to form the broad base of the Peelite machine were left to the care of local party leaders. The Carlton never paraded as a National Registration Society. Tory hatred of centralization in all its forms would not have tolerated it for one moment. Any interference by the agents of a London headquarters would have been intolerable, and even the elusive Mr. Spofforth perforce walked warily in Beaufort or Cecil territory. There was the power of Princes ; when the Court went down to the Pavilion, Brighton Conservatism waned ; when the Court went away it waxed strong again.[1] It was well known that the Marquess of Exeter held Stamford in the hollow of his hand. The Bedford influence over Bedford town was enough to get a local curate into serious trouble with his bishop for making a covert reference to ' a Lamb (certainly not without spot) ' at a meeting of the County Conservative Association.[2] It was not till long after the collapse of Peel's great political amalgam, that close contact between party headquarters and the constituencies was effected ; and by that time the centre of gravity of the Conservative organization had shifted from Pall Mall to Bridge Street, Westminster.

Between the years 1832 and 1841, Peel established the

---

[1] Bonham (J. B.) to Peel, September 23, 1837 (Addit. MSS. 40,424), on the subject of the East Sussex Conservative Association : ' You will not be surprised,' writes Bonham, ' that this association is now on the wane and requires every artificial support, the more so as a rival association formed within the last month has for a patron the Duke of Sussex, who is entirely unconnected with the place, and *therefore* is supposed to represent the feelings of the Palace.'

[2] *Times*, December 2, 1840. The ' Lamb ' was Lord C. J. F. Russell.

three powerful instruments of party action : a Press, an effective party headquarters, and a network of associations in the constituencies. As far as we know, Peel had nothing to do with the control of newspapers for party purposes. Attempts had previously been made by successive Governments to enlist the services of the Press. The Liverpool administration had made a practice of subsidizing certain amenable newspapers in Ireland. Responsible ministers coolly defended the outlay as a necessary means of influencing public opinion, and division lists prove that the expenditure was successfully justified in Committee of Supply.[1] But Liverpool himself admitted the virtual failure of the practice. Proprietors and editors not unnaturally ran away to the party which paid them best. The purchase of an entire party press was unattainable for the reason that bad papers which would sell themselves to the highest bidder were useless as party organs, while good papers (he probably had the *Times* in view) found it paid better to give the public what the public wanted irrespective of the wishes of the party leaders.[2] Peel, the unpopular joint-leader of the enemies of Reform in 1830, could scarcely depend upon a single Tory newspaper ; Peel, the triumphant leader of the Great Conservative Party of 1841, the Man of Destiny, found himself so encumbered by suppliant editors that he

[1] Torrens (W. M.), *Memoirs of Viscount Melbourne* (1878), vol. i. p. 248.
[2] ' You refer to our not having a newspaper. This is not enough. Why have we not one ? Why is it worth no newspaper's while to take up our cause ? It is with them a mere question of trade, and can only be referred to the fact that there are not buyers of newspapers enough of our opinion to make it worth their while.' (Lord Beauvale to Lady Palmerston, December 1, 1834 ; Airlie (Mabell), Countess of, *Lady Palmerston and her Times* (1922), vol. ii. p. 37.)

could actually choose his newspaper following.[1] Meanwhile the Whigs had been finding one newspaper after another deserting their side.

In place of a party press in the strict sense of the term, political leaders aimed rather at individual newspaper patronage. Brougham and Palmerston each had his periodical satellite, until the Master's public reputation suffered eclipse. John Walter of the *Times* was bound by ties of personal friendship to the Stanley group. So when Stanley and his friends came over to the Conservative side, John Walter and the *Times* came over too. On Peel's hurried arrival from Rome in December 1834, he found a letter from the proprietor of the *Standard* offering his services, adding that, if an agreement were reached, he would buy up two evening papers, the *Albion* and the *Courier*, to act as satellites, into the bargain.[2]

Perhaps Peel's strength lay in the somewhat austere attitude he adopted towards the press magnates of the day. While there is no reason to believe that the proprietors of favoured newspapers went unthanked for their services to the party, Peel drew the line at favouritism. He gave the monopoly of Government intelligence to none. C. E. Michele of the *Morning Post*, whose relations with Peel were singularly unhappy, wrote soon after the election campaign of 1841 complaining that his newspaper, a faithful party organ, was left in the dark by party chiefs. To which Peel replied : ' Complaints of the same nature

---

[1] When Michele, editor of the *Morning Post*, wrote to ask ' whether something might not be done which would promote the efficiency of the Conservative press as a political engine,' *i.e.* by encouraging the *Morning Post*, Peel's reply was frigid and aloof. (Peel to C. E. Michele, August 10, 1841. Addit. MSS. 40,486.)

[2] S. L. Gifford to Peel, December 8, 1834. (Addit. MSS. 40,404.)

with that which you addressed to me, were received by me from other parties connected with the public press, to whom you suppose undue preference to be shown, within two or three days preceding the date of your letter.' [1]

With an efficient headquarters at their command, the Conservative leaders were now free to turn their attention to the provinces. These years of Conservative opposition saw the organization of local Conservative Associations up and down the country.

It is not, of course, to be assumed categorically that the idea of local Conservative Associations originated with Peel. Some of those in existence during the Reform Struggle of 1832 may possibly have been able to trace their ancestry to the days of Reeve's Association, which rose during the period of Pitt's coercive legislation as a counterblast to the Jacobin societies inspired by the French Revolution. In Bristol a Constitutional and a Whig Club were active in the Election of 1780.[2] It is related by a contemporary that candidates for vacancies on the Infirmary staff had no chance of success unless they had the approval of the Tory Club at the White Lion.[3] Little enough, however, is heard of Tory Associations until 1831. The earlier societies and clubs of Tory gentlemen were scarcely continuous organized agencies of party propaganda.

---

[1] Peel to Michele, January 2, 1842. (Addit. MSS. 40,486.) Peel lived to rue the day of his estrangement from the *Morning Post*. One month after writing that reply Michele was attacking Peel's Sliding Scale.

[2] Smith MSS. (Bristol) quoted in Latimer (J.), *Annals of Bristol, Eighteenth Century*, p. 446.

[3] *Ibid.*, p. 447.

Such Tory societies as there were by 1831 seem to have been in the main confined to the larger boroughs. A group of young Norwich tradesmen founded the Eldon Society on October 8 of that year, on the day on which the Reform Bill had been rejected. The Leicester Conservative Club, another tradesmen's society, seems to have been well established by 1832. In common with universal practice these societies transacted their business at a public-house.

Tory societies which grew up under the stress of Reform agitation may summarily be divided into two classes : those conducted by tradesmen and those which accommodated the city or borough operatives. Of the first class it may be said that they were in every way respectable bodies providing social amenities and scarcely touched by the imputation of corruption. Select Committees on Bribery at Elections had little to report to their discredit. And it was this type of tradesmen's society, the child of the years of Reform, that was to provide Peelite Conservatism with a model for the Conservative Associations which were soon to cover the face of the British Isles.

When Peel in April 1835 retired after a short season of precarious power, the new Conservative machine was running smoothly. Throughout the spring Conservative Associations were springing up everywhere and at a rate which dumbfounded the enemy. It seemed that a vital spirit had entered the old Tory party, giving it a new store of energy.

The movement began in South Lancashire, the home of a particularly virile form of local Toryism. Political association in the district was no novelty. Manchester

Toryism had been long united, while the Liverpool Tradesmen's Conservative Association may well have had its beginnings in the days of George Canning's fierce campaigns. In November 1834—months before the neighbouring counties had founded their societies—the South Lancashire Conservative Association was meeting to welcome an Irish Protestant delegation.[1] By the following April a Liverpool Conservative paper was urging the formation of Conservative Associations on the South Lancashire model.[2]

In point of fact, April 1835 was a fruitful month for Conservative Associations. A Loyal and Constitutional Society was founded by the Birmingham Conservatives as a set-off to Attwood's Political Union.[3] The movement had already spread to Ireland and Scotland. While T. Hamilton was engaged in mobilizing the No-Popery votes of the Irish constituencies by means of Conservative Associations, the party leaders in Edinburgh were founding similar associations throughout Scotland.[4]

In the agricultural constituencies Conservative Associations are found to have become the fashion in a score of districts. The Conservatives of South Hampshire formed themselves into an Association as early as April,[5] though of the smaller boroughs Deal and Walmer seem to have

---

[1] *Times*, November 4, 1834.

[2] *Liverpool Standard*, quoted in *Times*, April 23, 1835.

[3] *Times*, April 25, 1835.

[4] ' To-morrow there is to be a private meeting here to settle the plan of a Conservative Association which shall have branches in every town and county in Scotland.' (J. Mackenzie to Peel. Addit. MSS. 40,309.)

[5] *Times*, April 25, 1835.

45

led the way.[1] Yorkshire followed hard on the example of Kent. Thirsk had its Association by July.[2] Guildford founded its Association in the New Year of 1836.[3] Ludlow followed [4] during the course of the next two months.

The county constituencies were relatively late in following the lead of South Lancashire, South Hampshire and the county pioneers of 1835. Oxford did not possess its City and County Conservative Association until 1838 ; [5] Cambridgeshire seems to have taken precedence for some years.[6]

The General Election of August 1837 put the new Associations to the test. From all accounts they thoroughly justified their existence. Scottish Conservative Societies exerted considerable influence in the Municipal Elections of 1835.[7] By 1837 their usefulness to the party was apparent. The successful Conservative candidate for North Nottinghamshire wrote to Peel asking that he be allowed to acknowledge the value of the assistance he received from the local Associations during his electoral campaign.[8] In a confidential letter to Peel, F. B. Bonham of the Whips' Office reports a steady Conservative

[1] The Deal and Walmer Association held its first anniversary early in 1836. (*Times*, January 3, 1836.)

[2] *Times*, July 28, 1835.

[3] *Times*, January 20, 1836.

[4] Founded by John Brook Revis, a local journalist. Report on Election Petitions. Ludlow. (1840, ix.), Mins. of Evidence, Q. 3188.

[5] *Times*, July 9, 1839. It had just celebrated its first anniversary.

[6] Cambridge town enjoyed a wide reputation for its political efficiency. One of the pillars of local Toryism was the banker, Field Dunn Barker, Chairman of the Municipal Registration Society. (Parl. Papers, 1840, ix., Cambridge.)

[7] *Times*, November 12, 1835.

[8] H. G. Knight to Peel, August 19, 1837. (Addit. MSS. 40,424.)

reaction in East Sussex. The Tory success in that constituency was achieved solely, so he states, by the good management of the Conservative Association.[1] A score of letters couched in similar terms are preserved among Peel's correspondence for this year.

The new movement was not confined to the forming of Conservative Associations among the county gentlemen or the shopkeepers of the boroughs. ' The formation of Conservative Associations,' writes an exuberant pamphleteer, ' quickly gave birth to the idea of extending the principle to the other classes of society, and accordingly, in process of time, the labouring classes and the tradesmen followed the example. Thus was the system of organization rendered complete, and now we behold the peer, the tradesman and the operative firmly united in the bonds of union and good fellowship.' [2]

A common tradition ascribes the origin of Conservative Operative Societies to Lancashire and the West Riding. In none of these things did London lead the way.[3] The foundation of the northern societies is attributed on doubtful grounds to the example furnished by Lord Brougham, whose solicitude for Mechanics' Institutes and Useful Knowledge was invariably regarded by contemporary Tories as a bid for popular support.[4]

[1] F. B. Bonham to Peel, September 23, 1837. (Addit. MSS. 40,424.)
[2] *Thoughts on the State and Prospects of Toryism, etc.* By ' R. S. S.' (1837).
[3] *Ibid.*
[4] The author regarded Mechanics' Institutes as thinly-disguised operative political clubs which Tories might with advantage imitate, and on which Operative Conservative Societies were actually modelled. ' Lord Brougham taught the Conservatives a new plan of disseminating their principles among the people, and the establishment of Conserva-

Leaving aside the exultant ecstasy of the pamphleteer there is a grain of truth in his remarks. The foundation of Mechanics' Institutes all over the country, though the movement failed completely in the rural districts, certainly made a considerable impression upon Tory thought of the day. Up to the period of the Reform Bill no Tory could possibly have conceived, much less tolerated, the idea of his party actively enlisting the assistance of the working classes in maintaining party supremacy in the constituencies. Such was outside his political comprehension until the presence of the Political Unions confronted him as an accomplished fact. Any apologist of Conservative Operative Societies before 1832 would have been dismissed as a dangerous revolutionary. It is significant that our pamphleteer of 1837 assumes that he is dealing with a novelty and must therefore explain how it was that ' we had taken up a weapon which we had always condemned.'[1]

Peel had nothing whatever to do with the creation of the original Conservative Operative Societies. These were begun in the boroughs and owed their origin to the threat of Reform. And it is worth while noticing that when pamphleteers of 1837-38 talk of the ' present spread of Operative Societies throughout the kingdom,' they appear to have forgotten that similar societies had been in existence in several of the greater boroughs since 1831 and may well have existed long before.

There is a tempting explanation of their lapse of memory. The early societies, those of the years of the

tive Associations and reading-rooms among the working population throughout the country has been the result.'

[1] *Thoughts on the State and Prospects of Toryism, etc.*

Reform struggle, were not simply 'Operative Societies' in the sense accepted in 1837. They were created for a much more sinister purpose than the alliance of peer, tradesman and operative ' in the bonds of union and good fellowship.' They were partly formed as auxiliaries to the Tory interest in the boroughs for the simple purpose of creating Tory freemen votes and for mobilizing a counterforce to Whig and Radical mobs.

It was this class of Tory society which principally exercised the attention of the Select Committee of 1835. The Bristol Society of Tory Freemen was formed in 1832, and, according to a witness, was a ' mere nucleus until the Reform Bill was passed.' The rules of this body loftily disclaim the least connection with party agents or election committees, but as this disclaimer was a political convention of the time, little reliance need be placed upon its literal accuracy. The rules state further that the aim of the Society was to secure employment for free burgesses in preference to strangers, which a hostile witness interpreted to mean that Tory voters might never lack employment.[1] Nominally, at any rate, this body claimed to be a Friendly Society, with the usual paraphernalia of sick, funeral and maternity benefits and scales of relief. Actually this branch of the Club's activities appeared to be completely dormant. It was governed by a joint committee of operatives and gentlemen in whom the property of the Society was vested. The latter were trustees.

One aspect of the activity of the Conservative Operative Societies was scarcely influenced at all by the passing of

[1] Roebuck in presenting a petition for Bristol, alleging Tory bribery, was perhaps nearer the mark when he declared that ' the object of this society was to " conserve " the mechanics of Bristol and to procure their services at future elections.' (*Hansard*, xxvii. 833, April 6, 1835.)

the Reform Bill. Not many weeks had elapsed since the General Election of January 1835, when the electors of Coventry received the following circular letter, dated the 2nd April of the new year, and of interest to electors and non-electors alike :—

> SIR,—A Society is commenced for the purpose of raising a fund to assist those friends of Conservative principles, who have not the means to take up the freedom of the City, in order that they may have a vote at an election, to add to the strength of that party . . .
>
> Mr. JOHN HUDSON, *Secretary*.[1]

The Bristol Society, founded in 1832, performed identical functions.[2] It was not the first time that Bristol Toryism found a political use for beef and beer. In the election of 1780, Burke found that he could do nothing against the Tory candidate, Lord Clare, who, during his long tenure of the City representation, made himself welcome to the lower class of voters by copious entertainments.[3] Nor was the progress of bribery in Parliamentary elections at first much affected by the Reforms of 1832. As the basis of the representation was broadened the influence of corruption was proportionately extended. The creation of freemen went on as before, and the methods of accommodating the middle-class voter were modified to suit new conditions.

---

[1] Report on Bribery at Elections (1835, viii.), Q. 1080.

[2] *Ibid.*, Q. 6578. Bristol Toryism had at least one virtue : when it sinned, it did so in public. After the result of the poll of January 1835 had been declared the *Bristol Journal* announced that over £800 would be distributed as Blue beef to Tory operatives to mark the triumph of their principles. The distribution of Blue beef, according to a witness before the Select Committee of 1835, was effected on the plan that ' they get no beef, those that split their votes.' (*Ibid.*, Q. 6830.)

[3] Latimer (J.), *Annals of Bristol, Eighteenth Century*, p. 444.

CONSERVATIVE PARTY ORGANIZATION

The Tory members for Liverpool seem to have found great favour among the old freemen of the town. The Shipwrights Club was a pseudo-Tory society, perhaps for the reason that Sir Howard Douglas' Committee had devoted large sums to the entertainment of the poorer voters. When a Select Committee of 1833 read from the statement of the accounts of recent Liverpool election costs that £196 appeared under the heading ' music,' and that a sum of £366, 4s. 6d. was devoted to the purchase of flags and ribands, members not unnaturally became suspicious.[1]

The work of placing freemen on Corporation rolls and mobilizing the Church-and-King rabble for Nomination Day could not be undertaken without cost. The Operative Conservative Society of Bristol was rightly suspected of doubtful practices. But like the old Conservative Societies in the other municipalities it owed its origin entirely to local influence.[2] Its funds were supplied by honorary members.[3]

The passing of the Reform Bill brought new problems of party government to the fore. Peel was among the first to recognize the tremendous potentialities of one of the direct consequences of Reform—the registration of voters ; and he made provision accordingly.[4] In the battle of the registration the Operative Society had a

[1] Report on Election Petitions, Liverpool. (1833, x.)
[2] Report on Bribery at Elections (1835, viii.), Q. 6803.
[3] *Ibid.*, Q. 6598.
[4] See his much-quoted letter to Arbuthnot, November 8, 1838 (in Parker's *Peel*, vol. ii. p. 368). Peel however was merely advising a course already adopted by the other party. A Reformers' Registration Committee began to serve out notices of objection to Conservative voters soon after the Reform Bill was passed. (Seymour (C.), *Electoral Reform in England and Wales* (1915), p. 134.)

definite part to play. 'My acquaintance with the Operative Conservative Societies,' wrote the author of the pamphlet quoted above, 'has taught me that active employment is highly necessary to their prosperity, if not to their future existence. Like a giant machine, they must be kept constantly in motion, or some part or other will become rusty.' [1]

The function of these societies is then set forth. They might assist the tradesmen's societies in attending to the borough registration. The tradesmen, with the assistance of legal agents, might form registration committees, while the Operative Societies might take upon themselves the responsibility of canvassing those parts of the town 'where the lower class of voters reside.' [2]

Thus by 1838 the Conservative party, pocketing its pride, was concentrating seriously upon the registration. All over the country societies of working men were coming into existence for the purpose. Even the agricultural constituencies were not excepted. Lord Chandos frankly told an audience at Brill in Oxfordshire the true reason for his coming to them : 'We have formed a Conservative Association for the district, having for its main object the placing on the register of electors all Conservatives qualified to be there, to defend the votes of those who are unfairly objected to, and to strike off as many of our opponents as are actually disqualified from being on that register.' [3]

The truth was that the forming of this obscure registration society among the humbler inhabitants of

---

[1] *Thoughts on the State and Prospects of Toryism, etc.*, by R. S. S. (1837).   [2] *Ibid.*
[3] *Times*, October 24, 1838.

the Chilterns was but one symptom of a movement proceeding parallel with that which brought to birth the Conservative associations among the gentry and the tradesmen. The Conservative Operative Society of 1835 had nothing in common with its less reputable predecessor of 1832. While the old True Blue Clubs, according to the needs of the time, served the interests principally of the Tory freemen of the boroughs, the new societies concentrated upon the Registration and the maintenance of party prestige. So great was the gulf between the old, unreformed societies of the boroughs and the recent creations of 1835, that the panegyrists of the latter imagined that the new type of Operative Conservative Society was the work of their own hands.

The distinction of being the first Conservative Operative Society under the new dispensation is claimed by Leeds. The printed rules of this society are dated February 1835.[1] The Society possessed a club-room of its own and rendered useful service in the municipal elections of 1838, when the first reformed Corporation was chosen. The rules afford a valuable indication of the point of view of the working-class members. After a preamble in which the operatives of Leeds ' acknowledge the Government and Being of God,' the rules proceed :

> We reverence the king and all in authority, and pay due deference and respect to all who are in high stations . . . because we believe that the different degrees and orders in Society are so closely united and interwoven with each other that, while we exalt them, we raise ourselves ; as,

[1] Paul (W.), *A History of the Origin and Progress of Operative Conservative Societies* (Leeds, 1839).

should we depress them, we proportionately lower ourselves. While we maintain their rights, we secure our own, and while we defend their privileges, we increase our own. We profess no sympathy with those persons who think they degrade themselves by giving ' to every man his due.' . . . We invite persons of true Conservative principles to unite with us ; especially we address this invitation to our brethren, the operatives. We ask them to aid us in our efforts to defend the rights of ' the ALTAR, the THRONE and the COTTAGE.'

Behind this crude, bombastic language there is a touch of native, West Riding fervour. Richard Oastler might well have inspired the framer of those rules.

After the example of Leeds, Operative Societies arose during the same year at Salford, Ripon, Barnsley, Bradford and in the surrounding villages.[1] In July the recently formed Manchester Operative Society announced its first public dinner.[2] The South Lancashire Conservatives founded an Operative Society—an offshoot from the parent body—in December.[3] Liverpool founded its Conservative Operative Society during the autumn.

Meanwhile the movement had travelled further afield. Throughout 1836 Operative Societies in a hundred centres were holding their first anniversary.

The subsequent history of these societies may be traced in the columns of provincial and London newspapers. In 1837 Leicester had Operative Committees in every

[1] Paul (W.), *A History of the Origin and Progress of Operative Conservative Societies.* Two years later the Barnsley Society, now equipped with library and news-room, was appealing for subscriptions and ' the patronage of those who move in a sphere of life above that of the ordinary run of its members.' (*Times*, September 9, 1837.)

[2] *Times*, July 29, 1835.

[3] *Times*, January 5, 1837.

ward, as well as a central body.[1] Next year Sir Francis
Burdett, now acclaimed as a ' perfect specimen of an
English country gentleman,' attended the third anniversary dinner of the Manchester society.[2] Salford held its
Operative Conservative Tea Party and Ball, which more
than 3000 guests attended, nine-tenths of them ladies,
so states the report.[3]

An important function of many of these Operative
Societies survived all the changes which came over
political party organization after 1832. This was the
prudential function. Not a few of the new societies
copied their forerunners of Unreformed days in maintaining club funds for the relief of sickness and unemployment. In 1842 the Conservative member for Lewes, in
evidence before the Select Committee on Election Petitions,[4] stated that there were about ten different benefit
clubs in Lewes, to all of which political necessity compelled him to subscribe. Chief among these were the
Constitutional Pruning Club and the Liberal *Bundle of
Sticks Society*, the earlier of the two. The Constitutional
Pruning Club was reputedly a benefit society for poor
men ; of 850 electors in Lewes between 100 and 200
were members.[5] An ordinary labouring member paid
2s. or 2s. 3d. a month. If disabled he was allowed a
guinea a week ; if his wife died he got £5 to bury her,
or if he himself died his wife could claim £7 to bury
him. Surpluses, if any, were divided yearly and there
was an annual dinner. Obviously a club run on these

---

[1] *Ibid.*
[2] *Times,* April 20, 1838. [3] *Times,* April 23, 1838.
[4] 1842, v., Q. 1163 (H. Fitzroy, M.P.).
[5] *Ibid.,* Qs. 1473 and 1474 (Briggs).

lines could not pay its own way. Richer Conservatives, in fact, provided most of the funds.[1] With a few notable exceptions the new Conservative Operative Societies were subsidized from outside. The ' Blue Beef ' tradition of former days continued with some persistence. No one could imagine that the sumptuous dinners provided by the operative Ward Committees of Leicester were not paid for by the wealthier Townsmen.[2] Nor would it be concluded that many members of the Operative Conservative Society of Oldham were expected to pay the five shillings a head for their third anniversary dinner.[3]

In attempting to discover who provided for the running expenses of the new Operative Conservative Societies, we touch a leading principle of Peelite party organization. A prevalent contemporary opinion credited the Carlton Club with bearing the burden of the subsidy. At present there is no evidence to point one way or the other.[4] There are no grounds for supposing that the Carlton Club, in its collective capacity, was in the habit of contributing to the maintenance of any particular local society. There are fairly solid reasons for the assump-

[1] 1842, v., Qs. 1480-1485 (Briggs). Banbury Conservatives founded a Conservative Friendly Society in 1837. Its members seem to have been working men. (*Rules for the Regulations and Government of a Conservative Friendly Society, etc.*, 1837.)

[2] *Times*, January 5, 1837. (From the *Leicester Herald*) ' We understand the dinners at each house are to consist of roast beef and plumpudding at the top of the table, and a boiled leg of mutton and turnips at the bottom. What can be better ? '

[3] *Times*, January 8, 1838.

[4] Further light may be thrown on the matter when the remaining volumes of the Peel Papers, now being catalogued in the British Museum, are rendered available for research. The existing catalogues of the Carlton Club Library offer no clue.

tion that subsidies proceeded from another source. It is probable, judging from the general temper of Tory politics in the constituencies, that any systematic payment by the Carlton Club would have been regarded as an unwarrantable arrogation of authority by a London political organization, and would have been bitterly resented by local Tories, who still almost universally held the view that local patronage begins at home. The assumption therefore is that the local gentry, members of the well-to-do Conservative Associations, and not the party headquarters, found the money. The work of the Carlton Club in the provinces was limited to the management of elections ; beyond that its authority was at an end.

It is to Peel's credit that, in constructing his vast political machine, he carried out the work with the minimum of error. The greatest mistake which he could possibly have committed would have been that of over-centralization. Had he attempted to make his London headquarters an absolute bureaucracy, he would soon have broken the Conservative party in pieces. How nearly the party approached disaster may be estimated from the following letter from Bonham to Peel. Referring to certain advances which were being made by one Hunter, a disreputable newspaper promoter, he writes : ' I hope that Lord Sandon has not allowed himself to be duped by him as (between ourselves) *he was* about a National Conservative Association, of which many of us, under the sanction of his name, have not yet absolutely escaped the consequences in the shape of various threatened actions.' [1]

[1] January 7, 1838. (Addit. MSS. 40,424.)

Another portentous piece of folly (had it succeeded) would have been the attempt made by a group of Young Tory hotheads to outrival the Reformers' Registration Committee by a central organization to control the Conservative registration campaign from London. 'Perhaps you may have heard,' Bonham continues, 'that some more zealous than wise friends of ours, Lords Strangford, Exmouth, De Lisle, Bob Scarlett, Disraeli, formed themselves into what they called a " Registration Committee " to *manage* the registration of the Empire !!!' [1]

By avoiding such mistakes as these, and by that untiring energy which Peel and his Whips devoted to the party machine, Peelite Conservatism marched towards office in 1841. In that year the fortunes of the Conservative party were at their highest. Marked approval was coming in from unexpected quarters. From its editorial offices in Leeds O'Connor's *Northern Star*, while confusedly denouncing the Cobbettites and Tory Chartists, found itself bound to cater for a working-class public which was by no means hostile to a return of political Conservatism to power. Even O'Connor made friendly reference to Disraeli's Shrewsbury candidature in the election of July 1841. [2] The Chartist Pitkeithly in his political addresses, while rabidly attacking the Whigs, had nothing bad to say of the Tories. [3]

A fortunate coincidence added strength to the Conservative position during the last years of the tottering administration of Melbourne. This was the Tory-Pro-

[1] January 7, 1838. (Addit. MSS. 40,424.)
[2] *Northern Star*, July 3, 1841.
[3] *Ibid*. Despite his friend O'Connor's dislike of Cobbett, Pitkeithly was 'somewhat of the Cobbett school of Politics' himself. (Gammage (R. G.), *History of the Chartist Movement* (1894), p. 64.)

testant connection. Protestant England had for some time murmured against the reputed Popish sympathies of the Whig Government. The Conservative Opposition, hard on the heels of Whig policy in Ireland, automatically drew towards itself considerable Protestant support in this country. People had not forgotten Catholic Emancipation—they had temporarily forgotten Peel's part in it—and the Protestant cause possessed an electoral value of which Peel was quick to avail himself. Next to denouncing the New Poor Law there was nothing a Conservative Operative Society enjoyed better than to welcome a Protestant delegation hot from Ireland. Formerly, in the days when Reform was the one great question for election campaigns, Tory candidates and their followers were accustomed to explain that the issue was between the friends and the enemies of the Church, when a Sandon or a Douglas would assure the Liverpool Freeman that ' Real True Blues and Loyal Jacks would cut a nice appearance by being represented by Radicals —Chaps without Religion or Loyalty.' [1] By 1838 the field of battle had narrowed and the issue was now between Protestantism and Popery. In this year we find the South Hampshire Conservatives deciding to celebrate their recent electoral victory by building a church, a work ' more congenial with those Protestant and Christian principles which form the basis of true Conservatism.' [2] Indeed, there are cases in which it is difficult to distinguish Conservative and Protestant societies. Conservative Associations, meeting on Monday evenings, so

[1] From a Poster. (Report on Election Petitions, Liverpool, 1833, x., Q. 5847.)
[2] *Times*, January 15, 1838.

often reappeared as Protestant Societies on the following Thursdays. For years there existed the closest amity between the Protestant Associations of London and the Metropolitan Conservative Society.[1]

At the same time the official Conservative party organization held scrupulously aloof from a formal union with the more extreme Protestants who followed the Duke of Cumberland. In 1835 the equivocal activities of the Orange Societies were made the subject of Parliamentary inquiry.[2] Documents printed with the Report confirm the opinion of the Committee that in 1833 the Orangemen were making desperate attempts to create a Conservative-Orange alliance. The Committee cite an ' Address to the Members of the Carlton Club and the Conservatives in England ' in support of their contention.[3] This Address makes a political and not a religious appeal. ' The Orange Institution is the only society peculiar to Great Britain and Ireland, which already includes individuals of every rank and grade, from the nearest to the Throne to the poorest peasant. This society is useful for the purposes of intercourse between the higher and lower orders . . . a time may come, nay is not far distant, when a combination against all property . . . must be repelled by organized loyalty ; what better means of co-operation can be offered them than the Orange Institution ? '

This does not imply that the Conservative party leaders and the Carlton Club in any sense desired to be parties to such an alliance. When Colonel Fairman, a leading

---

1 *Church of England Quarterly Review*, October 1838, p. 625.
2 Parl. Papers (1835, xvii.).
3 Parl. Papers (1835, xvii.), Report, pp. xvii-xviii. The Address is reprinted in full in App. xiv. p. 114.

Orangeman, told the Committee that the Loyal Orange Institution and the Carlton Club were so interwoven that the difference of name was of no consequence, he was artfully attempting to gain prestige for Orangeism by connecting it with the Conservative party.[1] The Committee declined to make much play with the Judas-kiss of this doubtful friend of Conservatism. Even Hume, who raked among the appendices of the Report for evidence of a Tory-Protestant union, contented himself with the mild allegation that the Duke of Cumberland's party in 1831 had contemplated the political use of No-Reform mobs in the service of No-Popery.[2] None of the correspondence quoted by Hume indicates the least connection between Orangeism and the Conservative Operative Societies. Peel's own attitude towards the Orange movement removes the last suspicion.[3]

The alliance between the friends of the Church and the Conservative party is but one of many illustrations of the centripetal action of Peel's Conservative policy. The great interests making for law and order gradually awoke to the fact that they were not alone. The popularity of the new Conservative organization in the provinces, especially among the working classes, revealed that Peel was riding in the saddle of a nation-wide reaction against the insecurity of unlicensed Radicalism and Reform.[4]

---

[1] *Ibid.* Mins. of Evidence, Q. 472.

[2] *Hansard,* xxxi. 779, February 23, 1836.

[3] The Committee of the Protestant Operative Association and Reformation Society abused Peel for referring disparagingly to numerous addresses which that body had sent him. (Addit. MSS. 40,540.)

[4] For a treatment of this theme from the side of religion, see Halévy (E.), *Histoire du peuple anglais au xixe siècle,* tome iii. (1923) ; and from

TORYISM AND THE PEOPLE

It is not easy to point to the first rift appearing in the fabric of the Conservative party. Long before 1845 prophets foretold the dissolution of the bonds which held the party together. It was, in fact, at the very moment when Peelite Conservatism appeared to have reached its maximum degree of efficiency that the first symptoms of cleavage appeared.

Looking over the panorama of years between 1832 and 1846 and attempting a just survey, one may take it for granted that a break was bound to come. In the complicated structure which Peel had built were two components mutually incapable of amalgamation—the older Toryism and the new Progressive Conservatism. Once the storm arose the structure would crash in pieces. ' On reflecting on all that has passed,' wrote Peel after the crash had come, ' I am much more surprised that the union was so long maintained than that it was ultimately severed.' [1] It was due to the genius of Peel that the end was so long delayed.

It is conceivable that Peel sacrificed too much in his efforts to build up a powerful party machine. He was, of course, tactless. He was tactless in small matters. When the whole Tory world was protesting that ' Brougham's ' Mechanics' Institutes represented an ideal in education to which Tories were strangers and which Tories literally loathed, Peel must needs blunder into the Tamworth Reading Room to make a speech upon the glorious fruits of Useful Knowledge. Newman's friends of the *British*

the legal side, Dicey (A. V.), *Lectures on the Relation between Law and Public Opinion in England during the Nineteenth Century* (1905), Lectures VI., VII.

[1] Parker's *Peel*, vol. ii. p. 347.

Critic hinted that ' if all the Institutes in the kingdom were to putrify into " Operative Conservative Clubs," and in that happy state of perfection were able to turn the scale at the election, Sir Robert would be the last to deplore so sad a reverse to the cause of science.' [1] Peel might have realized the dangers involved in a break with Oxford and the greater part of the Clergy.

The work of keeping the party together was not always unhindered by signs of mutiny within. It seems hardly to have been realized at the time how near the party came to disaster during the summer of 1835, when the Right Wing, exasperated by the Corporations Bill, threatened to leave their official leaders to range themselves behind Sir Richard Vyvyan. More trouble came with the Irish Corporations Bill in 1837. Again in 1841, hardly a month after the General Election, the Tory malcontents were showing their teeth.[2]

Nor did the party mechanism at Westminster always run smoothly upon its way. The General Election of August 1837 had revealed a certain animosity existing against the personnel and the tactics of the Whips' Office. There were complaints of the autocratic behaviour of William Holmes,[3] Peel's trusted henchman, which may have been by implication a complaint of Peel's high-handed discipline. Sir George Clerk, the Conservative Chief Whip, had been defeated for Midlothian, and hostile sections of the party feared that Holmes would succeed him. By a timely concession Peel relegated Holmes to

[1] *British Critic*, vol. xxx. p. 86, July 1841.
[2] Arbuthnot to Peel, August 6, 1841. (Addit. MSS. 40,484.)
[3] Lord Granville Somerset to Peel, August 9, 1837. (Addit. MSS. 40,424.)

a secondary position in the Whips' Office and placed Sir Thomas Freemantle over them both.

By the time of Peel's Corn Bill of 1842 it became apparent to all the world that something was not working properly in the Conservative machine. Rumours of dislocation were reaching the enemy's camp ; and those who in 1840 had been lamenting the apparent permanence of Peel's power and ' the docile idiots behind him who cheered his platitudes,' now in 1843 were exulting over the unpopularity of the Prime Minister among even his own followers.[1]

Signs of unrest among the members of the Parliamentary party there certainly were. On February 25, 1842, Peel carried his Corn Resolutions by an immense majority. Sir Richard Vyvyan, Mr. Blackstone, and Lord Ossulston left the House together, determined no longer to support their leader.[2] In the same month the Duke of Buckingham resigned the Privy Seal. Disraeli talked disconsolately of a thunderbolt in the summer sky and wrote to his wife—' Before the change of Government political party was a tie among men, but now it is only a tie among men who are in office.' [3]

Sir Richard Vyvyan typified the grievances of the rebels in a letter to his Cornish constituents written within a few weeks of his break with Peel.[4] This letter was the herald of the Tory revolt from Peelite discipline,

---

[1] *Lady Palmerston and her Times*, vol. ii. pp. 65, 96.
[2] Monypenny (W. F.), *Life of Benjamin Disraeli, Earl of Beaconsfield* (1912), vol. ii. p. 125.
[3] *Ibid.*
[4] A letter from Sir Richard Vyvyan, Bart., M.P., to his Constituents, upon the Commercial and Financial Policy of Sir Robert Peel's Administration (1842).

and the specific charges which it contains were to be re-echoed three years later by Disraeli and Bentinck in their fierce tirades. Vyvyan complained of the dictatorial influence of the party whips and of the iron discipline exacted by the Minister. He condemned the Conservative party as an attempt 'to convert a body of high-minded noblemen and gentlemen into a regiment of partisans.' And as for the Carlton Club and the 'cabals' which tended more and more to direct the political life of the country, 'they have extended the influence of party, and brought it upon the hustings of almost every constituency in the United Kingdom.' It was only too clear that Peel, in spite of Arbuthnot's advice that 'it always gives satisfaction to the supporters to appear to be consulted,'[1] did not trouble the party with over-consultation in 1842, when he passed measures which three-quarters of them heartily disliked.

In the constituencies political discord began to raise its head. Scottish lords were writing apprehensively of the drift of Peel's fiscal policy.[2] And in the industrial North Tories were beginning to feel the strain of confinement within the narrow bounds of the Peelite machine. Had the Conservative leaders but realized it, Toryism, though crushed in the enlightened centres, still lived on in those obscure country places where the organizing skill of the party agent had never made headway. There were wild places along the Pennines and on the moors where the names of Progress and Reform were accursed of the people, districts in which the rude populations had

---

[1] Arbuthnot to Peel, August 6, 1841. (Addit. MSS. 40,484.)
[2] *Ibid.*, March 31, 1842. (Addit. MSS. 40,484.)

never acquiesced in the Industrial Revolution. Northern Toryism had little in common with the new commercial policy of the Conservative leaders ; and Richard Oastler, speaking to a generation of rough, common men who had not yet lost all trace of their connection with the land, drew large mobs into railing against the times. 'Loyal and Constitutional' Conservative Associations as far back as 1838 were opening their doors to the militant and resentful Toryism of the West Riding orators.

Oastler's Toryism must have sounded strange to the ears of the new *bourgeoisie* which Peelite Conservatism in fact originated to attract. At an annual dinner of the Huddersfield Conservative Association Oastler, to the delight of his audience, gloried in the gulf which a wise dispensation had placed between the ' snod-faced Dissenter ' and the Tory ' who lived a healthy and moral life, though when he did transgress he sinned openly.' [1] And after fulminating in this vein against the ' modern days of Whiggery and Dissent ' he soundly trounced the aristocracy for their refusal to lead the people. So Richard Oastler was anticipating Young England by five years.

In 1843 the Peelite machine became deranged in all its parts. The strain upon it was excessive. The Conservative Operative Societies, fostered by the party leaders for the purpose of adding strength to their provincial following, showed no sign of accompanying the Peelite members along the road to compromise and ultimate Free Trade. For the greater part they remained staunchly

---

[1] Speech of R. Oastler, Esq., April 20, 1838. (Home Office Records, 40, 453.)

CONSERVATIVE PARTY ORGANIZATION

Protectionist, not only in the northern districts directly under the regal sway of Richard Oastler and the Tory squires of Yorkshire and Lancashire, but among the agricultural counties of the South and Midlands.

With 1844 came a host of Protectionist pamphleteers violently denouncing Peel.[1] Men were beginning to ask for what purpose the Peelite machine was maintained. Tory members were chafing under the despotism of the Carlton Club and hardly disguised their anger.[2]

Disraeli, who during Peel's ministry had maintained close contact with Vyvyan and the Tory malcontents, saw that the end was not far off. The future master of political organization poured mild scorn upon a party machine founded on no coherent principle. A passage in *Coningsby* reflected something of the feeling within the party when the machine began to run out of gear.

' " You are in as great peril now as you were in 1830," said Coningsby.

' " No, no, no," said Lord Monmouth ; " the Tory party is organized now ; they will not catch us napping again : these Conservative Associations have done the business."

' " But what are they organized for ? " said Coningsby. " At best to turn out the Whigs." ' [3]

---

[1] Including several in which Peel, Industrialism, and Political Economy are condemned without discrimination. Of these see, *Is the strong Heart of England broken that she does not rise ? Being a few words upon the want of high principle exhibited by the public men of the present day ; and some remarks upon the tergiversation of the periodical press* (1844).

[2] *A Letter from Sir Richard Vyvyan, etc.,* p. 32.

[3] Disraeli (B.), *Coningsby* (1844), bk. viii. ch. 3.

' " How pitiable," reflected Newman, " that such a man should not have understood that a body without a soul has no life, and a political party without an idea no unity." ' [1]

The opening of 1846 saw the machine irremediably broken, and the Tories had the mortification of observing that the builder and the destroyer was the same person. The Carlton Club, the very headquarters of the machine, became the seat of disaffection and confusion. So great was the ruin that Bentinck, Stanley and Disraeli had to begin rebuilding the Conservative party from its foundations.

From the foregoing review of the relation between the Tory party and the Conservative political machine three conclusions follow :—

The first is that the development of Conservative Operative Societies and Working Men's Conservative Associations was not an isolated event in the domestic history of the party, but an integral phase of Peel's policy for widening the basis of Conservative support in the constituencies.

The second is that the unstable character of Peel's connection with the Tory group, combined with Tory prejudice against highly developed party organizations, rendered any full co-operation in working the Conservative party machine, and with it the Conservative Operative Societies, increasingly difficult.

The third is that the nature of these Operative Societies, their composition, their function, and position in the

[1] (Pseud. ' Catholicus '), *Letters on an Address delivered by Sir Robert Peel, Bart., M.P., on the Establishment of a Reading Room at Tamworth* (1841), Letter VII.

party, precluded their reflecting in the constituencies the trend of Tory policy in Parliament.

It may be asked whether, had the old Tory wing of 1832 possessed the semblance of a political organization, it could have escaped the fall, and maintained its integrity as a definite party in the State.

It was clearly impossible. Where even the will to organize was lacking there could be no talk of an active, consolidated Right Wing. The Tories of 1846 felt that the very ground on which they stood was being cut from beneath them. They were unskilled in fostering popular movements and ignorant of the arts of propaganda, and in consequence they were politically impotent.

The Tories had gone into the Reform struggle with a bias against organization. For twelve years Peel had forced them to organize for their very lives as a parliamentary party. And now, when 1845 gave way to the fatal year, they found that the disintegration of the party was at hand. Left to themselves they were incapable of political union. With redoubled energy, Cobden smashed them with his Free Trade press, his propaganda and his campaigns. With no defence against the dialectical supremacy of their opponents, they sought refuge in a blind and hopeless resistance.

Peel's political suicide wrought havoc in the party machine. With a forgivable excess of piety a kinsman wrote of him that ' he touched the dry bones of the Tory party, giving thereto a new life and a new name, and, if it might be, a wider purpose.' [1] Tories who lived nearer the time knew better. ' He has divided you,

[1] Summary of the life of Sir Robert Peel by his grandson, the Hon. George Peel. (In Parker's *Peel*, vol. iii. p. 561.)

and sunk you, and made you ashamed of your name, and that is all which Peel has done for the very party which worships him.' [1]   Richard Oastler came nearer to the truth.   Toryism by 1846 was fast becoming a memory, and memories cannot be organized.

[1] ' To the People of England ' (1838) in Home Office Papers, 4040.

CHAPTER III

TORYISM AND THE POLITICAL
ASPIRATIONS OF THE WORKING CLASSES

THE Tory party no longer showed a solid phalanx to the
world when the forces of Reform opened their overwhelming assault in 1830. It was rather a demoralized
rabble which had with difficulty dragged itself from the
disasters of 1827 and 1829. The memory of Canning
and Catholic Emancipation had left it broken by domestic
convulsion. The condition of the Tory party when
Reform became the paramount political question was
one of impotent distress.

The short but bitter struggle over the Reform Bill
provides useful material for the study of political propaganda, one of the chief destroyers of the Tory party.
During the few months of high excitement which preceded the passing of the Bill, Reform had become a
national obsession. Oastler, at this time working for
the Factory Bill, told Sadler's Committee that it was
almost dangerous in a popular assembly to propound
any question but that of Reform.[1] It was a period in
which emancipation from the boroughmongers became
the theme of every Reformer. Political emancipation

---

[1] Report on the Regulation of the Labour of Children in Mills and
Factories in the United Kingdom (1831-32, xv.). Mins. of Evidence,
Q. 9802.

captured the imagination of the public to an extent which made Catholic or Slave Emancipation seem paltry and insignificant. To the orator the subject of Reform possessed untold dialectical advantages over any other question. Commending Brougham for his recent pamphlet, *Thoughts on the Aristocracy*, which Brougham had published under the pseudonym of *Isaac Tomkins*, James Mill drew attention playfully to the honour which came of being a Reformer : ' These emancipations are the things to get permanent glory by, and Isaac Tomkins knows it.' [1]

In the general heat of public passion all sense of proportion was lost. Birmingham politicians took upon themselves the responsibility of dictating terms from home. Moralists pointed sententiously to the signs in the sky. ' A great change,' wrote one, ' is working over even the surface of things. Fashion within the last twelve months has been shaken on her throne. Among the great events of the time frivolities have ceased to charm. People talk no more about Almack's and fine ladies ; and Agitation, which works in good as in evil, has done this much—it has called forth the higher, the graver, the steadier properties of the English character.' [2] A host of local poets, in wretched verse, adjure the people of England to defy

' the scoffing sneers
of heartless placemen and tyrannic peers.' [3]

The tyrant was to be made aware of his impending

---

[1] Mill to Brougham, June 1833. (Bain (A.), *James Mill, A Biography* (1882), p. 380.)

[2] *Sheffield Courant*, January 6, 1832. (Quoted from *New Monthly*.)

[3] *Sheffield Courant*, June 8, 1832. By Ebenezer Elliott.

doom.   On the eve of the Bristol riots Alderman Daniel, the leader of the local Tory party, went down to William Herapath, ' the president of a numerous working-class organization known as the Political Union,' bearing from the Common Council a request for help in keeping public order in the event of emergency.   His appeal was scornfully refused.[1]

When the result of the Lords' division in June 1832 became known, the country went mad with exultation. Even the intellectuals were carried away in transports of enthusiasm.   ' They are gone,' cried a Sheffield orator, ' Gatton and Old Sarum, Middlehurst and the rest of them with their appurtenances.'   Their ruins ' will be devoted to the pasturage of sheep instead of to the septennial orgies of political usurpation.'[2]   And the party rhymster babbled in precarious rhapsody of :

> ' Mind's great Charter !   Europe saved !
> Man *for ever* unenslav'd ! '[3]

' In this country,' wrote Lord Talbot mournfully to Mr. Secretary Gregory, ' the Conservative interest is beaten out of sight.   The Radical is the strongest interest of the day.'[4]

The Reformers, being men of faith, took themselves very seriously.   They had an unquestioning confidence in the rectitude of their cause, which from a distance of almost a century seems almost incredible.   In their

[1] Latimer (J.), *Annals of Bristol, Nineteenth Century,* p. 149.
[2] *Sheffield Mercury and Hallamshire Advertiser,* December 15, 1832.
[3] *Sheffield Courant,* June 22, 1832.   By Ebenezer Elliott.   The last ' *Mind's great Charter* ' had been peremptorily thrown out by the Lords in the preceding October.
[4] December 24, 1832.   (*Mr. Gregory's Letter-Box, 1813-1830* (1898), p. 323.)

simplicity they imagined that all events of the past two centuries were working up to the climax of Reform. There was a universal desire to make history accord with the new facts, and Reform brought with it nothing less than a new interpretation of history. There was much talk of ' awakening the masses of the people from the political slumbers in which they had lain since the time of Hampden and Cromwell.' [1]

A distinguishing mark of the political outlook of the Liberal and Reforming school was its tendency towards a rationalizing of political principles. Though the Reform Bill, purely from the necessities of the case, partook of the character of ' a patchwork of opportunism,' it was generally recognized that the solution of 1832 was only the first of a long chain of franchise reforms.[2]

And yet, for all the rationalizing tendencies of the time, there was no school of political thought which was productive of more obscurantism than that of Liberalism in the early nineteenth century. Nobody was readier than Jeremy Bentham to detect mysticism and metaphysics in political science and in jurisprudence, yet it was Bentham's immediate disciples who evolved one of the most portentous of politico-metaphysical systems since the time of Rousseau. There may be said to have existed during the greater part of the nineteenth century a ' metaphysics of Reform.' Mill, in his *Essay on Liberty*, excelled himself in building those impalpable castles in which contemporary writers upon representative institu-

---

[1] It is surprising to find that Redlich treats this passage not as reflecting a prevalent sentiment of the time, but as a statement of fact, and incorporates it in his text. (*English Local Government*, vol. i. p. 61.)

[2] *Ibid.*, vol. i. pp. 82, 83.

tions delighted to dwell. Even Cobbett, who set out to be a realist, who despised shams, more than once fell a victim to the intellectual shortcomings of his age and concealed himself in the twilight of mysticism and mental obscurity.

Here, however, was an end to the vagueness of their political speculations. In their day-to-day political activity the adherents of Liberal Reform were, as a body, eminently practical men. The triumphant party of 1832 was moderate in all its actions. A middle-class electorate, though swelling with pride at its newly-won electoral importance, dared not afford itself the luxury of political violence. It is open to serious doubt whether the threat on the part of Political Unions to take up arms if the Lords threw out the Bill would ever have been translated into terms of direct action. It can scarcely be believed that the Birmingham worthies, Joseph Parkes, Thomas Attwood, and their friends, though they took themselves so seriously, were prepared to be shot on the barricades for the sake of Schedule B or the ten-pound freeholder. To suggest that, as a nation, we mean what we say in election campaigns, is to mistake the character of Englishmen. One can no more imagine Muntz fighting his way to Westminster than imagine the hot-headed Duke of Cumberland appearing in the Mall at the head of a Protestant and Ultra-Tory army to place himself on the throne of the young Victoria.[1] Even the Birmingham Political Union, the one body in the country, if there was one, which might be thought capable of a military revolution, stopped far short of musketry. ' I know

[1] The possibility discussed in Halévy (E.), *Histoire du peuple anglais au xixe siècle*, tome iii. (1923), p. 180.

every leader of the Union,' wrote Parkes to George Grote, ' I know they do not mean to lead the people, and will not.' The reason was plain enough, as this ardent Reformer added in the same letter—' there is not sufficient virtue in even the best part of the people to resist and to enforce their rights.' [1]

During the Reform struggle the corporate political intelligence of Labour may safely be regarded as dormant. The working classes produced no theories of consequence that were not coloured by bourgeois ideals. The working classes had, in fact, little or no independent notions on political subjects. At Birmingham the Trades followed in the wake of Attwood, Muntz and Scholefield, and joined the Political Union ; at Bristol the Trades were for no one party.[2] Of the daily thoughts of the working classes on the point, we have little enough of evidence. So far as they thought at all on political matters they appear to have given general approval to the Reform Bill. Occasionally there was an outburst of extremism ; a Richard Carlile or an Orator Hunt would appear for a time and then go forgotten. But, generally speaking, the labouring classes accepted without question the Reformers' interpretation of the controversy. Anti-bourgeois, anti-capitalistic literature was then scarcely noticed by the masses, although Tom Paine was everywhere quoted.

The attitude of the popular tribunes towards the

---

[1] Buckley (J. R.), *Joseph Parkes of Birmingham* (1926), p. 89.

[2] The Sheffield Trades with their regalia made common causes with the local Political Union in Reform processions (*Sheffield Courant*, June 8, 1832). The Bristol Trades were divided, and held rival Whig and Tory meetings. (Report on Bribery at Elections, 1835, viii., Q. 7007.)

question of the political representation of the labouring classes hardly gave cause for confidence. The leaders of the local Political Unions were, often as not, bourgeois. Hunt, who has been called the first authentic representative in Parliament of the Radical masses, spent all his force denouncing the Bill up and down the country, telling the workers that they were being betrayed. Then, when the Bill came before the House, Hunt meekly voted in its favour. Even the Birmingham Political Union had nothing positive to contribute ; the reputation of having successfully intimidated the Government lay heavily upon its provincial soul.

All the intellectual impetus of the Reform movement was provided by bourgeois leaders, while the actual framing of the Bills themselves owed much to aristocratic draughtsmanship. The ideas of the working classes who supported Reform had been prepared for them by others. A mere remnant, even of the crowd which met at the Rotunda, took their catchwords from Hunt and Carlile. Cobbett alone of the people's orators came forward with a coherent democratic plan of Reform— universal manhood suffrage and the removal of pecuniary qualifications for members of Parliament.[1]

The master spirits of the movement, whether of the group of Lord John Russell, of Brougham, or of Joseph Parkes, were not prepared to pay too heavy a price for the co-operation of the working classes. Cobbett and Hunt might talk as they wished of universal manhood suffrage, but any practical step towards the establishment of an electoral democracy was immediately arrested by the Parliamentary leaders of Reform.

[1] *Political Register*, October 1830.

Political Reform, in the sense understood by the Moderates, implied anything but universal suffrage. Roebuck, in the course of an exposition of Radical-Liberal electoral views, thus explained his faith : ' Although I be one who believes that no good Government can be attained without the concurrence of the people . . . still I am far from believing that the golden age will be attained merely by creating a democratic government.' [1]

' You never heard me,' Cobden told the House of Commons, ' quote the superior judgement of the working classes in any deliberations in this assembly.' [2] James Mill, a pupil of the strictest school of Benthamism, had nothing but contempt for the popular movement which Attwood led. He would have the newspapers ' suppress all knowledge of these rascally meetings by abstaining from mention of them.' [3] So much for the views of two avowed disciples of Political Reason and Liberal Reform.

Alison's conviction that the downfall of civilized society would quickly follow the political ascendancy of the masses was shared by a large body of educated Radical opinion.[4] While the prevalent Liberal doctrine, that universal suffrage was the guarantee of governmental authority, enjoyed widespread popularity, expediency demanded an educated body of electors, and the educated— even the readers of Roebuck's *Political Pamphlets*—were by no means universal. No wonder that an illiterate

[1] *Hansard*, xx. 145, July 30, 1833.
[2] *Hansard*, lxxxiv. 281, February 27, 1846.
[3] J. Mill to Brougham. In Bain's *Mill*, pp. 363-4.
[4] Except that Allison based all true authority on an undefined aristocracy of rank and intelligence, while the moderate Radicals, by implication, placed authority on a very definite aristocracy of the educated middle classes.

son of the people complained to Place that Roebuck's *Pamphlets* had become 'the Instrument to publish the Opinions of a set of Starving Political Economists,'[1] or that the Handloom Worsted Weavers' Central Committee drew up a manifesto on *Political Economy versus the Handloom Weavers*, with special reference to Roebuck.[2]

In one particular only were the Reformers prepared to accept a radical change in the generally current electoral doctrine received in this country. And this was in the function of the elected representative. Was a member of Parliament to be regarded as a representative or as a delegate?

Adherents of the theory of delegation stoutly denied that they were sponsors to a revolutionary principle. Antiquarians among the Intellectuals of the Reform movement produced historical evidence to prove that Parliament had only of recent time ceased to be a delegate body, and that the supersession of its ancient representative function by the grosser prejudices of a corrupt age was due to the monopoly of the representation by boroughmongers and placemen.

In spite of its alleged antiquity the delegation theory has rightly been considered as Radical in its origin. However limited may have been the restrictions placed by a Plantagenet shire or borough upon its representative at Westminster, the fact was the Plantagenet Parliament was in no sense a sovereign body. And when Reform candidates appeared on the hustings in 1831 and 1832 assuring their potential constituents that they were but instruments whereby to work the will of the electors,

---

[1] Cray (R.) to Place (F.), undated (1835) in Place Collection, vol. 52.
[2] *Weekly Police Gazette*, May 11, 1835, in Place Collection, vol. 52.

scandal was caused among the adherents of the more Conservative doctrine.

To this the Tory party had nothing to say. It was the party attacked, and not the attacker. It had no time for speculation or indeed for attending to the literary merits of policies. To the average uninstructed Tory the doctrines of Reform were unintelligible, the delegation theory positively dangerous. The Tory view of the British Constitution had the disadvantage of being clear in all but theory. Had Tories found a suitable phraseology expressive of their ideas in 1832, the subsequent history of Electoral Reform might have told a different tale.

Ultimately the attitude which the Parliamentary Tory party adopted towards the whole question of Reform, whether towards the ' Meliorist ' reform proposed by the friends of Grey and Russell or that so passionately advocated by O'Connor and the *Northern Star*, depended on the Tory conception of political authority.

Bentham implied that the guarantee of the governor's authority lay in the expressed consent of the governed. His Whig and Liberal disciples, in varying degrees, placed what his contemporaries called sovereignty in a duly-elected Parliament. They looked upon law as the reflection of the universal will of the people, and though their politicians expressed themselves in cruder terms, this was their belief.

Tories approached the problems of Government authority from another angle. Authority to the Tory was not a matter of a general election at all. Sovereignty, if that elusive idea was to be found anywhere, lay in the mixed constitution of King, Lords and Commons. The electorate was too vague a conception for use in the world of political fact. There was no greater danger in Reform than the tying of the hands of Parliament, which after all was only half of it elective. Reformers in placing undue emphasis upon election were faced with the possibility, which they scorned to consider, that a reformed electorate might, after all, be no more representative of the whole people than the old corrupt, exclusive electorate of unreformed days. There was no adequate guarantee that a body of representatives drawn from the mercantile and middle classes would consider the interests of the classes above or below them any more than those servile, nominated members whom Reformers justly detested. In other words, the Reformed Parliament of Grey and Russell and Brougham might well be as much a class Parliament as that of Liverpool, Eldon, and the Duke. Universal suffrage, condemned by Tories as a form of political madness based on a fundamental ignorance of the structure of English society, was at least intelligible. Suffrage confined within the limits of the ' respectable classes ' was certainly not.

The difference was one of political values. To the Reformer election by the people was the hall-mark of authority and the *sine qua non* of legitimate Government. To the Tory election meant little more than an unseemly, though necessary, formality to enable the natural leaders of the people to assume control—a formality which did the elected member little temporal good and a great deal of moral harm. The one regarded the exercise of the franchise almost as a sacred political rite ; the other viewed it as a minor evil, one of the petty shortcomings of an otherwise perfect Constitution in Church and State.

TORYISM AND THE PEOPLE

Tories were condemned for their failure to appreciate the necessity for Reform. But this argument is superficial. There were deeper reasons why to the Tories Reform should appear as a second-rate political question. The Tory regarded the problem of government from an angle entirely different from that of the Reformer. His idea of the respect which should be paid to authority in political life was widely different also. Authority with the Tory was not looked upon as a power vested in the people as a sacred right. On the contrary, authority with him was a concrete, tangible thing, a matter of men and vested interests. The Tory sought the mainsprings of political power, not in the suffrages of respectable voters or in other generalizations of this kind, but in the tangible persons of the King and his Ministers. If a convenient distinction may be drawn between the rival attitudes towards the problem of authority, the Tory view may be called organic as opposed to the Liberal view, which may be called inorganic or mechanical. One depended upon the person of a visible ruler, the other upon the form of a political concept.

The Tory view of the function of the representative follows accordingly. Now the Tory was frankly doubtful whether it was at all possible for a number of men (an amorphous mass of individuals, not one-tenth knowing anything of the problems of government at all) to rule *through*, or by means of, an individual. Just because they happened to choose that individual was not to affirm that they, collectively, were ruling through him. For, to state that a mob of men were capable of ruling was to him sheer imagery.

He would, of course, admit the utility of the ruled

being able to criticize the conduct of the ruler. He had often done so himself. But for a member of Parliament to set up as a delegate, to reflect the collective will of a Birmingham or Manchester mob, however respectable, the Tory would have none of it. The *Quarterly Review* noticed with some alarm : ' another novel circumstance, and one which shows a most important change already effected in the constitution of the country, is that the House of Commons has virtually become an assembly of " delegates." ' [1]

There was not a Tory who did not deplore the change as inimical to the government of the country and sub-versive of all authority. Old Lord Eldon saw the hand of the devil in it. ' To convert a member of the other House of Parliament into the mere representative of the peculiar place for which he was returned, instead of the representative of the whole of the Commons of England, was a perversion of one of the best principles of the constitution.' [2] In the Commons Sir Robert Inglis had said the same at an earlier stage of the debate on the Bill. ' This House is not a collection of deputies as the States-General of Holland, and as the assemblies in some other continental countries. We are not sent here day by day to represent the opinions of our constituents. Their local rights, their municipal privileges, we are bound to protect, their general interests we are bound to consult at all times ; but not their will, unless it shall coincide with our own deliberate sense of right. We are sent here with a large and liberal confidence ; and when elected, we represent, not the particular place

[1] *Quarterly Review*, No. cxviii. p. 555, October 1837.
[2] *Hansard*, xii. 391, April 13, 1832. Reform Bill, 2 R.

only for which we are returned, but the interests of the whole empire.' [1] Parliament, wrote Sir John Walsh in a reasoned apology of the unreformed system, should be independent of the ebb and flow of popular hysteria ; ' it is the guardian of the interests, not the echo of the will, of the people. It is composed of representatives, not of delegates.' [2]

Tory detestation of the mere thought of delegacy was not confined to speeches in Parliament. It was a dogged prejudice which was ingrained in all who had not fallen to the new political tendencies. During the summer of 1835, certain young hotheads of the Carlton Club had taken it upon themselves publicly to reprobate a couple of Conservative members, Pusey and Young, for voting against the majority of the party in one of the crucial divisions of the Irish Church Tithe Bill. Pusey, thoroughly frightened, offered to resign his seat. Croker held up hands of horror ' that a Conservative should give the example of offering to resign his seat for a vote, thereby establishing the principle of delegation.[3] And when the appearance of the Chartist Convention in London further roused the Conservative party to apprehension, it is clear from contemporary speeches that the delegates of the people were considered to be dangerous men. Tories feared them, not because they were Chartists only, but

---

[1] *Hansard*, ii. 1095, March 1, 1831. Inglis was on the subject of intimidation from Reforming mobs outside the walls of Parliament which might 'entirely annihilate our deliberative character, and will reduce us to the mere function of speaking the wills of others from day to day.'

[2] *Popular Opinions on Parliamentary Reform considered* (1831), p. 38.

[3] Croker to Peel, July 30, 1835. (Addit. MSS. 40,321.)

because they were delegates. The awful consequences which followed the meeting of the States-General fifty years before might be repeated in London. Fires which gutted the Châteaux of the Loire might even yet destroy Longleat and Bowood.

The victors of 1832 were forced into the position of delegates. They could not help it, if they followed their Reformism to its logical end. Reform candidates were the first to explain that a change in the representation of the House of Commons was not a question of a few Whig and Radical leaders who happened to conceive of the benefits of the change to the country. It was rather the outward form of a spontaneous movement of the English public of whom they were but the humble mouthpiece. With their reverence for the body of electors and for the inherent virtue of its decisions they showed an enthusiasm equalled only by Frenchmen of the Revolution. Their faith in the inherent rectitude of the Public Meeting surpassed the faith of the Tories in the legal omniscience of Quarter Sessions. The Reformers contemptuously abandoned the old view of the State as a pyramid of vested interests for the newer and more metaphysical conception of equality.

Electoral humility such as this made little way among Tory opponents, who would declare, consistently with their faith, that the only really independent members were those who came from the close boroughs. All others were fettered by the interests and claims of local and parish politics.[1]

In their electoral theories, the politically-minded working classes borrowed wholesale from the general stock

[1] Shelley (J.), *Hansard*, ii. 1160, March 2, 1831.

of Reforming ideas. Their Chartist Convention of 1839 was but a replica of the elected House of Commons on the morrow of the General Election of 1832, except that Chartists took William Cobbett rather than Lord John Russell as their guide. In fundamental principle, both assemblies rested on the same basis. The Convention, conceived after the first heat of the Parliamentary Reform movement had cooled, never evolved anything approaching a syndicalist conception of government; [1] the delegates to the Convention, like the members who sat in the Parliament of the Oppressors, were elected on a geographical, not on a syndical, principle. There is not a scrap of evidence to show that the most anti-Parliamentary of our working-class leaders before 1848 conceived even the shadow of a Commune, least of all a system of Councils of Soldiers and Workmen. The Parliamentary idea permeated the political notions of the leaders of the working classes.

There was something of greater consequence than the clash of political creeds which shook Toryism to its foundations. There was the clash of social ideals. The victors in 1832 represented the middle classes in more than political outlook ; their victory meant the domination of middle-class institutions, middle-class manners, and middle-class ways of thinking. But for the mere matter of dates the Victorian Age began in 1832.

This will partly explain the reason why Tory resent-

[1] It is interesting to recollect that Sir William Harcourt's proposal for a central syndicate of County Councils represented one of the nearest approaches in this country to the introduction of the machinery of the Corporative State.

ment, in the face of the triumph of middle-class intelligence, equalled in rancour the resentment harboured by the working classes when the true significance of the Reform Act was realized. Tories hated the supporters of Reform even more than they hated the Reform Bill. The middle classes rightly prided themselves upon their rational political intelligence ; Tories looked suspiciously upon the application of rationalism to politics. The middle classes in their ascendancy introduced new standards of public and private morality, from their ranks arose philanthropic busybodies who were to make the life of the succeeding generation a burden. The adherents of Reform (it was a reiterated grievance of the *Morning Post*) drank tea. In all things the old school of Tories detested the new regime.

Their hatred transcended the limits of impartiality. While the New Ten-Pounders were denouncing the heartless tyrants who begrudged them their votes, the Tory newspapers were fulminating against the Ten-Pounders, ' grasping, greedy creatures, who pick up money here and there by a sort of half-labour, half-gambling, who care not a doit for anything but their own gain.' [1]

It would be misleading to consider Reform merely in its English perspective. The triumph of bourgeois ideals extended over Europe. Here and there a solitary observer would turn from the battle to ask himself whether the victory had not been bought too dearly. De Tocqueville, himself a man of the Orleans Monarchy, and the correspondent of the leading English Utilitarians, reflected mournfully upon the disappearance of the old

[1] *Morning Post,* January 20, 1841.

order and the arrogance of the new.[1] The patriots on the barricades of 1830 hardly died to place Louis Philippe and the Paris Capitalists in the seat of power.

Nearer home the timid voice of the doubters was drowned by the bull-roar of triumphant optimism. A few protested, but they were laughed at. The Parliamentary Conservative party dared not protest at all. Those who objected did so knowing that they had no real defence against the dialectic of Reform. 'I care not who dislikes the declaration,' grumbled the Duke of Newcastle, 'I openly avow that I am not a Reformer; and more, I declare that I have my suspicions of all men who profess themselves to be Reformers.'[2] Prejudice alone, however, will not win victories in Parliament.

The Reform Bill became law. Utopia was not proclaimed. The British Constitution in Church and State was not destroyed. Peel and the Parliamentary Tories wisely acquiesced in the Reformers' victory. It would have been extremely difficult to have resisted the spirit of the age. Toryism had lost and the party had no right to commit political suicide in reckless adherence to a lost cause.

The next few years of opposition gave Peel the opportunity he needed for the creation of an efficient party machine to cater for the change. But Tories were under no doubt as to the effects of the Bill. More than one Tory candidate in 1835 and 1837 must have grieved bitterly over the fact that the working classes were not represented. Wortley at Halifax in 1832 found himself surrounded by cheering Short Time Committeemen and

[1] *Memoirs* (transl. 1861), vol. ii. p. 19.
[2] *Thoughts in Times past tested by Subsequent Events* (1837), p. xi.

factory operatives, while his opponent vainly promised to vote ' for the extension of political rights amongst the Independent and Intelligent classes of the Community.' [1] Michael Sadler came very near the truth when he said to a crowd at Huddersfield eighteen months after the passing of the Act—' Gentlemen, to make use of a Yorkshire term sufficiently intelligible, you have been bamboozled.' [2]

Toryism never had anything in common with what is generally understood as Democracy—the right of all, irrespective of property or function, to a share in government. Toryism accepted the Reform Bill grudgingly and from sheer necessity. Had there not been such an overwhelming mania for political Reform the Tories would have had no Reform Bill, or if they had, it would have been conceived on lines far different from those laid down by Grey and Russell in 1831-32. Only the whip-hand of the master, Peel, availed to make Tory opinion amenable to acquiescence in the clauses of the Bill. To the principle of Reform as laid down by the Whig leaders the Tory party was almost unanimously hostile.

Subsequent movements within the Conservative party show to what extent the year 1846 marks the death of Toryism. Young England was not interested in Democracy as a substitute for the industrialism against which it took its somewhat lofty stand. And Randolph Churchill's Tory Democracy represented a point of view with which stalwarts of 1846 had absolutely nothing in common.

[1] *Halifax and Huddersfield Express*, July 7, 1832.
[2] *Leeds Intelligencer*, December 14, 1833.

Mental obscurity is even encouraged by the fact that the term ' Democracy ' has no definite meaning. In 1846 it meant something sinister : in Randolph Churchill's time for Toryism to adopt it was a novelty ; to-day the masses are universally attached to Democracy, though nobody cares exactly to define the term ; only the younger prophets are doubtful and suspicious.

The Tory party was never fully representative of the middle-class political attitude either before or after 1832. Tories in fact conceived it to be part of their faith to suspect the classes which had become so powerful. A reason given for the desire of the middle classes for Municipal Reform was that they were largely townsmen who wanted a higher standard of public order and public health,[1] a generous assumption which the verdict of history has not confirmed.[2]

It followed *a fortiori* that the Tories were, as a party, even less inclined to repose a monopoly of power in the hands of the people at large, irrespective of rank or function in the State. The Tory idea of the nature of government was wholly incompatible with the granting of power to such an abstraction as ' the people.' [3] With Sir Francis Burdett they applauded the benefits which proceeded from ' this free and paternal Government.' Burdett, after his so-called conversion from the Radical

[1] Cf. Redlich, vol. i. p. 113.

[2] The demand for Corporation Reform was mixed with the demand for economy, often at the expense of municipal and parish social services. (Webb (S. and B.), *English Local Government : The Parish and the County* (1906), p. 271.)

[3] Sir John Walsh (*Popular Opinions on Parliamentary Reform considered* (1831), p. 38) praises the unreformed House of Commons on the ground that it did not re-echo the voice of the people.

cause, told the Wiltshire Conservatives that 'the advocates of Democracy were like those whose Gothic ignorance would propose to raze some noble structure to its foundations. . . . The absence of orders and degrees in society would be fatal to liberty and incompatible with civilization.' [1]

Alison's melancholy prophecy, that an English reformed Parliament would be directed in times of tranquillity by the financial interests of the majority of electors and in the times of suffering by the passions of the majority of the people, was never realized, for the reason that the triumphant party of Reform kept 'the majority of the people' at arm's length.[2] Distress, too, was not sufficiently acute to goad the people to try their strength with the *bourgeoisie*.

Democracy was as a red rag to a bull wherever Toryism was concerned; for the Democrats of the day mixed Secularism with their Democracy. Socialism, as advocated by the modest Robert Owen, was merged in the greater terror; and even Ashley, who was not easily deceived by appearances, who lashed contemptuously at the dream of Conservative Democracy, fulminated with all his strength against Socialism and Chartism, 'the two great demons in morals and politics' which would rend society from top to bottom.[3] The *Morning Post* com-

[1] Speech at a Conservative dinner, Devizes (*Times*, September 20, 1837). Although this was spoken in the later years of his conversion to the Right Wing, his opinions on Democracy, which were those of any high-minded country gentleman of the time, had not changed since his Westminster days.

[2] *Some Account of my Life and Writings* (1882), vol. i. p. 311. Alison was moralizing upon the election of 1835.

[3] Hodder (E.), *The Life and Work of the Seventh Earl of Shaftesbury* (1886), vol. i. p. 322.

mented apprehensively upon the desire of some portion of the lower orders beguiled by wicked men to convert the Government of England into a pure, unmitigated democracy.[1]

Attempts were made throughout the nineteenth century to identify Democracy with Toryism. But it must be borne in mind that, after 1848, both terms, buffeted in the rough-and-tumble of changing circumstances, altered their form and acquired a new meaning. A romantic Toryism, academical, and not too closely defined, became the political faith of young Conservative statesmen, bored by the political drabness of the age. Democracy was beginning to assume its modern significance of representative government based upon equal civil rights. Perhaps, since Toryism after 1846 had ceased to count as a serious political force in Parliament, it was not difficult to point to the appropriate moral. As for the old Toryism, that instinctive faith which once led a powerful party, it was already dead when Lord Randolph Churchill and Tory Democracy entered the scene.

Dominating the attitude of the Tory party towards the labouring classes was the idea of ' vested interest.' That which resisted most persistently the efforts of the Liberal Reformers to mould public administration on intelligible rational lines, was the old eighteenth-century prejudice in favour of the ' interest ' rather than the state as the unit of government—the extra-Parliamentary interest rather than the interest created by, and under the tutelage of, Parliament.

Were it possible (and I have attempted to show that it was quite impossible) to imagine a Tory Utopia, the

[1] *Morning Post*, January 1, 1840.

'vested interest' would occupy a principal place in the machinery of government. Besides the 'landed interest' and the 'city interest' there might be a trades or crafts interest. Actually the idea of government by interest held sway in the minds of many, even when the Corporation Reform of 1836 had swept the second most powerful of vested interests out of the way. When Croker complained to Burdett that the Reform Bill had taken the direction of affairs out of the hands of the property of the country, Burdett replied that the new Parliament had more property in it than the last. But Burdett meant 'wealth,' and Croker lectured him on the difference.[1] There were many, unconnected with the violence of the party war, who would, if given the choice, have preferred the older 'interests,' with all their corruption, before the new and purer Government Commissioners and public bodies. They preferred the stodgy security of the one to the brilliant insecurity of the other. The Tory idea of government by interest found expression in adherence to the traditional conception of a mixed government of King, Lords, and Commons, at once monarchical, aristocratic and democratic—a conception which Blackstone had done much to define and Burke to popularize.[2]

It is only to be expected that a group imbued with a conception of society which found expression politically

---

[1] Croker to Burdett, March 3, 1833. (Addit. MSS. 40,320.)

[2] One of the many interpretations of the system of checks and balances, a conception which formed the stock-in-trade of Church-and-King speeches before 1832. A Hampshire parson speaking at a dinner of the North Hants Conservatives lamented that the traditional view was coming to be looked upon as 'mere antiquated nonsense.' (*Times*, January 30, 1837.)

in 'mixed government' and socially in a hierarchy of classes and interests, should adopt towards the masses an attitude of paternalism. It was the taunt of Cobden that the Tory party would allow everything to be done for the people and nothing by the people themselves. Cobbett had said the same of the school of Buxton and the sisters More, the 'humanity-mongers' of twenty years before; and the taunt was not without justification. After all, to personify a class of people and to assert that the working class was capable of positive action of its own volition, was nothing less than to create a conception, fashionable among Radical speculators, but wholly new to the political practice of the time. Tories may be excused their inability to differentiate the growing tendency to endow classes with personal attributes from what they honestly believed to be mystical claptrap. Ashley was roused to anger at the thought of the ignorant multitudes being ' surrendered, almost without a struggle, to the experimental philosophy of infidels and democrats.' [1] And yet these experimental philosophers were called Rationalists, and theirs the Rationalist movement, in politics and public administration. Nothing was more certain than the ultimate conflict between this curious view of rationalism and the reactionary political notions sponsored by the Tory party.

The idea of efficiency as applied to the problems of public administration does not precede the generation of Edwin Chadwick. The new passion for efficiency demanded two changes : instant and drastic reforms of local government coupled with the placing on a rational

[1] *Quarterly Review*, No. 134, December 1840. Quoted in Hodder, vol. i. p. 322.

basis of the essential social services of the nation. Rationalism in administration was desired if only on the grounds of economy : centralization was the means of attaining it.

The power of the Central Government grew under the shelter of political reform. All the time the adherents of Reform believed that administrative reform was the best cure for reactionary tyranny, they were unconsciously placing enormous powers over themselves in the hands of the central authority. Under cover of taking the control out of the hands of privileged classes and securing them under popular Parliamentary supervision, they were creating and augmenting a force which grew into a Colossus before the eyes of their immediate descendants. If the middle classes of the thirties and forties would not themselves shoulder the responsibility for an advanced social bureaucracy, they were content to confer the honour upon the next generation by preparing the way.[1]

The tendency towards centralization is frequently treated as a phase of a wider revolt against the over-extension of the principle of *laissez-faire*.[2] The defect of such a view lies in the fact that it is concerned only with appearances, and not with reality. Centralization can scarcely be considered as a movement necessarily hostile to *laissez-faire*, since the centralization which Bentham and especially Chadwick meditated did no more than touch the dominant middle classes. Centralization, swept clear of theory, meant centralization of those services which affected the labouring classes. Centralization, it

[1] Chadwick by no means had his own way with his contemporaries. (Redlich, vol. i. p. 144.)
[2] *Ibid.*, vol. i. p. 136.

cannot be doubted, was never intended to curtail in the slightest degree the economic and social freedom of the more respectable classes. Nor did it.

In their fight against anomalies the Utilitarians did not object to the imputation of favouring the State before the local interest. They became Centralists, not because Centralism was a necessary part of their political system —far from it—but because they championed the application of rational principles to the problems of government. Although Edwin Chadwick stands somewhat apart in his romantic reverence for the mechanism of the State, it may be said with certainty that the authors of the Poor Law Amendment Act had no intention of favouring *étatisme* in any form. It is in perfect keeping with this view that those who supported the reform of the New Poor Law and opposed the reform of the Factory system would have indignantly replied that it was not they but their political opponents—the Ashleys and the Owens, the Socialists as they were curiously called—who sought to magnify the State.

Championship of the principles of abstract political reason properly accompanied a demand for the abolition of the old structure of local government. The heads of the State had too long neglected the problem, and their neglect had given rise to chaos. The structure was assaulted from all sides during this period, and by the middle of the century the country had passed through a mighty change. Already the local supremacy, and to some extent even the local prestige, of the county magistracy faded in the glaring splendour of Whitehall.

This efficient central organ which the disciples of Bentham were evolving in England possessed no authentic counterpart in the past. The very meaning of the expression centralization, as Chadwick understood it, may well have been unintelligible, for instance, to the Speenhamland magistrates of 1795. The new state was an abstract, rational thing, unrecognizable to those who still clung to the mental habits of unreformed days. To reactionaries the worst features of this state was its merciless omnipresence, its cold impersonality, and above all its amazing exactitude. Nothing seemed outside its purview. Commissioners had their feelers everywhere ; they represented in tangible form Bentham's ' new principle of inspectability,' which in Bentham's own mind implied the subordination of the local authority. When the Boroughreeve, Constables, Churchwardens and Overseers, and Select Vestry of the Borough of Salford respectfully protest against incorporation in a Union, and pray the Commissioners ' not to fetter the good sense, humanity, and discrimination of the gentlemen who constitute these boards,' they are answered by an impersonal official letter intimating that ' their communication had been received.' [1] The Board of Guardians of the Wangford Union had granted the paupers of the Shipmeadow Workhouse a Christmas dinner of roast beef and plum-pudding ; to which manifest breach of the dietary regulations the Commissioners replied that they felt it to be their duty to withhold their sanction from the proposed festivity.[2]

Against these impersonal manifestations of the Ben-

---

[1] Poor Law Commissioners for England and Wales. (Minute Book, vol. x., April 12, 1837.)
[2] Poor Law Commissioners for England and Wales. (Minute Book, vol. viii., December 17, 1836.)

thamic State in practice was ranged the humanitarian feeling of the people. Opposition to centralization was frankly reactionary in essence, and on that account had the usual double-headed form in Radical and Tory opposition.

Radical and Tory each approached the problem of centralization from a different angle. To the Radical the omnipotence of the Central Government would produce in a country tending to Liberalism the omnipotence of Capital or Privilege. Parson Lot doubted whether after 1832 any other force than Capital was adequately represented in Parliament.[1] Radicals, therefore, questioned the legality of Commissions and Commissioners.

Tory sentimentalists objected to centralization because centralization tended to destroy the traditional fabric of local government, the regional autonomy which was an integral part of the ' Constitution in Church and State,' which they revered. Alison, a realist among Conservatives, attributed the Rebecca Riots of 1843 to the neglect of the Central Government in remedying a legitimate local grievance.[2] John Walter spoke of the New Poor Law as ' a plan which might draw the country yet further from its ancient habits, and ultimately change the character of Englishmen.'[3] Disraeli harped on the same chord during the debates on the continuance of the Poor Law Amendment Act, when he lamented that the union of parishes constituted a total revolution in the ancient parochial jurisdiction of England, and outraged

[1] *The Christian Socialist : A Journal of Association,* vol. i. p. 50, December 14, 1850.
[2] *History of Europe, 1815-1852* (1854), vol. vii. p. 86.
[3] Quoted in Baxter (G. R. W.), *The Book of the Bastilles* (1841).

the manners of the people.[1]   The essence of the British Constitution, contended Oastler, is self-government ; the tendency of every plan of the Reformers is centralization, or, in other words, despotic power. ' Does it never strike you, Sir, that such a change cannot take place in England, without an entire destruction of the present social system ? ' [2]   Oastler and the Anti-Poor Law leaders spoke darkly of Senior and Chadwick as the Empson and Dudley of Somerset House.[3]

There seems to have existed a general opinion among reactionary leaders that the executory powers claimed and wielded by the series of Commissions after 1832 were illegal. Lord Abinger and Sir William Follett both entertained serious doubts as to the strict legal position of these Commissions. In Lord Abinger's opinion the granting of executive power to the Poor Law Commissioners represented a delegation of authority unknown to the constitution, making the Commissions ' a sort of *imperium in imperio* I can never bring myself to allow.' [4]

A rooted distrust of Commissioners was, in fact, among the first manifestations of the Tory revolt from political Benthamism. A hostile feeling among other parties showed itself during the debates on the Poor Law Amendment Bill in 1834. In the Commons Sir Samuel Whalley, though he would gladly see the last relics of the feudal system swept away—a phrase thoroughly in the fashion—was against the arbitrary power of Commissioners.[5] Colonel Evans disliked the proposal to

[1] *Hansard*, lvi. 375, February 8, 1841.
[2] Fleet Papers (1841), vol. i. No. 16.
[3] Baxter (G. R. W.), *The Book of the Bastilles* (1841), p. 234.
[4] *Ibid.*
[5] *Hansard*, xxiii. 807, May 9, 1834.

erect a central Poor Law Board and, even if it were erected, he doubted whether Parliament had power to vest the Board with so great authority.[1]

It is a curious circumstance that, in fighting the centralizing tendencies of Reform legislation, Tories and Radicals were alike led in the direction of *étatisme* of another kind. Disraeli would check the overweening power of Parliament and the Cabinet by exalting the Sovereign. Richard Oastler would appeal to the good sense of the young Queen to limit by her prerogative what he called the power of the Commissioners to inflict cruelty, and the cry was still heard when Oastler had sunk into old age. It was Kingsley and the Christian Socialists who would now exalt the Queen. Parson Lot boils with indignation at the thought of the Crown ' practically in commission, as the representation of the People is.' [2]

There was no particular reason why individuals who, for the most part, were bound up with the old tradition of local government, should specially welcome the weakening of local autonomy. It was a common complaint against the Tory party, during the years of the struggle over the Reform Bill, that it was the party of privilege. To the Tory it was the cause of much bitterness to find, after the Reform Bill had become law, that the increasing centralization of administrative functions was accompanied by an extension of the opportunites for Government patronage. Why should the Ministry of the day possess the scope for patronage denied to political parties or to great landowners ? Tories entertained small respect

[1] *Hansard*, xxiii. 805, May 9, 1834.
[2] *The Christian Socialist*, vol. i. p. 50, December 14, 1850.

for the Ministerial powers of patronage. They were
inclined to regard the tendency towards centralization
as an attempt to weaken the local authority of the
Justices ; Brougham's reforms in the Law of Real Property received the same bad name.

Englishmen have not taken kindly to all the implications of bureaucracy, and champions of local rights have
arisen to defend their cause with vigour. The period
which began with Cobbett and ended with Toulmin
Smith is rich in literary exponents of local autonomy,
the first principle of Tory political doctrine.

The old Parliamentary Tory party still clung to the
antique notions of government by interests. By 1832
the new doctrines, based on ideas radically different,
secured their first victory. Within twenty years the last
of the old Tory school were passing away from the scene
of political activity. Their views and prejudices fell on
ears which were accustomed to another language. The
old territorial constitution of England, solid and un-
wieldy, but not without merit in its day, gave place to
a complex and efficient machine. Government by the
sole sanction of the franchise, held impossible by a less
intelligent age, became a working system. Universal and
equal Parliamentary suffrage, formerly the Utopia of
cranks, became the great end of Political Reform.

Whether the extinction of the older idea of government
by vested interests and its supersession by the idea of
government by the elected representatives of a political
democracy was a sign of progress or of retrogression, it
is no part of this inquiry to determine. It seems that
the change has scarcely strengthened our Parliamentary
institutions for their journey through the present century.

TORYISM AND THE PEOPLE

It would be unfair to the giants of nineteenth-century Political Reform to condemn their vision of the Democratic State as a dissipated dream. But there can be little question that the Tory conception of government by interests has returned with a vengeance into the arena of practical politics. The politico-democratic structure erected by the Reform Acts totally ignored the social and economic elements in the life of society. One may take the liberty of a hazard that the transition to-day might have been less disconcertingly sudden had the triumph of Political Reform been less overwhelmingly complete. The all-wise Sidonia warns the youthful Coningsby that the Spirit of Progress is unmoved by prayers and that she is doubly intolerant of Progressives.

As we see that the Barons, the Church, the King, have in turn devoured each other, and that the Parliament, the last devourer, remains, it is impossible to resist the impression that this body also is doomed to be destroyed; and he is a sagacious statesman who may detect in what form, and in what quarter the great consumer will arise.[1]

1 Disraeli (B.), *Coningsby* (1844), bk. iv. ch. 13.

CHAPTER IV

TORYISM AND THE ASSOCIATION OF LABOUR

INTRODUCTION

THIS chapter concerns the reaction of Tory ideas to the problem of the association of labour, and attempts an investigation of the clash of Tory doctrines with a new and perplexing feature of the time : the non-sovereign labour group associated within the pale of the State.

I have found it convenient to consider each separate kind of working-class association roughly according to its function. For the purpose of exposition I have examined four principal types of associations in the following order :

(*A*) Trade Unions : associations existing for the purpose of raising or maintaining the economic status of their members—associations which seek to attain their end through aggressive economic means.

(*B*) Factory Short Time Committees : associations formed for furthering a specific reform of the condition of industrial labour by means of peacefully influencing Parliamentary and public opinion.

(*C*) Friendly Societies: associations founded and maintained for the purposes of mutual benefit, but which avoid the weapon of direct economic action.

(*D*) Mechanics' Institutes and Working Men's Clubs :

associations formed for educational or social purposes only. The division of working-class associations into four types is arbitrary and approximate. There is a considerable difficulty in providing an adequate distinction between those associations which combine a multitude of functions. The period is replete with instances of quasi-industrial Trade Unions which, but for the name, might be as easily classified as associations of good fellowship and might well be placed in the category of Friendly Societies. Similarly there were so-called Friendly Societies which were in reality little else than subsidized clubs of city freemen, their sole claim to the title of Friendly Society consisting in their receiving supplies of beef and beer during critical periods which immediately preceded Parliamentary elections.

For the rest I have taken refuge in the accepted definitions of the nature and function of the various types of association with which I deal.

(A) INDUSTRIAL ASSOCIATION : THE TRADE UNION

At the end of the last chapter I suggested a reason for the bitter feeling engendered in the struggle which surged round the Reform Act of 1832. I attributed this feeling to the conflict of two incompatible attitudes towards the whole problem of civil government : the one placing supreme authority in the hierarchy of rank and estate, the other reposing sovereignty in an intelligent electorate.

The following chapter is concerned less with political theory and more with concrete associations of working

men. A study of the relation between the Tory party
and the Trade Union movement introduces a type of
working-class group unlike that which embodied the
political aspirations of the common people during the
period of Reform. The difference between the Political
Union and the Trade Union is basic. Membership of a
Political Union was free : any one might find himself
elected to the highest offices within it. It represented a
political opinion rather than an economic necessity.
The Trade Union, on the other hand, drew its membership from one class and its policy from the immediate
needs of its members. While the Political Union embodied the political opinions of men who happened to
think alike on political questions, the Trade Union arose
from a sense of common interest in the bitter struggle
for wages.

The rise to power of organized labour as an integral
part of the structure of society was one of the principal
features of the period. The fourteen years of Peel's
Great Conservative Party—' that mighty mystery of the
nineteenth century ' [1]—coincided with one of the most
critical formative periods in the history of the Trade
Union movement.

At the present day society recognizes the position of
the non-sovereign group in and co-existing with the
State. The attitude which contemporaries adopted
towards the problem of association was obscure and
confused. Public opinion during the twenty years succeeding the abolition of the Combination Acts in 1824
seems to have regarded the labour group either as an
anomaly or as a positive evil, feared by some because

[1] *Sybil*, bk. iv. ch. 14.

it constituted a potential rival to the supremacy of the State, by others because its existence transgressed a fundamental law of Political Economy. The early nineteenth century was never quite at ease in the presence of self-governing combinations of workmen.

It is not true that the received legal opinion of the time found no place for the trade association of workmen. The framers of the Act of 1625 knew perfectly well that combinations both of masters and men had for long been an accomplished fact, and that, in certain trades, it had been the practice for the associated masters periodically to meet the associated workmen—the name Trade Union was scrupulously avoided—for the transaction of business and the settlement of trade disputes. There is no denial that the Act of 1825 still left considerable room for trade combinations of labourers.

The industrial-labour group owes its origin to the consequences of the Industrial Revolution. The requirements of the new industry brought into existence an industrial proletariat. It gradually became apparent that the changed conditions of life left the operatives without the means of corporate self-defence. Hence the origin of combination.

The Select Committee on Artisans and Machinery which recommended the repeal of the Combination Laws emphasized the absolute necessity of enacting a law to punish either masters or workmen who ' should interfere with that perfect freedom which ought to be allowed to each party, of employing his labour or capital in the manner he may deem most advantageous.' [1] Whatever may have been the construction subsequently placed upon

[1] Parl. Papers (1824), v.

the words, ' employing his labour or capital in the manner he may deem most advantageous,' it is doubtful whether the Select Committee of 1824 calmly regarded Trade Unions on the one hand and Trade Cartels on the other as the logical and legitimate consequence of the freedom of labour and capital. Indeed, their point of view was rather the reverse ; they would abolish the Combination Acts in the hope that combination would itself ultimately disappear. They changed their minds next year.

None of the parties interested in the repeal of the Combination Acts were in the least aware of the place which combination must necessarily take in the type of society which had come into being. While the lawyers were able to define and circumscribe the legal position of the early Trade Unions, they were unable to grasp the significance of the principle of association in the Leviathan of the body politic. The Progressives of the Liverpool administration adopted, at best, a negative attitude. Huskisson and the promoters of the Bill of 1824 could not conceive of an industrial combination other than as a combination in restraint of trade or as a disagreeable necessity. Nor can it be said of Place, the power behind the Bill, that he rose above his contemporaries in his appreciation of the intimate connection between industrial society and the principle of industrial association.

The makeshift social structure of the early nineteenth century was inadequate to accommodate the changes which had taken place in the relation between masters and men engaged in industry. The Industrial Revolution had come upon a nation still thinking in terms of the old domestic economy of semi-feudal England.

Attempts were made at the outset to meet the consequences of the change by adopting the ancient expedients of wage and price regulation. Then, as these expedients were one by one allowed to drop, the new individualistic principles took their place. Men contemplated the change and rationalized upon it. The transition from a basis of status to a basis of contract, which Maine noticed in the development of legal ideas, was closely paralleled by the transition from status to contract in the industrial operatives' economic position.

The contractual basis upon which the relations of the classes in industry were now established was generally accepted as a necessary, if not a beneficent, change. It is true that neither society as a whole nor industrial labour in particular accommodated itself to the new conditions with the readiness which the school of *laissez-faire* implied in their writings. The Combination Acts were repealed in 1824, not because it was felt that the Trade Union principle had become an integral part of industrial society, but because Trade Unions had become a problem which baffled even the farthest-sighted of Huskisson's generation.

The one thing lacking in the contemporary attitude to industrial questions was the capacity to take a broad view of the problem of association. There was wanting a synthetic mind which would grasp the significance of the new industrial relations and attempt a specific remedy for the ills which the change engendered. Towards the end of a stormy career Stephens, the Tory Chartist, recalled the industrial chaos of his early days. He thus states the problem with great precision : ' Of all organizations in this country that which was least of all brought into usage was the organization of factory labour. They had organizations in almost everything else; but in important and vital matters affecting the existence of labour on the one hand and capital on the other, they seem to have arrived at no fundamental law; they seem to be unable to bring any principle to bear on it; and the consequence was throughout the whole of these islands, where capital had established so many manufactures and where the labour of tens of thousands is gathered together, they had nothing but strife, disunion, and division.' [1]

Stephens would have had to go far even in the days of his old age to find the industrial synthesis which he sought. The men of the early nineteenth century had no leisure and no inclination to pause and examine the machinery which created the national wealth. Their sons were much too busy to indulge in self-criticism. Early Victorians were the last in the world to admit that they had made mistakes. They were certainly not prepared to admit that their whole attitude towards combination was wrong. One cannot imagine Early Victorians at Canossa.

Tories shared the universal ignorance of the true nature of combination. The chances were overwhelming that, whenever a Tory member was addressing the House of Commons on the subject of Trade Unions, he was borrowing his ideas from a Liberal source. Eldon and the Intransigents based their condemnation on the fear that Trade Unions with their violent methods were threatening the supremacy of the Government. The argument which Coleridge applied to the Roman Church

[1] Speech at Dewsbury, December 1865. (Holyoake (G. J.), *Life of Joseph Rayner Stephens* (1881), p. 132.)

was applied by almost universal Tory consent to the Trade Unions. 'If I met a man who should deny that an *imperium in imperio* was in itself an evil, I would not attempt to reason with him; he is too ignorant.'[1] Prejudice was the death of argument.

The progressive elements within the Tory party were no more enlightened. The group of Sadler and Ashley had no solution to offer. Ashley himself, in spite of his lifelong contact with organizations of working men, never seemed to appreciate the importance of those innumerable grades and associations of which organized labour was composed. In his criticisms of the industrial action of the Trade Unions he forgot that his skilled-artisan friends who sat on Short Time Committees were but Trade Unionists in their Sunday clothes.[2]

Although Tory opinion on the problem of combination groped in the dark, there was a distinct difference between the motives of Tory and Liberal hostility to Trade Unionism. The task here is to discover what this difference was and to examine how far the Tory attitude to the whole problem of the Trade Union movement was part of what may be called the Tory philosophy of labour.

It was the destiny of Sir Archibald Alison to have spent the greater part of his career among the chaos of the new industry. The Recorder of Glasgow was almost alone among the Tories to attempt a literary apology for the attitude of his party. Alison, however, did not try to formulate a Tory Trade Union policy.

[1] Prose Works, vol. i. p. 347 (ed. 1876).
[2] Ashley was hardly familiar with the term 'organized labour,' and the phrase is rarely found in his speeches and writings. In a speech on agricultural gangs he uses the term 'organized labour' to convey apprehension. (*Hansard*, clxxxvi. 1465, April 11, 1867.)

THE ASSOCIATION OF LABOUR

In the course of his judicial work in Glasgow Alison saw much of the more repulsive aspect of labour unrest. Giving evidence before the Committee on Combinations of Workmen [1] he showed some hostility to the then constituted Trade Union movement among the Glasgow cotton operatives. He believed that combination, no less than violence, was the cause of drunkenness. ' I think combination has an evident tendency to increase the drinking of spirits ; the tendency to combination is in the lower ranks of life very similar to that of the establishment of clubs with respect to the higher ranks in London, but unhappily they do not associate together merely to read the newspapers, or to converse, but it is constantly followed by drinking.' [2] In essence, he declared in a further statement, combination was ' just a system of the aristocracy of skilled labour against the general mass of unskilled labour '—an observation which, if true, demolished the argument that the Trade Union movement of the time was anti-capitalist in its policy.[3]

Alison was ready to give tribute where tribute was due. He admitted that the Unionists in his district were drawn from the better class of skilled workmen. Most important of all, he conceded the point that peaceful combination was actually useful to the trades and ' indispensable to a just balance between master and workmen.' Although he naturally objected to the violence with which combination was attended through the rowdiness

[1] Parl. Papers (1837-1838), viii.
[2] *Ibid.*, Q. 1910.
[3] Oastler, similarly opposed to combination in theory, admitted its necessity in existing industrial instability. (Parl. Papers (1831-1832), xv. p. 455.)

of drunken souls, he was ready with constructive suggestions for Trade Union reform.[1]

He would make a beginning by shortening the hours of labour. He would grant the Unions the right to sue and be sued in the persons of their officials. He would have the officials registered annually. He would guarantee the status of the Unions, and their power to sue and be sued, by Act of Parliament, since by that means rather than by common law would the respect of the artisans be gained for the measure. Coming as they do from a Glasgow Tory, who walked in the strictest Tory faith, these suggestions are of considerable interest.[2] ' Combinations,' he writes, ' are the natural resource of the weak against the strong, the poor against the rich, the oppressed against the oppressors. As such they have been known in all countries and in all ages, and have often rendered important, sometimes beneficial, services to society.' [3] As for abolishing combination, he told the Select Committee of 1838, they might as well talk of Utopia.

But combinations for the purposes of strikes were a different matter. These he loathed beyond measure as ' worse than plague, pestilence or famine.' Strikes affected not only the body but the mind. ' They utterly confound the ideas of right and wrong among immense

---

[1] Parl. Papers (1837-1838), viii., Q. 1967.

[2] Alison elsewhere records his impatience of the inactivity of this Committee ' which took a great deal of important evidence on the subject, and ended by recommending nothing ; the usual results when a great social evil not immediately affecting the interests of any party is under consideration.' (*History of Europe, 1815-1852* (2d. 1854), vol. vi. p. 305.)

[3] *Ibid.*, p. 298.

numbers of the people, and by arraying them in hostile
bands against their fellow men, induce a *bellum plusquam
civile* in the heart of peaceful society.' [1]

In industry there was a considerable cleavage between
these points of view. The newer captains of industry
were, in the main, new to the handling of men and the
wielding of authority over large bodies of employees.
They had for the most part retained the habits of mind
of their pre-industrial fathers. In their relations with
their men they went often to the extreme of paternalism.
The Truck system, the close supervision of the moral
and social relations of their workers, and a dozen other
practices which later grew into the most flagrant of
abuses, took their origin from the farm, kitchen and
parish church of an earlier day.

To rural Tories, who were not directly in touch with
conditions in the industrial areas, the apparition of the
Trade Union caused unbounded apprehension. So long
as the Trade Union movement remained limited to the
workers in the large towns, the Tory cannot be said to
have been hostile. Alison has been shown to have
given conditional approval of combination; and well-
instructed Tories, conversant with the condition of the
industrial labouring classes, had long held the same views.
As early as the debates on the Act which repealed the
Combination Laws in 1824 Tory members of Parliament
had expressed strong doubt as to the wisdom, much more
the possibility, of abolishing combination. And when
the frightened Progressives of 1825 were meditating the
repeal of the Enabling Act of the year before, General
Gascoyne from Liverpool—the seat of a strong Trade

[1] *Ibid.*, p. 306.

TORYISM AND THE PEOPLE

Union movement and of an equally strong local Toryism
—asked the Commons ' was it not justifiable, fair and
legal, if men thought they were entitled to larger wages
than they received, to unite together for the purpose of
accomplishing their object ? ' [1]
It was when the Trade Union movement departed
from that which some Tories seem to have held to be its
legitimate course, and spread over the rural districts,
that Whig and Tory landowners, tenants and parsons,
rose to a height of fury. The Dorchester prosecutions
of 1834 provide a specific illustration of the attitude
which a group of provincial gentry and their following
adopted towards Trade Unionism among the agricultural
working classes.

It is possible to regard the Dorchester prosecutions
from three different points of view. There is that of
the Dorchester Committee, a body hastily assembled to
open a campaign for quashing what Lovett and Owen
believed to be a monstrous legal iniquity. There is the
usually accepted modern view, based upon the Committee's condemnatory attitude, and reinforced by an
appeal to modern standards of social justice. Thirdly,
there is the point of view of those who took part in
prosecuting the labourers or who, at the time, approved
of the sentences meted out to them. It is with the
third point of view that this inquiry is necessarily
concerned.

In order to form a just estimate of the Tory attitude
towards the Dorchester incident, it will be necessary to
recall the nature of the association which Loveless and
his fellow-Unionists wished to establish. By this means

[1] *Hansard*, xiii. 356, May 3, 1825.

the Tory objection to the Unionists' project will be more
clearly understood.

From evidence given at the trial it appeared that prisoners
were engaged in forming a Friendly Society of Agricultural
Labourers affiliated to the Grand National Consolidated
Trades Union.[1] It is evident, if the statements of the
accused are to be taken into account, that the Tolpuddle
Friendly Society of Agricultural Labourers was not a
Friendly Society in the accepted sense of the term. It
was more. Local gentry could have taken little exception to the formation of a Friendly Society pure and
simple. Already the country was honeycombed with
Friendly Societies. There were over fifty registered
societies, and a far larger number of small, non-registered
provident clubs in Dorsetshire alone.[2] At Milton Abbas,
not ten miles from Tolpuddle, a Society of Agricultural
Labourers had been enrolled in 1833. If Loveless and
his fellow-prisoners had wished to found a Friendly
Society among the labourers of Tolpuddle, their action
would have been perfectly legal. They were however
prosecuted, not on the ground that they were forming a
Friendly Society, but that they meditated a Trade Union.
A Trade Union, in fact, they were.[3]

[1] Webb (S. and B.), *The History of Trade Unionism* (revised ed. 1920),
p. 145.
[2] A Parliamentary return of 1837 shows most of the enrolled Friendly
Societies in the county to have been registered before 1835. (Parl.
Papers (1837), li.) See p. 133 below.
[3] A form of association which came under the notice of a Select
Committee some time before. (Report on the Laws respecting Friendly
Societies, 1825, iv.) ' The Committee regret to find from the evidence
that Societies, legally enrolled as Benefit Societies, have been frequently
made the cloak under which funds have been raised for the support of
combinations and strikes.'

The weight of evidence given at the trial supports this conclusion,[1] and the tenor of the *Rules of the Friendly Society of Agricultural Labourers*—a document produced in court—places the matter beyond all doubt.[2] A decisive factor in the case lay in the character of Loveless's Union; it was admittedly not autonomous, but was a branch of a National Union. This of itself raised an insuperable prejudice in Tory minds. National Unions of all kinds, even though formed for purely provident and humanitarian purposes, were anathema to Tory doctrine—a prejudice manifested with equal force in the relations of Toryism and the Friendly Societies movement.

There appears to have been a reversal of modern legal values in the circumstances that the secret oath administered by the officers of the Dorchester Union was made a principal part of the prosecution. But even this apparent injustice becomes intelligible in the light of contemporary feeling in the matter. The sinister significance of the secret oath was brought home to those who had bitter cause to remember the incendiary career of 'Captain Swing' barely four years before. A cloud of mystery enshrouded the disturbances of 1830-31 out of all proportion to the realities of the trouble. Swing still represented the very spirit of anarchy, and there seems to have been a vague notion that the conspiracy of Loveless and the apparently harmless labourers behind him was a reappearance of the dreaded Captain, the

---

[1] Evidence of John Lock from an account of the trial in the *Times*, March 20, 1834.

[2] From a copy of the Rules printed in Bland, Brown and Tawney, *English Economic History : Select Documents* (1914)

destroyer of society. Care must be taken in applying to the circumstances of the trial the sensitive standards of modern morality. The Tolpuddle Unionists with their secret oath were suspected of bringing into a tranquil, if distressed, countryside the dreaded war of classes which had already convulsed the factory towns. The existence of the secret oath was considered by the presiding judge of far greater import than the existence of combination. It was admitted by the prosecution that, since the Combination Acts had been repealed, associations for the purpose of raising wages were no longer illegal. But the oath was held inexcusable. At another trial the judge gave what seems to be a replica of contemporary legal opinion when he stated the incompatibility of secret oaths and ordered government. '. . . It is impossible that any well-ordered state of society could tolerate the existence of confederacies bound together by secret compacts and oaths not required by law ; one of the obvious consequences of such confederacies being to deprive the State of the benefit of the testimony of those who are engaged in them—a state of things injurious to individuals, subversive of public order, and striking at the very existence of the State.' [1]

In contemplating the prosecution from the point of view of the Dorchester Committee it is not easy to resist the suggestion that there were political interests in London which found little cause for resentment against a Dorchester jury for providing them with an occasion for attacking a Government which they believed (not without justification) to have betrayed the working

[1] Bosanquet (J.) in *Rex* v. *Dixon*. (Carrington and Payne, vol. vi., 1833-35.)

classes in 1832. The Government could hardly have been popular with a class which the *bourgeoisie* were thought to have consciously excluded from power. The bitterness which Loveless harboured against his oppressors was natural, though rancour made him sententious. He writes in the strain of one who regards his ill-treatment as the beginning of a literary career. The Dorchester Committee provided the opportunity and the funds for making his complaints public. Loveless seems to have been sedulously instructed and encouraged in his new character as a political pamphleteer. His imprisonment and subsequent transportation furnished the theme of his first pamphlet, ' The Victims of Whiggery,' a laborious and uncouth compendium of grievances against the many petty occurrences of prison life. He criticizes the legality of the trial. He criticizes prison arrangements both before and during his voyage to New South Wales. He criticizes the administration of the Colony.

Heartened by the reception of his first venture Loveless turned again to his pen. Next year followed a diatribe against Church and Poor Law entitled ' The Church Shown Up,' in a work which bears manifest evidence of collaboration with a more skilled controversialist. It is significant that Hartwell, Secretary of the Dorchester Committee, wrote the preface at his Holborn office. He played the part of Las Cases to the Dorchester Napoleon.

The Dorchester incident had two consequences unnoticed at the time. It was proved that the existing machinery of Trade Unionism was totally unfitted for application in the rural areas ; and it was shown that the feeling of the agricultural interest—landlord, tenant and labourer—was totally unprepared for the introduc-

118

tion of the Trade Union principle. Many years later Joseph Arch learnt by bitter experience in organizing a discontented peasantry that a union of farm labourers and a union of industrial operatives have little but a name in common. With centuries of custom at his back, the agricultural labourer requires more than a single generation of hard times to make him politically a proletarian.

In spite of repression and poverty the farm labourers of the period declined to absorb the revolutionary doctrines then current in the industrial areas. Had they imbibed revolutionary ideas, their attitude towards the New Poor Law would have been far different than it was. The labourers clung in fear and resentment to the Old Law which, with all its abuses, enshrined the remains of a feudal-labour system, and they ranged themselves with the stubbornness of despair against the innovations of 1834.

Agricultural England was not ready to shoulder an organization created for the proletarian conditions of factory populations. A wholesale syndicalization of the countryside was out of the question. Even where the new principles of *laissez-faire* and the doctrine of the Freedom of Labour had never penetrated, the opportunity for extending rural Trade Unionism was still less favourable. In the country districts there was but one recognized group, and that was the feudal group, the antique hierarchy of landownership, tenancy and labour. All other groups either conformed to this threefold association or were considered superfluous.

In the industrial areas the change to a proletarian society was almost complete. The outer forms of a proletariat, at least, were there. A race of workmen had grown up, little acquainted with the rural economy of their fathers, and divorced from the soil.

The condition of this proletariat at the time may be illustrated from the letter of a Litchfield correspondent, who wrote to Place in 1838 that 'All the old sets of intelligent, clever, and able workmen have long since been broken up and scattered abroad or annihilated; and the younger ones, they tell me, are reckless slaves —dissatisfied (as they might well be) but for the present, mindless.' [1] From Lancashire and the West Riding come equally sinister forebodings. One hears much, about this time, of 'the long-continued jealousies and animosities which exist between the masters and workmen.' [2]

It is of course well known what was the attitude of the Grey and Melbourne administrations towards the industrial situation. Coercive legislation against combination was contemplated. In 1834 troops were lavishly used for quelling disturbances in the crowded Northern and Midland cities. And more than this : the espionage system was maintained under the patronage and direction of the Home Secretary.[3]

There is ample evidence to indicate that, up till a period which outlasts the fourteen years of this study, the industrial working classes looked beyond their own ranks

---

[1] Price (H.) to Place (F.), February 22, 1838. (Place Coll., vol. 52, p. 356.)

[2] Lord Duncan to Major-Gen. Sir H. Bouverie, July 26, 1834. (Home Office Papers, 41. 12.)

[3] 'Lord Melbourne directs me to repeat that any expense you may incur in obtaining information will be immediately reimbursed if you will inform him of the amount.' (Melbourne to Bouverie, March 22, 1834. Home Office Papers, 41. 12.)

in their attempts after a juSt and coherent relationship between themselves and their employers. That they looked to the Parliamentary Radicals when once the excitement of 1832 was over is doubtful. The economic principles of the Radical group proved a bar to their reconciliation with the masses ; and, as we have shown, Political Economy was anathema to the working classes. Here and there operatives write to Francis Place to ask him to influence Mr. Hume or Mr. Roebuck in the direftion of the Faftory Bill or a similar measure. But organized labour steered clear of the Parliamentary Radicals, perhaps because the workmen knew that their cause could hardly be aided by those who entertained doubts on the compatibility of that cause with the principles of Political Economy. When leaders of organized labour associations correspond with Place it is rather to complain of the unsympathetic attitude of one of Place's Parliamentary friends. The Trade Union movement owed little to the Parliamentary Radicals. Radicals served willingly enough on the DorcheSter Committee ; but there they Stopped.

Trade Unionism had little cause for gratitude. The very Reform Aft which the Unions had largely helped to bring into force did them neither good nor harm. They gained nothing from its provisions. They owed it neither admiration nor respeft.

Nor did they look with feelings of friendliness towards the Parliamentary Conservative party, which shared the patronizing aloofness of the other parties.

Northern Toryism, on the other hand, in closer contaft with the induStrial labourers and their working conditions, adopted a Stronger and more positive attitude. The great

Tory newspaper of the North, the *Leeds Intelligencer*, continually preached a more generous regard for the right of labourers to combine. Tory candidates from Yorkshire constituencies, who were credited by Liberal newspapers with the boisterous support of rowdy mobs of operatives, held views on the matter of combination far less academical than those of their political friends in the South. An instructive, and somewhat ludicrous, incident took place at the hustings during the Leeds Election of February 1834. The three candidates were facing the questioning of a howling mob below when a voice rang out above the noise of the crowd. ' Gentlemen, I beg leave, in the name of the operatives of Leeds, to request an explicit reply from each candidate to the questions which I have to propose. Sir John Beckett, will you support a bill, or help in bringing one in, which shall secure to the British labourers, as quickly as possible, the privileges of the emancipated slaves in the British Colonies ? . . . Do you approve of the operatives being peaceably and lawfully united to prevent a ruinous reduction of their wages, which some of the manufacturers tend to reduce ? '

SIR JOHN BECKETT : ' I have no difficulty in saying that I do not object to their so meeting.' [Bravo and cheers.]

MR. BAINES : ' I do.' [Disapprobation.]

MR. BOWER : ' Gentlemen, I agree to this ; I do approve of it.' [Cheers.] [1]

The Parliamentary attitude of the Conservatives was strictly circumspect, and Peel relegated combination to the limbo of second-rate questions which might well wait

---

[1] *Leeds Intelligencer*, February 15, 1834.

on one side. It was left to one group alone within the party to formulate the principles of what might have been an industrial policy. But the influence of Young England was transitory. Young England with its feudal ideas of labour could do nothing against the onward march of accomplished facts which Peel was both unable and unwilling to resist.

(B) POLITICAL-INDUSTRIAL ASSOCIATION : THE FACTORY SHORT TIME COMMITTEE

A second type of workmen's association with which Toryism came in contact was the Short Time Committee which occupied a prominent place in the factory operatives' side of the movement for Factory Reform.

Short Time Committees, throughout the greater part of their career, enjoyed the reputation of being thoroughly respectable bodies. Into the Factory Reform movement came the best elements of Trade Unionism. Short Time Committeemen were never in imminent danger of proscription from Whitehall.

On one occasion only was there a tendency on the part of Short Time Committeemen to work in the dark. It was in 1833, during a year of unprecedented Trade Union activity, when the slightest mistake of policy might have exposed them to the suspicion of the Home Secretary. Trade Union activity throughout 1833 was fraught with considerable difficulty, amounting almost to positive danger to Unionist leaders, and the bourgeois supporters of Factory Reform were justifiably careful in their dealings with working men's Committees. In giving evidence before Sadler's Committee of 1831-32 a

Glasgow operative inadvertently let out that the Glasgow factory workers had determined to combine to agitate for shorter working hours. Sadler felt called upon to explain hastily to the Committee his abhorrence of the sentiments expressed by the witness. He discreetly disclaimed all knowledge of such a Combination as that referred to, nor had he any intention of forming one.[1] He sought to make it perfectly clear that Factory Short Time Committees formed no part of Trade Union activity.

Ten years passed before witnesses attending Parliamentary Committees felt themselves free to describe the history and mechanism of the Short Time organization. During the interval committees of operatives had spread over the industrial areas and had become an integral and recognized element of the Factory Reform movement. Evidence given before the Select Committee on the Act for the Regulation of Mills and Factories [2] by John Lawton, a member of the Manchester Short Time Committee, affords valuable information of the strength of the movement among the cotton-spinners of South Lancashire. It appears that the Manchester Committee had been in existence since 1814; witness had been periodically a member of it ever since.[3] Its operations were not at all secret. Visitors might attend the actual sittings of the Committee.[4]

The elder Sir Robert Peel seems to have been ignorant of its existence when he began his labours on behalf of the factory children. His language in 1816 suggests

[1] Parl. Papers (1831-1832), xv., Q. 6457.
[2] Parl. Papers (1840), x. [3] Ibid., Q. 8475.
[4] Ibid., Q. 8477.

either ignorance or perhaps a desire for a politic silence on the matter. Indeed, his chief difficulty came from the other side, from the embarrassing over-eagerness of certain Tory country gentlemen, ignorant of factory conditions, to impose impossible restrictions on the mill-owners.[1]

The activity of Sadler and his friends in bringing the Factory question into greater prominence revealed the existence of local federations of Committees in Lanarkshire, Lancashire, Yorkshire and in the lesser factory areas. Delegates from these local federations began to meet annually. The movement continued to expand until, in 1845, a delegate meeting of the Short Time Committees of Lancashire, Yorkshire and Glasgow came to a decision to take over offices in Manchester and employ a permanent secretary.[2]

The development of the Factory Short Time Committee has no parallel within the Trade Union movement. The Committees were constituted differently from Union Lodges. Their functions were different. Though both types of association owed their origin to the harsh demands of industrial necessity, the resemblance ended here.

From the Tory point of view the difference was fundamental. The contact of the Tory party with the Factory and Trade Union movements during the fourteen years of this period was regulated by a vivid consciousness in Tory minds that the two movements had nothing whatever in common.

[1] Quoted in Alfred, *History of the Factory Movement* (1857), vol. i. p. 30.
[2] *Morning Post*, November 3, 1845.

First : the Factory Short Time Committee, though a workmen's association,[1] was in no sense a weapon of industrial aggression. It was a peaceable body formed for the purpose of maintaining existing law. Its functions in this respect were twofold, inspectorial and propagandist. It was a vigilance Committee existing to safeguard the operatives from breaches of the Factory Acts on the part of employers and managers. In 1836, reported a witness already cited, the law was so badly carried out that the Manchester Committee thought it necessary to appoint two individuals from their body to look after the mills, and to give information to the superintendents and inspector ' as things might occur.'[2] It was also a propaganda Committee for disseminating information to the operatives and to the public at large. In 1833 the Leeds Short Time Committee was issuing broadsheets and posters to the operatives warning them of the ' snare ' of an Eight-Hour Double-Shift Bill, which it was feared Ministers were about to introduce.[3]

Secondly : the Short Time Committee was, in fact, a Committee and not a comprehensive association of operatives. The Manchester Committee was a most Conservative body. Eleven members were first appointed at a general meeting and were given power to

1 The Rev. G. S. Bull was Secretary of the Lancashire Central Short Time Committee (Alfred, vol. i. p. 300). ' The local leaders were supported by committees consisting of the principal operatives of their districts ; they were supported by the body of beneficed clergy, by ministers of various other religious denominations, most of the respectable medical practitioners and the influential gentlemen.' (*Ibid.*, *p.* 215.)
2 Lawton (J.). (Parl. Papers (1840), x., Q. 8471.) The Committees also kept a careful eye upon Parliament, keeping the Factory question alive at Westminster by numerous petitions.
3 Circular and Poster. (In Place Coll., vol. 52.)

add to their number. There seemed to be no question of periodic elections. Members, apparently, were allowed wide liberties in co-opting others whom they thought fit.[1] Thirdly : it has been observed that the procedure of the Short Time Committees of Manchester was public. There were no secret oaths or ceremonies of initiation, and no processions. The Short Time Committee was a purely business body.

Fourthly : though the Short Time Committee organization was wholly in the hands of factory operatives, the organization was not regarded as self-contained, as the Trade Union organization was, but as an integral part of a movement in which members of other classes were invited to join.[2] From 1831 the Factory Reform question became the object of a national movement which rendered more public the activities of the Short Time Committees. In its character as a component part of the national organization for Factory Reform the Short Time Committee came into closest contact with the Tory world.

Thus neither the structure nor the procedure of the Short Time Committee bore any relation to that of the Trade Union. In purpose only were the two types of association moving on parallel lines—the betterment of industrial working conditions.

There was a sentiment, attributed by political opponents to the body of the Tory party, that the essence of Tory social ideas was that everything should be done for the workers and not by the workers themselves. It is Miss Martineau's theme, through many laboured pages of her

[1] Parl. Papers (1840), Q. 8478 (Lawton).
[2] Alfred, *passim* ; membership of the actual Committee rank and file, however, was confined to operatives.

History of the Peace.[1] Like many catchwords it had a basis of truth. On the other hand, nobody within the Tory party seems ever to have suggested that Tory assistance should be withdrawn from the Short Time Committees because of some vague theory or catchword of the theorists. It will be sufficient to show a continuous and intimate connection between Toryism and the Short Time Committee organization during the years of Factory Reform activity.

In his relations with the Short Time Committees Ashley had no need of Sadler's circumspection. There was no object now in affecting to deny that the Committees existed. The Tory Sabbatarian, Sir Andrew Agnew, brought G. S. Bull to Ashley's notice. Bull was himself not only a delegate from the Lancashire Central Short Time Committee but its Secretary. Two confirmed reactionaries, Peach and Scarlett, urged Ashley to take up the question of Factory Reform.[2]

The intimate connection between the unofficial Tory party and the Factory Reform movement was quickly recognized by opponents of the Ten Hours Bill. The Short Time Committees were called a Tory device for spreading discontent among the workmen of mill-owners who happened to be largely Liberal in sympathy.[3] The whole movement received the stigma of being a manifestation of Tory spite against the Reform Act.

Apart from the taunt of Tory revenge there was the insinuation of Tory ignorance. Tories, especially those residing in the agricultural areas of the South, could

---

[1] *The History of England during the Thirty Years' Peace, 1816-1846* (1850), vol. ii. pp. 519, 551.
[2] Hodder, vol. i. p. 148.   [3] Morley, vol. i. p. 289.

have known little of industrial conditions. This was a favourite complaint which, on the face of things, was partly justified. Ashley admitted that he had heard nothing of the Factory question before 1832, and that his attention was first drawn to it by a chance reading of the *Times* reports.[1] Oastler was not brought into contact with the Factory system until his visit to John Wood of Horton Hall in 1830.[2] He had previously nothing to do with factories, and the question had simply not occurred to him.[3] G. S. Bull, the parson of Brierley, probably joined the movement in December 1831,[4] although he had discussed the matter with Sadler as long ago as 1823 during a convention on Sunday Schools in which they were both interested.[5]

Neither taunt goes very far. For one thing, political opponents are, it seems, in the habit of ascribing everything their enemies do to a trick. The Carlton Club was a trick, the Tamworth Manifesto was a trick, in fact the whole Tory party was a trick.

Even so, a persistent suspicion remained in the minds of conscientious Reformers, in the full flush of their victory, that Toryism, beaten in politics, was reappearing in industry. ' The hydra may have lost some of its heads,' writes a provincial journalist, ' but others have risen up in their stead, varying in shade and colour, and adapting themselves to altered circumstances.'[6] And when local

---

[1] Hodder, vol. i. p. 148. Memorandum written in 1838.
[2] Alfred, vol. i. p. 95.
[3] Though his letter on ' Yorkshire Slavery ' was written immediately after his visit. (*Leeds Mercury*, September 29, 1830.)
[4] Alfred, vol. i. p. 215.
[5] *Ibid.*, vol. i. p. 220.
[6] *Halifax and Huddersfield Express*, July 7, 1832.

Tory leaders in Yorkshire and Lancashire were seen supporting the Short Time Committees the suspicion deepened. At a Bradford Factory meeting in January 1833, John Doherty, the Ultra-Radical delegate from the Manchester Short Time Committee, had to make a specific disclaimer on the matter.[1]

The Tory complexion of these Northern Factory meetings added colour to the rumour. The meetings had been held throughout the years of 1831-32, when the Reform agitation was at its height. A gentleman at a meeting at York called out ' Reform and Retrenchment ! ' and ' he was desired to go out of the yard.'[2] Operative speakers were telling their audiences that the Ten Hours Bill would give them solid benefits, whereas the Reform Bill gave them nothing at all.[3]

In after years the Anti-Corn Law League found Factory Reformers indifferent to their appeals. The Factory system, the Reformers pointed out, sweated children's labour before Corn Laws existed.[4] Corn Laws, in fact, had little to do with Factory system.

It was to be expected that all mention of Political Economy was banned at Factory meetings. A local grocer at a Leeds meeting held in 1833 gave vent to the sentiment that they should go to the root of the matter and make labour free and unrestricted.[5] He was hissed

---

[1] *Halifax Guardian*, January 19, 1833.
[2] Parl. Papers (1831-1832), xv., Q. 9802. Evidence of Oastler (R.).
[3] *Leeds Intelligencer*, March 16, 1833. Meeting of Operatives at Court House, Leeds.
[4] The Address of the Operatives of England and Scotland to all ranks and classes in the land. Manchester, April 25, 1833. (Actually from the Lancashire Short Time Committee.) Hodder, vol. i. p. 159.
[5] *Leeds Intelligencer*, March 16, 1833.

for his pains. The address which the Lancashire Short Time Committee drew up in 1833 emphasized the necessity of 'staying the plague of Political Economy and all-engrossing covetousness.'[1]

No purview of the relation between the Tory party and the Factory movement would be complete without a survey of the field occupied by Conservative party organization in its contact with the factory operatives. The survey leaves little in doubt as to the position of the Parliamentary leaders of the party. No attempt seems to have been made to bring the Factory Short Time Committees within the ambit of the Conservative party machine, or to accommodate them within the ranks of the new Operative Societies. There was every reason why this could not be done. The Conservative party had no Factory policy ; nor were the party leaders unnecessarily prejudiced against the factory owners. The further the Conservative party moved away from the Reform Act the more Conservatism as an active political force sought the sympathy of the manufacturing interests. When Peel began to cover the land with his provincial associations, he did not intend to run the risk of offending the very interests he laboured to conciliate. Peel's attitude towards the Factory Short Time Committees was already determined when he drafted the Tamworth Manifesto.

[1] Hodder, vol. i. p. 159.

TORYISM AND THE PEOPLE

(C) Provident Association : The Friendly
Society

If the Tory attitude towards the Trade Union movement
was largely compounded of mistrust and repression, it
was far different in the case of the Friendly Societies.
As early as the last quarter of the eighteenth century,
the Friendly Society possessed a legal status in the
country. Benefit Clubs grew in popularity among the
hard-pressed armies of skilled labour during the period
of the French wars, and they retained their popularity
all through the dark days of economic instability and
Pittite repression. It is of interest to note that Friendly
Societies were at no time regarded in the same light as
combinations even by the reactionary legislators of the
Combination (Amending) Act of 1825.[1] None of the
arguments of the rising school of *laissez-faire* were ever
seriously applied to combinations for mutual benefit.
In an age when the administration of the Poor Law
had become an intolerable burden on the public, voices
were heard in praise of Friendly Societies as efficacious
instruments for restoring what contemporary idealists
considered to be the spirit of the Poor Laws of Elizabeth
—the independence and morality of the labourer.[2]
Evidence given before a Select Committee of 1825, then
considering the state of the law respecting Friendly
Societies, proves clearly that combinations of working

[1] Though the Tory General Gascoyne feared that the Committee
investigating the consequences of the Act of 1824 intended to interfere
with *bona fide* Benefit Societies. (*Hansard*, xiii. 356, May 3, 1825.)
[2] Report on the Laws respecting Friendly Societies (1825, iv.),
Minutes of Evidence, p. 31. (Rev. J. T. Becher of Southwell.)

people and others along these lines were thoroughly in accord with the prevailing notions of the time.

Among the agricultural districts especially the idea of the Friendly Society took firm root. Landlords even went so far as to encourage the formation of local clubs. Round about Nottingham the farm labourers subscribed in large numbers.[1] Prebendary Becher, giving evidence before the Committee, advised, in cases of emergency, an extension of the methods adopted by the justices of Hampshire in granting such clubs an aid from the County rate.[2]

The first thirty years of the nineteenth century saw a rapid increase in the number of the Societies in the predominantly agricultural counties. A Parliamentary Return of Friendly Societies, compiled in 1837,[3] reveals a total of over a thousand registered societies covering England and Wales, not to mention a host of obscure clubs whose existence was unknown to the Actuary. In Hampshire alone the registered societies numbered 38, while in Dorsetshire, a county in which great distress was then prevalent among the labourers, there were 54 registered lodges.

The Societies, independent, autonomous units, grew by the thousand during the first thirty years of the century. The parallel growth of the Trade Union movement in no way hindered their increase. The better elements from the ranks of the skilled workers, who steadfastly refused to follow the politically-minded Trade Unionists into the doubtful ambit of Chartism, remained loyal to their Friendly Societies.

[1] *Ibid.*, p. 32.   [2] *Ibid.*, p. 32.
[3] Parl. Papers (1837), li.

The Societies were fraternities in every sense. If they excluded party politics, they provided a home for kindred spirits both in politics and in religion. Thus, while there existed often side by side in the same village Church Benefit Societies and Methodist Provident Unions, True Blue Clubs and Reform ' Friendlies,' the political element everywhere gave way to the social. Societies of all conceivable kinds were in abundance, and the friendly pint of ale formed the closest bond of union among all. The Parliamentary Return quoted shows that the rural or town working classes were not alone in availing themselves of the benefits of providential union. Landlords, tenants, shopkeepers, all had their societies. Shrewton in Wiltshire boasted of its Society of Gentlemen Farmers and Tradesmen, a society enrolled in 1831. There was a Cleveland Friendly Society, a convivial club of Yorkshire gentlemen founded in 1772, and rather more convivial than provident.[1] The City of Lincoln had its well-managed General Friendly Institution under the patronage of the local Tory gentry strongly represented by the Sibthorpe family.[2] Banbury, to its dozen or so Friendly Clubs existing in 1837, added a Conservative Friendly Society, strictly limited to one hundred members and meeting at Ann Burnham's White Hart Inn.[3] At Oxford there were three enrolled Societies accommodating Tory tradesmen, Reforming tradesmen, and young freemen, all three clubs enrolled before 1836. There

[1] Its constitution is given in Ditchfield (P. H.), *The Old English Country Squire* (1912), p. 226.
[2] Rules and Assurance Tables of the Lincoln General Friendly Institution. Established January 17, 1829.
[3] Rules for the Regulation and Government of a Conservative Friendly Society (1837).

THE ASSOCIATION OF LABOUR

was an Old Men's Club at Sandbach, a New Friendly Constitutional of St. Austell, a True Blue Society at the Plough Inn, Sandacre, in Derbyshire, and an Amicable Society of Women at Devonport. Lyneham in Wiltshire had its Mutual Subsisting Society, Chester its Harmonicons and Noah's Ark.[1] In Ramsbury, a remote village in the Kennet Valley, a place which then held little over 3000 inhabitants, the labourers and tradesmen could find accommodation in accordance with their political convictions. The Union Society, strongly for Church and King, and patronized by the parson, met at the Castle Inn, while the village Nonconformity resorted to the more liberal Friendly Union which held its meetings in the Wesleyan Methodist schoolroom.[2]

Side by side with the independent societies were lodges affiliated to federations of which the principal types were the Oddfellows and the Foresters. The idea of a union of lodges presented Tory thought with an entirely different set of problems. With the smaller, autonomous societies there existed no problem at all. Tory magistrates smiled upon them and gave them the countenance of Quarter Sessions. Tory squires and parsons patronized them and actively assisted their funds. It is noteworthy that most of the village Benefit Societies existing in 1837 had come into being long before the Reform Act.

In the case of the federated union the Tory was impelled by an inveterate prejudice, a lively suspicion of centralization of any kind. Applied to Friendly Societies it was a prejudice which extended beyond the

---

[1] Parl. Papers (1837), li.
[2] *Ibid.*, and from information derived locally.

135

limits of Toryism. Tidd-Pratt, the first Registrar of Friendly Societies, with a long life experience at his back, declared his opposition to the great Orders and encouraged local, autonomous societies.[1] One of the greatest difficulties which beset the missionaries of the Manchester Unity on their tours through the country lay in the half-hostile attitude of the local gentry. Not that hostility was universal in the country parts. Thomas Arnett, commissioned by the Quarterly Committee of the Manchester Unity to secure the allegiance of wavering lodges, and to make converts to Oddfellowship, seems to have encountered little opposition from landowners or tenants during his visitations of 1825 and 1826. From here and there, however, come indications that Oddfellowship was none too popular among the landed classes.[2]

Although the centralizing tendency inherent in the great federations of Friendly Societies provided Tory critics with a sound academical case against such a body as the Manchester Unity, there was a far deeper cause for Tory suspicion. Only once during its long career has English Oddfellowship had reason to fear trouble from the law. In the trial of the Dorchester labourers

---

[1] Contemporary feeling against the great Orders did not extend to the County Friendly Societies, which became very popular in agricultural counties towards the middle of the century. The Bishop of Salisbury recommended his clergy to support the County Societies on the ground that the village clubs were often financially unsound. (*A Charge delivered to the Clergy of the Diocese of Salisbury* (1848), p. 35.)

[2] See *Norfolk Chronicle*, October 25, 1856, for an instance at a later period ; also Daynes (A. W.), *The late Samuel Daynes : A Short Biographical Sketch with a Reprint of the Controversy with Lord Albemarle on the Stability of the Manchester Unity in 1856* (1892).

the legality of secret oaths administered by Trade Unions or Friendly Societies was called in question. The officers of the Manchester Unity flew into a justifiable, if unnecessary, panic. There was a foreboding that the sentence imposed upon the Tolpuddle Unionists might fall impartially on their heads also. If the labourers had received sentences of transportation for administering illegal oaths, was the elaborate ritual of the Unity wholly above suspicion ? At all events the directors of the Annual Movable Committee, who sat that year in Hull, resolved to abandon the more incriminating part of their ritual and to destroy the last traces of anything likely to compromise the Order.[1]

Whatever the law might determine, the attitude of the Order is clear enough. In the course of a statement compiled by order of the directors in January 1837, and laid before Sir John Campbell, the Attorney-General, for his legal opinion, the directors carefully define the attitude of their society in the matter of political intervention. ' The Order discountenances Trade Unions ; and does not allow assistance to be given to those who leave their employment in strikes or tumults—by this means promoting good will to all men.' [2] Actually the Order had no need to take these defensive measures, for no attack upon its constitution or customs seems to have been contemplated.

There was nothing in the domestic economy of the Friendly Societies, either autonomous or affiliated, to which Tory scruples might take exception. Throughout

[1] Lewis (A.), *The Complete Manual of Oddfellowship*, privately printed (1879), p. 76.
[2] Spry (J.), *The History of Oddfellowship* (1867), p. 39.

the period of Chartism and Corn-Law controversy the movement continued to gain ground. London and the Home Counties abounded in hosts of struggling, independent lodges, many unknown to the Chief Registrar. The number of district lodges affiliated to the Manchester Unity, to the Druids, to the Foresters and the Freemasons became prodigious. An Oddfellow with a taste for rhyme compiled a long inventory in doggerel of the London lodges of his Order, beginning :—

> I 'll sing you of our lodges, and thro' the district stalk ;
> Lord Byron is in Bermondsey, I think, in Page's Walk.
> In Greenwich Town the Men of Kent hard by the North
> Pole lay,
> And the Pride of Kent reposes at the Bells in Mary Cray.
> St. Saviour's in the Borough and the Bud of Hope so sweet,
> St. Olave's and the Philanthropic both in Union Street. [1]

With few exceptions the rendezvous of Friendly Societies at this time were public-houses, the usual resort of political and social clubs of all descriptions. Lodge members met to transact business over their ale, and the quantities of liquor which they consumed often had its natural effect : the brethren got drunk. Indeed, the drunkenness associated with lodge meetings occasioned much misgiving among religious bodies. A member of the Wesleyan Methodist Conference of 1830 drew attention to the injury to the faith in the Manchester and Huddersfield district owing to the convivial influence of the Independent Order of Oddfellows. He complained that this society began as a convivial

[1] Larkin (G. G.), *The Pleasures of Oddfellowship and other Poems* (1844).

fraternity and had only of late years become a mutual provident association. Unfortunately it still retained its primitive usages and character. He went on to say that these societies had during the Luddite Agitation been 'foci of a revolutionary propagandism.'[1] The Rev. G. S. Bull, the Tory Factory Reformer, likewise had occasion to admonish the brethren on their lapse from a state of godly temperance. He would have them remove the cause of temptation by withdrawing their meetings from public-houses. Fruitful sources of drunkenness in the industrial North were funeral feasts and tides, in which commiseration for a departed brother led to the intoxication of the mourning lodge members.[2]

The most orthodox Tory could scarcely accuse the Friendly Societies of clandestine and subversive political activity, and it seems that the complaint of the Wesleyan minister on the score of ' revolutionary propagandism ' was either based on confused evidence or on evidence inapplicable at the time of his complaint to the Conference. The *Manchester Guardian* of the day took every opportunity of criticizing the Manchester Unity, but the political neutrality of the constituent lodges was not impugned.

The emphasis which the Friendly Societies placed on the social side may be gathered from a review of the rules of the lodges compiled at this time. The Stamford Loyal Independent Society of Oddfellows heralds its Regulations by the preamble, ' The Pleasures of Good Company, The Improvement of Good Morals and the Relief of Every Afflicted or Distressed Brother, are the

---

[1] Gregory (B.), *Sidelights on the Conflicts of Methodism* (1898), p. 93.
[2] Bull (G. S.), *The Gospel of Christ recommended to Coal Miners* (1834).

Primary Objects of Oddfellowship.' The early rules of the Manchester Unity make no reference to the discussion of politics at lodge meetings, but in the ' Laws for the Government of the Independent Order of Oddfellows,' compiled in 1841, clause 18 declares ' that, if any member sleep in the lodge room during lodge hours he shall be fined threepence ; and any member swearing, singing any indecent or political song, or giving an indecent or political toast or sentiment, shall be fined one shilling.' So insistently was violence of speech, or anything bordering upon partisanship, reprobated, that it is recorded of certain over-zealous brethren of one of the Manchester lodges that they were brought to task for allowing the toast—' May our enemies be lathered with *aquafortis* and shaved with a hand-saw ! ' Political neutrality among the lodges seems to have been the normal attitude.[1]

The attitude of the Established Church towards the Friendly Societies is instructive. The truth was that clergymen knew better than to oppose the spread of the lodges. Here and there were instances of clerical bigotry. A Primitive Methodist minister would accuse the local Oddfellows of luring his congregation from the chapel, and thus reducing his stipend. A Wesleyan Methodist minister would bring the matter of lodge meetings and drunkenness before the notice of Conference. The Huddersfield Oddfellows were attending St. Paul's Church, when they were suddenly assailed by a torrent of abuse from the parson. ' What do you mean by coming here with your badges, collecting a multitude of people, breaking the Sabbath and keeping thousands from a place of worship ? . . . You are a disgrace to

[1] *Oddfellows' Magazine,* New Series, vol ii. p. 363, March 1834.

society—a scandal to the country you live in.'[1] Occasionally the brethren would invite a minister to deliver them a sermon, only to find that the worthy preacher had prepared a wholly irrelevant discourse, perhaps a homily upon the Fall or strictures upon the snares of riches.

In the main both clergy and ministers adopted an altogether different attitude. 'The first excellence to which your Society holds out most encouragement is industry,' declared the Rev. E. Greenshaw to the Oddfellows of Great Ouseburn, 'an active and unremitting attention to your duty in that state of life in which it has pleased God in His good providence to place you.'[2] A Cheshire parson preached to his flock upon the blessedness of fellowship : 'When we see an institution, the principal and grand objects of which are the cultivation of friendship, the improvement of morals, the unity of brotherhood, brotherly love, the rendering essential service to each other through all the varying vicissitudes of life, by the mutual aid and assistance of each other . . . such an institution seems to have all the appearance, not only of temporal, but also of eternal welfare.'[3] And the parson of Horton in Yorkshire dismisses the local Oddfellows with the benediction of the Church : 'The Lord God of your fathers make you a thousand times so many more as ye are, and bless you as He hath promised.'[4]

[1] Moffrey (R. W.), *A Century of Oddfellowship* (1910), p. 43. A sermon preached by the Rev. Mr. Bywater. This was in 1833.

[2] *Oddfellows' Magazine*, New Series, vol. iv. p. 353, June 1837.

[3] Moffrey, p. 45. Sermon preached by the Rev. J. Bostock, October 31, 1831.

[4] *Oddfellows' Magazine*, vol. ii. p. 269, June 1833. Sermon preached by the Rev. J. C. Boddington at Illingworth, Easter Monday, 1833.

It is clear that the Mutual Benefit Society, as a type of working men's association, fitted into the Tory scheme of things. In the sense that the Friendly lodge represented an ethical, rather than a political, idea, the Tory squire and parson found no difficulty in according their sympathy. That hostility to Friendly Societies found no place in contemporary Tory polemics is evidence of a spirit at least of toleration. Wherever objections and opposition arose it was the threatened bureaucracy of federated Unities that was called in question. Friendly Societies owed their success throughout the period no less to the fact that their insistence on prudence, thrift and self-help found equal sympathy with the prevailing moral doctrine of the day.

(D) EDUCATIONAL ASSOCIATION : THE MECHANICS' INSTITUTE

The struggle of rival educational theories during the second quarter of the nineteenth century never assumed in this country the proportions of an intellectual war. Fortunately for England the causes which aggravated the fierce conflict on the Continent between the partisans of secular and of clerical education were here almost wholly absent. The leaders of educational secularism were moderates and, what was more, they were bourgeois. They scrupulously refrained from any attempt to overturn the religious and moral basis upon which the existing system had for centuries reposed. And, in return, there were extremely few champions of the traditional order who were greatly concerned to find in the newer educational systems the anti-moral, anti-social nightmare which a de Maistre or a Polignac found in every little Secularist academy in France.

Fortunately, too, neither the zealots among the Radical extremists nor the enemies of the ' subversive system of Mr. Owen ' were taken too seriously. The country had other and more important problems on hand. It was due to the fact that reform in education was not in England considered a first-class political question that our educational methods have preserved a degree of continuity seemingly impossible in any other country.

This is not an assertion that moderate reform was everywhere accepted without question. The great changes which the quarter-century yielded, both in the practical methods of instruction and in the popular attitude towards the whole problem of education, were subjected to a stubborn resistance from defenders of the established system. And it was when that established system fell foul of a competitor governed by ideas and values fundamentally different from its own, that the strength of educational conservatism in England can best be realized.

It was a common gibe of Reformers of the time that the Tory party was actively hostile to all schemes for educating the working classes. The gibe was merited, though it was but a half-statement of the truth. It were better to have retorted that the Tory party was the uncompromising enemy to the spirit which influenced all contemporary designs for extending knowledge to the labourer. And not only the Tory party, but that more powerful force, Tory sentiment, was the enemy. It was a radical difference of principle that separated the champions of reaction and reform. ' Education ' in the hands of the two bodies of adherents meant two entirely different things.

What the Society for the Diffusion of Useful Knowledge meant by 'popular education' seemed to the National Society to connote a form of national apostasy, while to conscientious Secularists the work of the National Society was reactionary paternalism, a sop to the working classes.

It was unreasonable that the spirit of Reform, which had already begun to attack traditional political and economic principles, should abstain from undermining the foundation of the accepted system of education, so little in sympathy with the rising tide of opinion. Although care must be taken to avoid making *laissez-faire* the keynote to every change in every department of nineteenth-century existence, yet it is nevertheless true that the spread of Liberal ideas in Government and Industry was coeval—and not by chance—with the extension of Liberal Reform to the realm of popular education. *Laissez-faire*, as a leading political and commercial maxim of the time, had definite moral and spiritual implications. And this *laissez-faire* was not merely a vapid aspiration ; it was to Liberal Reformers a statement of fundamental law. Under the guise of extending the advantages of knowledge to the labouring classes lurked the reality of an individualist system of education.

The development in this country of the idea of Progress was accelerated during the nineteenth century. Progress dominated the new system of education, and with it came that curious blend of optimism and rationalism which characterized this period. The more enlightened teachers of the time held fast to a theory of progress which they applied with universality, which, to us of a more sophisticated generation, appears incredible. And belief in the illimitable possibilities of individual self-development leads straight to a state of mind similar to that which enabled the adherents of the *Rights of Man* to believe in the possibility of man's ultimate perfectibility. From perfectibility there is but a short journey to Reason.

The element of rationalism in education was not, of course, born with the generation which superintended the foundation of London University or sponsored the birth of Mechanics' Institutes. Full fifty years before James Mill subscribed £5 to Dr. Birkbeck's Plan, the young *Candide* had wandered disconsolately through the whole realm of experience to find refuge at last in the garden of Pure Reason on the shores of the Bosphorus. Fénelon's *Télémaque*, whom Bossuet justly suspected of being half a young Secularist, was contemporary with our Church-and-King Sacheverell. Laicism as a principle of education had been officially adopted by the First Republic. But education in England was practically untouched by rationalizing influence when the greater part of the Continent had already moved towards Secularism—a testimony to the national instinct in favour of conservative systems.

The belief that the diffusion of knowledge leads necessarily to the self-improvement of the individual is a form of philosophical optimism native only to an age which places the value of Reason very high. Yet this belief was the most powerful of the motives behind the principal educational reforms of the early nineteenth century.

From a belief in the reality of Progress and a reliance

on the beneficent influence of Reason came a naive theory of knowledge. The prevailing optimism led educational reforms to regard knowledge as something to be desired. No matter what kind of knowledge ; knowledge was education ; education was good. To increase facilities for popular education was to assist the march of progress. A rooted trust in the infallibility of Right Reason led them by easy stages into a haven of intellectual optimism. It was fitting that the nation which had led the way in removing restrictions to the freedom of trade should vie with foreign States in removing restrictions to the acquisition of knowledge. Hence the Mechanics' Institutes, the result of a brilliant idea of middle-class Intellectuals for furthering educational progress among the working classes by placing in their hands the means of imbibing Useful Knowledge.

Without doubt the founders of Mechanics' Institutes placed the value of Reason very high indeed. Birkbeck and his associates admitted their debt to Bentham's hard thinking, and Bentham's influence aided the rationalist tendency of our educational methods. Reason was the most powerful of all the weapons wielded by educational Reformers of the day. It was the principal gravamen in the Reformers' indictment of established institutions that they were contrary to reason.

When Reformers took their stand upon the rock of Reason, and from that strong position attacked the fallacies of existing educational systems, they felt themselves to be secure from counter-attack. They felt themselves to be logically unassailable.

The prevailing passion for rationalism in public instruction extended even to the education of the child.

A scholastic expert of the time reported to the Central Society for the Diffusion of Useful Knowledge his conclusions on the subject of juvenile education : that children prefer rational to irrational toys—wooden trucks to coloured dolls.[1] Another proposed that games of chance be abolished in adult schools and rational games —chess for example—be alone permitted. He would go even further and give it as his considered opinion that chess, a game of science and skill, if introduced even into schools, would ' have a great effect upon the moral and intellectual character of the nation.' [2]

Against this rationalizing movement in education was ranged the whole force of reaction.

One hesitates to tie down the Tory party of the early nineteenth century to the sponsorship of any one educational system, for the very good reason that the Tory party was not always fully representative of what may be called Tory sentiment in the country. But it must be admitted that Toryism, here as elsewhere, stood obstinately in the old ways. While the Liberal school saw tremendous possibilities in the progressive education of the masses, the Tory school emphatically did not.

There is little doubt that the Parliamentary Tory party, had it dared, would have resisted the introduction of a State-aided national system of education. The very idea of a national State system was abhorrent to Tory prejudices, not because the system was national, but because the State might impose educational principles which Tories held to be pernicious. Only with the greatest

[1] Duppa (B. F.) in *Papers of the Central Society of Education*, vol. i. (1837).
[2] Baker (C.), *Ibid*.

147

difficulty could Peel persuade his Tory followers to continue the Treasury grant to approved societies for the education of the poor. Of the Diffusion of Useful Knowledge, of knowledge for its own sake, the Tory knew little and cared less. And there was a reason. For between the Reformers' best intentions and the working classes stood the cumbrous bulk of the Church Establishment—Toryism on its spiritual side.

Toryism in education was no novelty. Whatever else the authors of the Reformation had jettisoned in response to the demand of exuberant nationalism, they left intact the clerical hegemony over the national education. So that Reformers in education who took upon themselves to oppose the monopoly over education exercised by the Established Church, who agitated for the admission of Dissenters to the universities or who favoured the 'national' education of the masses, were by implication questioning the validity of the basic principle upon which English education had rested since learning first appeared in this country.

This system, which had its roots far deeper in history than the scholarship of Erasmus and of Richard Hooker, survived in its theoretical essentials into the generation of Peel and Brougham. Little blame can attach to Reformers who, drawing their inspiration from a far different source, regarded the existing system of popular education as hopelessly inadequate for the time in which they lived.

Tory prejudice against what were then considered to be the progressive notions of education found itself at a loss for cogent argument why the labouring classes should not be admitted to those benefits of self-improvement which the Society for the Diffusion of Useful Knowledge laboured to obtain for them. Two circumstances supported the Tory view—the same two which provided the motive for much Tory action at the time—prejudice and the appeal to facts.

Prejudice is a political weapon not confined solely to the Right Wing. And prejudice was especially powerful in matters of educational policy. Reformers were detested not because, as Reformers, they were intrinsically bad, but because those who preached Reform were men whose whole outlook was poison to Tory prejudice. Without doubt much of the odium which Tories associated with the founding of Mechanics' Institutes arose directly from a rooted dislike of Henry Brougham, who figured prominently as a patron of adult secular education. In fact it was a common belief among members of the Parliamentary Tory party, both before and after the Reform Bill, that Lord Brougham's devotion to the cause of working-class education was prompted by the basest motives. Tories confessed to a considerable difficulty in denying themselves the conclusion that the establishment of Mechanics' Institutes was Brougham's way of collecting potential support for his Whig friends in Parliament —perhaps as a counterblast to the Operative Conservative Societies, lately launched under less intellectual auspices. The formation of Mechanics' reading-rooms was by some suspected of being a political gesture in disguise. Lord Brougham's self-improving labourers were not there, as it was said, to imbibe Pure Science but rather Reform, Radicalism, and Political Economy.[1]

There was a prejudice more profound than that which

[1] *Thoughts on the State and Prospects of Toryism* (1837).

sprang from a dislike or suspicion of Brougham's schemes of popular instruction. Tories believed that the New Knowledge tended to undermine the religious basis of English education. They had within their own recollection, as a stern warning, the collapse of religious education in Revolutionary France and the consequences which overtook Frenchmen under the rule of Hébert and Robespierre. The new educational tendencies were all Secularist, they represented a break with the clericalism of the past. Although in England the clericalism of the Church of England laid a yoke upon the national education not hard to bear, the Secularists chafed under the real or fancied burden.

Mechanics' Institutes were devoted wholly to secular education. Within the somewhat arid limits prescribed by public governing bodies the pursuit of knowledge was free to all ; provided there were teachers enough, members might learn anything. Coal-miners, seated within neo-classic porticoes of Halls of Science, might study the secrets of Marine Astronomy, skilled cabinet-makers were admitted to the realms of Physics and Hydrostatics, while to textile operatives, bent on self-improvement, it was given to acquire the rudiments of Algebra and Botany.

That which distinguished the Tory from the Liberal view of popular education was not so much a difference of method as a difference of aim. The two schools embraced two mutually hostile theories of knowledge. To the Reformers' principle of ' self-improvement through knowledge ' Tories might object that *laissez-faire* in knowledge brought about social consequences equally as disastrous as *laissez-faire* in industrial relations. The removal of all regulation of knowledge must lead to intellectual and moral anarchy. Education must have an *end* higher than self-improvement or it is but education in caricature. The Tory view was well stated by an enemy in the phrase that science—meaning his friends' views on science—was considered a form of sin.[1] Unregulated, uncensored science was assuredly considered a form of sin, not only by Tories, but by the body of Church opinion. The religious inspiration which prompted that sentiment came, not from Rome, but from Clapham Common.

But while the intelligent and public-spirited gentlemen who supported the Adult Education movement adhered to their views of the function of knowledge, they were impartial enough to leave room for the claims of sound common sense. Their belief in common sense brought them to desire that the principles of common sense should be placed within the reach of all. If one is in possession of the whole truth, the vehicle for imparting that truth to others is propaganda.

The reactionary Tory attitude to the educational principles of Reform can well be seen in the way in which Tories regarded the actual methods by which it was proposed to diffuse knowledge among the industrious classes. It will now be convenient to consider first the syllabus of training, including Political Economy, secondly the machinery by which this was to be accomplished.

The curriculum of the Mechanics' Institutes exhibited a propagandist tendency, not because there was anything harmful in teaching science to working men, but because

[1] The phrase is Holyoake's. Holyoake (G. J.), *The History of Co-operation* (1906), vol. i. p. 143.

the fundamental notion of knowledge-free-for-all inherent in the new working-class educational movements had not yet emerged from the battle-ground of controversy. The terms 'useful knowledge' and 'self-improvement' were not universally accepted in the vocabulary of education; they were still party catchwords of one or two hostile educational schools. In one instance particularly the New Education showed its teeth.

That instance was the teaching of Political Economy. Nowhere is the dogmatic certitude of the Age of Reform more clearly shown than in its studies. Not for the first time in English history a period of political development has accompanied a marked decline in the intellectual level of its instructed citizens. Up to the year in which the younger Mill began to entertain doubts upon the subject of the infallibility of Politico-Economic laws, it had become the habit of the orthodox schools to regard these laws much in the same light as religious belief. Either you accepted the verdict of Political Economy or you did not; for the intelligent there was no half-way house. Intellectual certainty was the desire of the devotees of enlightenment.

Members of the working classes, who thought of the problem at all, reasoned from a different point of view. When they were told by the unanimous voice of orthodox Political Economists that their own economic condition was governed by the laws of Competition and that industrial distress was capable of explanation in terms of the law of supply and demand, they came to regard Political Economy, not as an explanation of their evil case, but as an excuse for keeping them down.

Among the masses, and owing largely to the influence of Cobbett, Political Economy had come to be looked upon as a sort of black art. Rightly or wrongly the industrial operatives had convinced themselves that Political Economy was a weapon in the hands of their masters. It was in vain that employers retorted that their workmen were perfectly free agents to tolerate or avoid the system, as they wished. Working men simply could not see it. To the ill-educated and hungry reader of the *Political Register* or Oastler's *Fleet Papers*, Political Economy looked dangerously like a trumped-up, *ex post facto* justification of a policy of wage-cutting and labour sweating. The wretched handloom weaver who bitterly complained that Roebuck's *Political Pamphlets* had become ' The instrument to publish the opinions of a set of starving political economists,' in the same execrable hand wrote to Place : ' If I don't mistake Lord Brougham, Poulet Thomson and best part of the Ministry is Political Economist and if they don't advocate low wages, why punish men for trying to raise them ? ' [1]

The more instructed expressed the same sentiments with greater moderation. When a member of the Halifax Mechanics' Institute proposed that a class in Political Economy should be established, the Chairman told him that if they wished for peace in the Institute, Political Economy must not enter in.[2]

John Fielden, himself a mill-owner, would admit the contention that obedience to the rules of Political Economy might make England the workshop of the

[1] Cray (R.) to Place (F.), undated (1835) (in Place Coll., vol. 52). Cray apparently wrote the first letter to Roebuck, who passed it on to Place. [2] *Halifax Guardian*, January 12, 1833.

world. But the national vigour, he thought, would be destroyed in the process.[1]

The Tory attitude towards the subject of Political Economy may be dismissed very shortly. In Parliament Tory members had for many years been subjected to protracted lectures on Political Economy alternately from Huskisson on their own side of the House, and on the other from the whole Liberal-Radical following—those ' great luminaries of Political Economy,' Stanhope had once called them, ' who were considered as oracles.' [2] The Corn Law controversy saw the Tory party inundated by a torrent of Political Economy from all sides of the House. A Tory member lamented that, because Cobden was a Political Economist, he refused to be contradicted.[3] It was the intellectual dogmatism of men of this type which Parson Lot detested—men who ' arrogantly talk of Political Economy as a science, so completely perfected, so universal and all-important, that common humanity and morality, reason and religion, must be pooh-poohed down, if they seem to interfere with its infallible conclusions. . . . The Politico-Economical discoverer of twenty years ago solemnly forbids all future discoveries.' [4] In the debates on the Corn Importation Bill we find a member of the Country Party grumbling that the Political Economists, having abandoned their principles with regard to mines, railway regulation, and labour in factories, were now seeking to apply them in all their integrity to Corn.[5] The same member objects to the

1 *The Curse of the Factory System* (1836), p. 74.
2 *Hansard*, vi. 555, February 21, 1822.
3 Baillie (H.J.), *Hansard*, lix. 245, August 25, 1841.
4 *The Christian Socialist*, vol. i., No. 3, November 16, 1850.
5 Seymer (H. K.), *Hansard*, lxxxvi. 455, May 12, 1846.

application of Political Economy to the Corn Law controversy, and for this reason : that ' one man who wrote one book would give one set of definitions, whilst another would give a different set ; and they had no agreement. Their terms were not defined, their axioms were not universal, and their elementary propositions were not proved.' Hence the unfairness of dogmatizing. Dr. Chalmers throughout his life clung to the exalted ideal of the essential unity between the economic and spiritual well-being of society, between Political Economy and the Law of God. But even Chalmers could not resist a criticism of the assumed infallibility of those of the orthodox school who would by implication repudiate ' the moral ingredient.' [1]

Generally speaking, the most enlightened of the new era seldom paused to question any of their fundamental principles. Often the education of the working classes was given a political motive. The Central Society of Education in 1837 recommends that the study of Political Economy is particularly appropriate for those who attend Mechanics' Institutes. ' In towns where the working population forms a dense mass—where strikes, trade unions, and combinations have been so ruinous to the merchant, the manufacturer and the workmen—it is of the utmost importance that the principles which affect national wealth and industry should be most thoroughly understood.' [2] Elsewhere the Society proposes, by the influence of popular education, to counteract ' the propositions of Destructives for an agrarian law and a

---

[1] Preface to *The Christian Polity of a Nation* (Select Works, vol. xiv.).

[2] Baker (C.), On Mechanics' Institutions and Libraries. (*Papers of the Central Society of Education*, vol. i. (1837), pp. 247-248.)

community of property.'[1]   Place thought it worth while
to preserve among his papers a pamphlet entitled,
*An Address to the Labourers on the subject of destroying
Machinery*, published during the outbreaks of 1830-31,
under the authority of the Society for the Diffusion of
Useful Knowledge.   The old man (we may believe with
a smile) wrote on the cover that the writer was one
Henry Gawler, ' a good kind-hearted gentleman and with
the best intentions.'[2]   Thus was the New Knowledge
pressed into the service of the State.

Had Tories possessed the same confidence in the
sedative influence of Political Economy as an adjunct
to good government, their attitude might have been
less hostile.   For the most part, however, Tories ignored
the stabilizing, and saw only the disruptive, elements of
universal popular education.

While bishops were fulminating against the grant of
a charter to the ' godless ' London University, Tories
were denouncing Mechanics' Institutes as the breeding
ground of unrest.   They could not see why the friends of
the new order were condemning indiscriminate charity
(they had the New Poor Law in mind) while in the same
breath those same friends were loud in praise of a system
of indiscriminate education.

The theoretical objections of the Reactionaries were
not unreflected in the country at large.   Adult education, when by education was meant merely the teaching
of secular knowledge, failed hopelessly in the rural
districts, where the pristine spirit of Toryism was most
alive.   It was in vain that the Society for the Diffusion

[1] *Papers of the Central Society of Education*, vol. iii. (1839), p. 126.
[2] Place Coll., vol. 21.

of Useful Knowledge counselled agricultural labourers on the advantages of ' self-improvement combined with rational amusement.' [1] Here and there a local institute would flourish for a time, but the rot soon set in. Members would cease to yearn for Useful Knowledge, and their Institute would become a club.

This was in spite of the fact that the promoters of the movement set to work with the best intentions. Arrangements were made for the establishment of itine-rating libraries, after the example of East Lothian, to supply the needs of local branches. [2] Here and there a generous-minded farmer would be Secretary and Treasurer of the village Institute. [3] Chichester found itself the centre of a group of affiliated village branches.

The movement failed for more than one reason. The ordinary village labourer, faced with the alternative of imbibing Useful Knowledge at the Mechanics' Institute or beer at the local Conservative Working Men's Society, can never have been in much doubt. Workmen, in common with most men, find great difficulty in main-taining two objects of allegiance at the same time, and it may be noticed here that the years 1836-37, which marked the rise of popular Conservative Societies throughout the provinces, marked also the first decline of the rural Mechanics' Institutes.

The investigations set on foot by the Central Society of Education in 1837 into the state of Mechanics' Institutes and Libraries revealed a discouraging situation. [4] From Chichester, where high hopes had been entertained, came

[1] *Papers of the Central Society of Education* (1837), vol. i. p. 239.
[2] *Ibid.*, vol. i., art. ' Duppa.'   [3] *Ibid.*
[4] *Ibid.* (1837), vol. i. pp. 236 foll., art. ' Baker.'

doleful intelligence. Despite a large membership the Institute had failed to develop its intellectual side, owing, it was said, to the irregular attendance of gratuitous teachers. At Lewes, while membership was well sustained, the classes for instruction had altogether decayed. The Lincoln branch was sustained by local patronage, but at Hastings the Institute lamented the virtual death of its intellectual side ; lectures had been discontinued while, to the scandal of the investigator, no less than five libraries for ' fashionable visitors ' were maintained. From the agricultural regions of the North was heard the same tale of despair. Classes held under the auspices of the Ripon branch had been insufficiently valued by the local workmen. Most of the returns from Yorkshire speak of the ' deeply rooted ignorance of the value of the application of knowledge.' The returns from the West showed no happier result. The Exeter Institute, soon to be harassed by the attacks of a Tory bishop, was in a thoroughly bad way, ' it having degenerated into a news-room ; its philosophical apparatus was, a short time ago, for sale.' As a desperate remedy the author of the report recommended the exclusion of newspapers from the Institute ; newspapers vitiated the desire for Pure Knowledge.

The attitude of the landed classes is at least intelligible. They can scarcely have been expected to approve a system of popular education which they sincerely believed to be entirely unadapted to rural conditions. Nor can the Tory party, overwhelmingly representative of the Agricultural Interest, be blamed for holding the same view. The diffusion of Useful Knowledge in the resorts of industry had led to discontent and rioting. Why encourage the same disruptive movement in the country districts ? Besides, Brougham was known to be among the number of the new educationalists, and where Brougham was, there was no further need of witnesses.

The chief assault of Tory criticism was levelled, not so much against the abstract principles of popular education, as against the practical application of popular education in the interests of party. It was on this ground that the Bishop of Exeter condemned Mechanics' Institutes and Halls of Science in his Episcopal charges.[1] The Die-hard Duke of Newcastle, who now but rarely broke the silence of exile by oracular warnings, drew a lurid picture of Mechanics' Institutes becoming ' debating societies for Radicals, Republicans and Anarchists of various species ; for Atheists and for Dissenters of every description.' [2]

There were Tories who suspected that Mechanics' Institutes were teaching labourers to be discontented with their lot. They saw in secular education, whether of adults or children, a tremendous danger to the structure of society. Instruction in the Institutes was haphazard and unregulated. Anybody could get to know about anything. The Halls of Science threatened to become the schools of intellectual neurotics, who are the forerunners of social revolution. ' Our national diseases,' wrote Oastler, more than half realizing the danger, ' arise from misdirected science, philosophy having bewitched us.' [3]

Birkbeck, Place, and the founders of the movement for establishing the Institutes, laboured in sincere anticipa-

[1] *A Charge delivered to the Clergy of the Diocese of Exeter, etc.* (1845), p. 51.
[2] *An Address to all Classes and Conditions of Englishmen* (1837), p. 104.
[3] Fleet Papers, quoted in *Northern Star*, October 29, 1842.

tion that popular adult education would be a powerful means of uplifting the working people. In Birkbeck's time the classes and lectures were not yet monopolized by the middle classes, and the Institutes offered to labourers, men and women, the means of a solid, ' if somewhat arid,' education.[1] Nurtured among the plaster-of-Paris busts and models in Halls of Science, there arose that austere race of dogged, hard-headed, self-reliant thinkers whom modern satire typifies as the Victorian Rationalists. These represent, perhaps more adequately than any other school, the true character of the revolt in the nineteenth century against that ancient system of Church education of which the Tory party was champion.

[1] Ludlow (J. M.), and Jones (Ll.), *Progress of the Working Classes, 1832-1867* (1867), p. 86.

CHAPTER V

TORYISM AND THE 'CONDITION-OF-ENGLAND' QUESTION

(A) THE INDUSTRIAL SYSTEM

THE phenomenal rapidity with which industry developed in this country was fraught with consequences which might have been more alarming had they not been commonly unheeded. The break-up of the relatively stable social conditions of pre-industrial England was followed by the growth, and then by the concentration, of a landless, amorphous body of working people engaged in the new industrial undertakings. The discontinuance of the personal connection between employer and employed—a connection which Cobbett too freely idealized —made way for a relation based solely upon wages. The domestic, half-feudal, bonds which held together the various parts of old economy were being loosened. The definition which Maine gave to the transference of legal ideas from the static to the contractual might here have been applied in caricature to a parallel change in the basis of social relations. Master and man were now coming to recognize that their interests were connected by contractual, cash bonds.

Competition became the directing principle of industry. Its sway was exerted over the mind of the manufacturer and the imagination of the educated public. Except among the few extremists of the time—reactionary Tories and Social Revolutionaries—social considerations were confined within the limits of the competitive principle. And this great change was regarded by the greater number of contemporaries without undue misgiving. The age contemplated a mighty revolution in a spirit of complacency almost incredible.

There are, however, relative degrees of complacency, and it would be a gross misstatement of fact to assert that contemporary complacency, in the face of the consequences of the Industrial Revolution, was entirely untempered by feelings of doubt and fear.

A certain complacency there certainly was. The wealth and material power of the Empire, with a few trifling vicissitudes, had increased enormously since 1760. The world of Grey and Peel was a world of new ideas, new inventions, new men. With but a tithe of our experience of social questions, and no experience at all of the ultimate consequences of the vast revolution which had taken place, intelligent Englishmen of the early nineteenth century must be pardoned if, in moments of ecstatic self-congratulation, they descended to worship the Leviathan which their hands had fashioned. It was a complacency born of ignorance which made the social tragedy of the time.

Few contemporaries troubled to question whether the increase in the total of national wealth was necessarily accompanied by a corresponding improvement in the social condition of the labouring classes. It is remarkable to what extent even the most impartial and the most enlightened, in their speculations on the effects of the changes which were taking place around them, so frequently adopted an attitude of superficiality bordering almost upon intellectual levity. The newly-popular science of Political Economy was conceived to be limited in scope to an impersonal contemplation of the revolving wheels of industry. Few were concerned with the power which made the wheels revolve, or troubled over the precautions to be taken should the furnaces blow out or the boilers explode.

Political development lagged painfully behind the advances made in the industrial sphere. While the mill-owners, the iron-masters and the railway projectors were covering the country with practical evidences of solid enterprise, the politicians were busy inaugurating the period *par excellence* of political shams. There was no time for the era of Reform to produce its own traditions of government, and it was found impossible to adjust the social consequences of the industrial system to the bombastic political apparatus of 1832.

Nevertheless, a spirit of general acquiescence in things as they were may be said to have permeated those classes which gained most from the industrial and political changes of the time. But public opinion moved a long way during the twenty years which followed the First Reform Bill. In 1832 the middle classes had only just won a nominal recognition, even if the narrow limits of the franchise failed to make many of their members voters. At the time they were still too fresh from their victory to be complacent. Complacency set in only after it seemed that the intellectual domination of the middle classes had become a secondary law of Nature.

Even as late as 1846, it had not grown unfashionable to criticize the middle classes to the extent of doubting the inalienability of their right to their political inheritance. Five years before the final defeat of the landed interest the Tory press levelled against the *petite bourgeoisie* gibes which yielded nothing to moderation or delicacy.[1] Such outbursts from Conservative newspapers ten years later would have been inconceivable ; they would have scandalized the country.

Tory bias against the supposed arrogance of the middle classes was the cloak for a deeper feeling. It was the embodiment of a protest, not necessarily against the existence of a politically powerful middle class, but against the whole mechanism of industrial society. Industry and Capitalism might exist without a middle class at all. The protest was deeper even than class antagonism.

The few, half-comic, half-tragic, voices raised in gloomy prophecy against the consequences of the vast changes which were taking place, were heard on both wings of contemporary opinion. The remnant which vainly struggled against the inrushing flood of new ideas was both Tory and Radical : Tory, because it saw danger in the dissolution of the ancient ties which, for good or for evil, had formerly bound English society together, Radical, because it sought to obliterate the very changes by removing their cause. Throughout the period under investigation there existed a remnant which would not bow the knee to Baal. Cutting rudely across political and social divisions was this fanatical protest against the age—a protest ranging from timid doubts of its beneficence to a profound conviction of its inherent rottenness.

[1] E.g. *Morning Post*, January 20, 1841, in which retail tradesmen are designated thieves and gamblers.

THE 'CONDITION-OF-ENGLAND' QUESTION

The torrent of reactionary feeling found its way to the surface by the most unexpected channels. Here the outburst would appear in the form of anti-Capitalism— a movement directed against the new banking, ' Scotch finance,' as it was contemptuously called, in doubtful tribute to the genius of Paterson and Law. In another quarter a mighty, volcanic outburst would hurl itself against the New Poor Law or, by catastrophic impulse, rush to destroy machinery. In nearly every one of its various aspects the new age discovered its favourite principles and assumptions in danger of being overwhelmed by the reactionary flood.

Against the defensive barriers raised by a people satisfied with its progress the flood dashed itself in vain. To the brilliant results of the new capitalistic and commercial age the older Radical and Tory schools could oppose only prejudices and forebodings. The powerful interests behind the national prosperity could afford to ignore both Radical and Tory protests.

The theory and practice of currency and credit, and the fiscal policy which prevailed among those who directed the Government during the first half of the nineteenth century, were repeatedly, though fruitlessly, the objects of an attack by a group of Tories and Radicals whose financial notions coincided in a remarkable degree.

This coincidence of Tory and Radical thought had curious implications. Chief among the so-called Currency Men of the Birmingham School was the Tory banker, Richard Spooner, a personal friend of the Attwoods, a relative by marriage of the Wilberforces.[1] The currency views of Birmingham were shared by

[1] See Buckley (J. K.), *Joseph Parkes of Birmingham* (1926), p. 15.

many Tory back-benchers whose crotchets were a source of continual irritation to Peel during the fiscal debates of 1842 and 1844. Newdegate, the Warwickshire Tory squire, in opposing the Bank of England Charter Bill of the latter year, told the Commons that he was not in the least ashamed of his connection with the Birmingham men whose doctrines were closely identical with his own.[1]

Peel was further inconvenienced by followers whose views on the industrial system betrayed a certain reluctance to accept the conclusions of orthodox Political Economy. Throughout this period there existed a school of anti-industrial Toryism which showed a dangerous tendency to carry its prejudices into the realm of capital. Indeed there were antiquarians—Alison and Macqueen among them—who harked back reflectively to the days of *iustum pretium* and the Usury Laws.[2] Stanhope went to the length of urging upon the Lords the need for wage-stabilization by reviving ' those ancient statutes,' abrogated in 1813, which empowered justices to fix wages.[3]

Ethical standards were not always divorced from finance, and these protesting Tories and Radicals were probably influenced in their attitude towards the capitalist system by the survival of those standards from an age which preceded the era of the New Finance. A belated leader-writer to the *Morning Post*,[4] commenting upon the

---

[1] *Hansard*, lxxv. 830, June 13, 1844.

[2] James Mill was vehemently apprehensive that Tory projects, like those of Macqueen, ' to violate the currency,' would give vent to the belief that capital could be tampered with. J. Mill to Brougham, September 3, 1832. (Bain (A.), *James Mill: A Biography* (1882), p. 363.)

[3] 53 Geo. III. c. 40. (*Hansard*, lxiv. 1266, July 11, 1842.) Brougham's Motion on National Distress.

[4] *Morning Post*, October 10, 1844.

recent speeches of Young England at the Manchester Athenæum, regretted that the spirit of commerce assigned to usury a place among the virtues, and to usurers a controlling power over the destinies of England—a pathetic piece of antiquarianism in 1844. When Cobbett attacked those capitalists who were ' mere buyers and sellers ' he was by no means expressing a revolutionary doctrine. The mere buyer and seller was long an object of popular suspicion. Cobbett's ' stockjobbers ' were heartless creatures who battened upon the land, and were incapable of feelings of loyalty or honour. Capitalism (it was believed by sceptics in Cobbett's day) was deaf to national or domestic appeals because capitalists were men with none but a financial interest in the country. ' Tell me, sir,' cried Oastler, voicing this sentiment, ' in what age or nation was a Capitalist known to be a Patriot ?—I have heard of none.' [1]

Tories in Parliament were of necessity more discreet in their utterances, but there is adequate evidence to show that they did not all appreciate what they were told were the benefits of the new financial system.[2] During the debates on the Bank of England Charter Bill of 1844, Newdegate dwelt gloomily upon the threatened supremacy of wealth in the government of the country to the exclusion of birth and talent.[3] He was laughed at for his pains.

Although freed from strictly moral limitations, the new Capitalism, it was believed, exerted a sinister influence

[1] Fleet Papers, vol. 21, p. 168.
[2] Vyvyan (Sir R.), *A Letter . . . to his Constituents upon the Commercial and Financial Policy of Sir Robert Peel's Administration* (1842). A standard Tory critique of Peel's fiscal policy of that year.
[3] *Hansard*, lxxv. 824 foll., June 13, 1844.

upon the national morality. This was the Bishop of Exeter's contention in his continual denunciations of unregulated Capitalism. 'The very glut and surfeit of national wealth in which we are now revelling,' he told his Diocesan clergy—'the unparalleled activity of all our manufacturers—the growing demand for labour in all branches of our industry—are only accumulating materials for a more deadly explosion.' Then this vast artificial structure, which capital and enterprise had created, would come toppling down in 'the overthrow of this empire of Mammon by its own serfs, and with it, the extinction of the fairest form of polity.' [1]

Alison found it difficult to reconcile his belief in the rational operation of the principle of *laissez-faire* with the condition of the industrial world in which he spent his life. He drew ominous conclusions from the excessive multiplication of the poor and from the accumulation of vast wealth in a few hands. Ultimately, he thought, the chaos which lay before him might prove neither good nor evil in its consequences. He suggested the melancholy conclusion that this was one of the means by which Providence induces the decline of aged communities, and provides for the dispersion and renovation of mankind. [2] Early Tory critics of the industrial system saw in the blackened pall which overlay Birmingham and Staffordshire the spectre of the avenging angel. Alison praised Sismondi for insisting on the fundamental difference between *économie politique*, the social science, and *chrématique*, the art of accumulating riches in a state. Unhappily in England the difference was ignored and,

[1] *A Charge delivered to the Clergy of the Diocese of Exeter* (1845).
[2] *History of Europe*, vol. v. p. 481.

when a slump occurred, it was the poor who suffered. 'Society,' wrote Alison, 'has become a great gambling-house, in which colossal fortunes are made by the few, and the great majority are turned adrift penniless, friendless, to destruction, ruin or suicide.' [1]

The elder Sir Robert Peel had held the same opinion thirty-five years before, when the results of the introduction of machinery were not so fully evident. 'Such indiscriminate and unlimited employment of the poor,' he said in giving evidence before the Committee of 1816, 'consisting of a great number of the inhabitants of trading districts, will be attended with effects to the rising generation so serious and alarming that I cannot contemplate them without dismay ; and thus that great effort, whereby the machinery of our manufacturers has been brought to such perfection, instead of being a blessing to the nation, will be converted into its bitterest curse.' [2]

In his insistence on the essential difference between wealth and riches Alison is at one with Cobbett, who could never understand ' what the beastly Scotch *feelosophers* mean by their "national wealth." ' [3] 'If weavers in Renfrewshire,' wrote Alison, 'and cotton operatives in Lancashire are making cotton cloths at eightpence a day of wages, we are not to be deluded into the belief that society is prosperous, because every three or four years six or eight cotton lords buy estates for a hundred thousand pounds a-piece ; and one-half of the railways

[1] *Essays* (1850), vol. iii. p. 249.
[2] Report on the State of Children employed in the Manufactories of the United Kingdom (1816), vol. iii. p. 133.
[3] *Rural Rides*, p. 380 (1826).

in the kingdom are constructed with the wealth of Manchester and Glasgow. There are no two things more different than national riches and the wealth of the rich of the nation.'[1]

A somewhat dull, though intensely earnest little group, whose financial speculations lifted them clear of any one party tie, vigorously attacked the practical effects of the system. Cobbett, whose genius emphatically did not run to finance, utterly mistook the enthusiasm, and saw only the dullness of the Birmingham Currency men. It is a great pity that the old political bruiser never rose above invective in his mockery of the ' little-shilling project of Messrs. Attwood and Spooner.' But then Attwood had hardly gone out of his way to conciliate Cobbett, while Spooner, Attwood's Birmingham friend, was a Tory. That was enough to provoke Cobbett.

Away from finance Cobbett stood on firmer ground. He saw, almost with terror, the creation of an unstable, discontented proletariat on English soil. He must warn his countrymen while there was yet time, and the *Political Register* breathed fire against the manufacturers. But Cobbett's generation declined to discuss what it did not understand.

Cobbett prophesied truly. Observers in the industrial districts brought reports of a seething lowering populace, godless and landless. Commissioners appointed to ensure the carrying out of the ineffectual Factory Act of 1833, who may be presumed to have had some opportunity of studying at first hand the temper of the industrial population, failed to keep their alarm from the pages of their official reports. One of them, Inspector

[1] *Essays*, vol. iii. p. 236.

Rickards, whose area of inspection covered the toiling masses in Lancashire, might have known that the ideal state of society which was maintained by ' the salutary influence of the one class with satisfied subordination on the part of the other ' was gone for good. The old social hierarchy was being undermined and the forces of society appeared to be ranging themselves in two hostile groups. Contemporaries never would realize that the author of *Sybil* was telling them the story of an accomplished fact.

One of the worst features of the Mechanical Revolution was the distress consequent on the rapid displacement of hand labour by machinery. Here and there complaints were raised against the sudden introduction of machines or, when already introduced, against the unrestricted use of them, and feeling upon the subject found considerable expression within the ranks of the Tory party.

Oastler, ever resisting the conclusions of optimists who believed in progress, whimsically pointed out the fallacy in the railway promoters' argument that machinery spells increased leisure for the user. Machinery, on the contrary, produced even more hurry and less leisure than before. ' Count the hours you spend on the rails—they are more numerous than those formerly spent on the road.' Oastler would therefore prophesy a moral, if not an economic gain in the regulation of machinery.

There was a serious side to the question. A common explanation attributed many of the miseries of unemployment to the introduction of machinery without thought of the social consequences to which its introduction might lead. Some—the more discerning—deplored the indiscriminate introduction of machines where hand labour had previously existed, others went further and, without qualification, denounced all machinery as destructive of civil society and ruinous to the labourer. Though admitting the dangers of generalizing upon party tendencies, it may be affirmed that, while Radical objection was concentrated upon a sweeping condemnation of all mechanical appliances which tended to supplant hand labour, Tory objection was concerned rather with the immediate evils arising from the indiscriminate use of machinery.

Oastler joined with Cobbett in advising a partial return to domestic manufacture. ' Suppose,' the Chairman had asked Oastler in Committee, ' from a failure of the profits, that the millowners should give up their concerns, would not the result be great distress in the neighbourhood ? ' ' If some manufactories gave up,' replied Oastler, ' there are many that have small property, who would begin business. It would introduce domestic manufacture, which would be the greatest blessing that could be introduced into Old England.' [1]

Oastler clung to his views till the day of his death, and not all the prosperity of the fifties prevented the old hero from finding gaping flaws in the structure of industrial civilization which was too preoccupied to pause and to ask itself whither it was going. ' In the present,' wrote

[1] Report on the Regulation of the Labour of Children in Mills and Factories of the United Kingdom (1831-32, xv.). Yet M. H. Sadler of Leeds, in a letter to Place in 1835, complained that Oastler was obstructing his sale of looms to the Yorkshire weavers. Sadler's design was stated by himself to have been to mitigate the evils of the Factory system ' by the adaptation of factory machinery to cottage labour.' He added that the response from the operatives was not great. (Place Coll., vol. 52, p. 117.)

Oastler in 1860, ' I observe great and increasing powers of production ; but I look in vain for much wisdom in their application. . . . Be careful, I pray you, that the increase of your knowledge and your power does not have too great tendency to make the Strong stronger and the weak weaker.' [1]

The Tory attitude was made manifest in the Parliamentary debates concerned with agrarian discontent. A competent statement of the reactionaries' grievance against the application of the principles of *laissez-faire* to the introduction of machinery occurs in a speech by Lord Wynford. He attributed the distress of the winter of 1830-31 to over-production in certain trades. The glut of manufactures, he supposed, was partly due to the use of machinery unregulated in output by Parliamentary enactment. ' He was not so absurd as to propose to put a Stop to the use of machinery altogether, but its use should be regulated, so as not to interfere with the labour of the poor man.' [2] In the other House a member advocated that machinery, since it displaced hand labour, ought to be subjected to a moderate scale of taxation, in order to render an equitable return to the revenue for the number of persons who might be dispossessed of employment.[3]

It was extremely difficult in Wynford's day to question the benefits of the wholesale introduction of machinery. There was an air of mystery about a machine, and contemporaries regarded mechanical inventions in a spirit of

---

[1] *On Convocation* (1860), p. 48.

[2] *Hansard*, i. 828 foll., December 9, 1830.

[3] Macqueen (T. P.), *State of the Nation at the Close of 1830* (1831), p. 8.

respectful awe. ' One rarely finds anybody who ventures to deal frankly with the problem of machinery,' wrote a disconsolate Radical; ' it appears to infuse a certain fear. Everybody sees that machinery is producing the greatest of all revolutions between the classes, but somehow nobody dares to interfere.' [1] Conservatives could do little while their leader, somewhat after the manner of a showman, was exhibiting before the Tamworth Mechanics' Institute the overflowing benefits of Knowledge, Wealth, and Machinery—triple buttresses of the Great Conservative Party.

Meanwhile in Parliament the Tory followers of Sir Robert Peel were exercised by different thoughts. The attitude of the Tory group towards the problem of industrial distress was bound up with the problem of machinery ; and, when 1841 brought the party back to power, distress was everywhere.

The views which Tories held on the causes of distress, if impolitic, were eminently practical. Members who followed Ferrand, Miles, Palmer and Newdegate were impelled by a sound instinct to resort to causes. They began to give voice to sentiments which had lain in silence since 1832. These Tories were again asking whether the gigantic economic gains from the unrestricted introduction of machinery were not outweighed by the chaos which followed in its train. The universal distress which greeted them on their return to Parliament in the spring of 1842 gave opportunities for reopening the question. During the years 1835-37 the industrial boom had resulted in the usual fever of over-speculation.

---

[1] *Northern Star*, February 25, 1843 ; quoted in Penty (A. J.), *Protection and the Social Problem* (1926).

THE ' CONDITION-OF-ENGLAND ' QUESTION

Anticipating a yet greater expansion of trade, factories
had been built and machinery installed in the hope of a
quick return of capital. A horde of agricultural workers
were imported from the South to cater for the continued
industrial boom. All talk of restricting machinery was
ridiculed ; Stanhope confided his forebodings to a mildly
contemptuous House. Then came the slump, distress
and Chartism. The machinery question began to be
timidly re-introduced. After the appalling rigours of
the winter of 1841-42, Tory members were again begging
for a pause to take stock of the situation.

Adversaries were quick to notice this new outbreak of
reaction. The member for Manchester had discerned
with great regret ' a disposition on the part of certain
parties (he would of course exempt the Prime Minister)
to explain that manufactures should be checked ; that
large bodies of people in towns gave rise to changes in
the constitution, till the people became a body which the
institutions of the country were unable to govern. . . .
There were missionaries at work, taken from ranks from
which they were hardly to be expected, endeavouring to
impress upon the people the necessity of checking the
tendency of the British nation becoming the workshop
of the world.' [1]

This was exactly the Tory attitude. Stanhope, in a
speech of unaccustomed sagacity, marshalled the Tory
prejudice on property in urging what he called the
protection of labour. If compensation had been allowed
to the landowner for injuries to private property by the
construction of canals and railways, it was reasonable
that the labourer should receive compensation for the

[1] Gibson (T. M.), *Hansard*, lxv. 527, July 22, 1842.

losses he incurred through the supplanting of his labour by machinery. He concluded by the childlike argument, not unjustified by events, that the cotton manufacturers were speeding production at such a rate that soon the whole world would be clothed and a glut would follow.[1] In the other House Ferrand asked members to recollect that a whole generation had been swept from the face of the earth since the restoration of peace. Meanwhile through the free export of our machinery foreigners were beginning to prove dangerous competitors.[2]

Having attempted to diagnose the causes of distress, Right Wing Tories thereupon sought a remedy. Ferrand brushed aside all suggestions for a Royal Commission and boldly moved for an immediate grant of £1,000,000. Since Parliament had granted £15,000,000 in compensation to the owners of the West Indian Slaves, members could scarcely oppose his moderate request to feed starving Englishmen.[3] Peel, however, hardened his heart, and the unemployed masses went empty.

With the revival of trade all talk of restriction of machinery was virtually at an end. 1843 brought the Anti-Corn Law lecturers into the country districts and Tories were fully engaged in fighting their own battles. With the triumph of Free Trade in 1846 the industrial masses too were thrown back upon their own resources. The theme of regulating the productive forces of industry took its place among the economic heresies of the succeeding age.

Nevertheless it is in this aspect of the ' Condition-of-

1 *Hansard*, lxiv. 1265, July 11, 1842.
2 *Hansard*, lxiv. 1222, July 8, 1842.
3 *Hansard*, lxiii. 1640, June 16, 1842.

England' question that we discover the foundations of the Tory critique of the industrial system. The necessity of counteracting the harmful results produced by excessive hours of labour in factories called into play the positive qualities of social Toryism.

There was a weak side and a strong side of Tory criticism. It was ever the case with the Die-hard Tory —the realist of the day—that he was more effective in attacking a positive social evil than in attacking an academic social theory. Confront him with a tangible question and he will produce a tangible reply. Entice him into attacking an opponent's abstract principles or prick him with some catch-phrase or other about the 'freedom of labour' and you will find him floundering in useless and ineffective controversy. Academic battles reveal the Die-hard Tory on his weaker side.

The apologist of social Toryism need have no qualms in admitting the wild and reckless character of the general Tory polemic against the manufacturing interests throughout the earlier period of the Ten Hours agitation. Michael Sadler and his friends, in their zeal to conquer in a good cause, did not scruple from making allegations which came near to misrepresentation of the mill-owners' case.[1] Edward Baines had cause for his complaint that the Tory party was deliberately fomenting an artificial prejudice against the manufacturing interest. A 'conspiracy' which he attributes to the bad example set by Sadler's Committee.[2] 'The educated classes every-

[1] For a re-statement of the mill-owner's position, see Hutt (W. H.), *The Factory System of the Early Nineteenth Century* (*Economica*, No. 17, March 1926).

[2] *The Social, Educational, and Religious State of the Manufacturing Districts* (1843), p. 53.

where,' wrote an unknown Ten Hours man in an excess
of snobbishness, 'are almost wholly Tories, saving
perhaps a few large manufacturing towns filled with
Socinian mill-owners or slave-drivers, who have nothing
in common with us, and who, we trust, never will.' [1]

Misjudgments often arose out of pure ignorance.
Rural Tories were not always ready to face the fact that
they were to a great extent ignorant of industrial conditions and therefore incompetent to pass judgment
upon a technical question of this kind. No supporter
of the Ten Hours Bill could honestly burke the truth
that the factory masters were themselves in the grip of a
competitive system which operated with an intensity
unknown in the rural areas.

How difficult it was to form an unbiassed opinion
may be seen in the Tory attitude towards the problem
of Truck, the system whereby the worker purchased his
necessities from an establishment controlled by his
employer. It is hardly surprising that a generation of
mill-owners, whose immediate forebears had not shaken
off the last vestiges of the feudal economy in which they
were reared, should have carried into their industrial duties
something akin to the paternalism of their fathers. The
authority which they wielded over the operatives in their
employ was intensely paternal. Robert Owen was
the very incarnation of benevolent Toryism applied to
industry. Samuel Greg of Bollington, most patriarchal
of factory masters, proudly confided to Dr. Cooke
Taylor that he had built a schoolroom for the children
of his workmen, that he had equipped it with a piano-

[1] *Fraser's Magazine*, No. 49, January 1834, art. ' The State and
Prospect of Toryism.'

forte and busts—household gods of a patriarchal age. The mill-owner was of necessity an industrial *parvenu*. His class was new to its work of controlling industrial hands. It is a common experience that, of all employers of labour, the employer *parvenu* is the most resentful of interference and the most autocratic. Hence to the benevolent paternalism which they inherited from their ancestors and from their own home associations there were mill-owners who added the scourge of tyranny which commonly afflicts the new man in his first consciousness of power. Until 1847 restrictions to the industrial sovereignty of the mill-owner were few and his rule was in practice absolute. Dr. Gaskell drew sinister comparisons between factory masters and feudal barons.[1] The difference was this : that while the older paternalism (whether of feudal baron or country squire) was accompanied by certain social obligations, the new economic relationship of master and man recognized nothing but the cash bond between them. The factory master was as free to do what he willed with his own as his ancestors were with their estate, or freehold, or inn. And if the country squire were allowed complete freedom to manage his estate, why should not a like privilege be accorded to the cotton lord ?

Tradition exempted the landed gentry from outside criticism of their domestic economy, the condition of their cottages, or the extent of their charities. Mill-owners, in affirming their right to consider their employees as a vast household establishment, were asking only for the same consideration which was accorded to the landowners. They not unreasonably demurred when

[1] *Artisans and Machinery* (1836), ch. xii.

Tories, who had been all their lives paying their workmen partly in kind on estate and farm, voted hard for the abolition of Truck among the factory hands. Ashley's interference with their absolutism was resented as being flagrantly unnatural as well as economically wrong. The chagrin of the mill-owners on discovering that public opinion, mobilized by Ashley and his friends, refused to accord them even the domestic privileges of the land-owners, can well be imagined. There can be little wonder that they stood resolutely at the back of the Anti-Corn Law League, whose lecturers and agitators harried the life out of the squires who had presumed to cry for the Ten Hours Bill.

Away from the entanglements of controversy the Tory Factory Reformer stood on surer ground. The evidence of Sadler's Committee and the periodical reports from the factory inspectors—technical men disinterested in politics—brought the ' Condition-of-England ' question vividly before the public view. Here at last was a practical question for practical social reformers, a palpable evil, and not a controversial shadow, to attack. There was nothing about the Ten Hours movement of hopeless allegiance to a lost cause. Practical men, repelled by the vagaries of Poor Law opposition and Tory Chartism, might league themselves with Richard Oastler and Parson Bull without fear of being stigmatized as unpractical Utopians. The cause of Factory Reform was not revolutionary but conservative. The leaders knew precisely what they were fighting for ; they were confident that, if victory should come their way, they could produce a workable policy ready to hand.

A perverse fate had decreed that Tories who identified

themselves with Factory Reform should fail to convert the Conservative party leaders to their views. Measured in terms of positive legislation the contribution of the Parliamentary Conservative party to the betterment of the social and industrial condition of the factory operatives was not particularly valuable. Tories suffered from their fatal weakness ; they were politically inarticulate. For reasons which have at this point become evident Peelite Conservatism was not unanimous on labour questions. The attention of the official party under Wellington and Peel was engaged elsewhere. Reforms in the electoral machinery of national and municipal government, Canada Bills and the Corn Law, held a greater interest for members of Parliament than the sordid affairs of Manchester cotton-spinners and their children. The enthusiasm of Young England was spent in battering its force vainly against the stone wall of Conservative party expediency. And when Peel came back to power in 1841 in the character of a Saviour of Society, the pressing fiscal problems which faced the country absorbed the attention of the Minister and his colleagues. Peel was led away from the path of social reform into the great morass which ultimately overwhelmed his party. ' All Peel's affinities,' wrote Ashley in his diary, ' are towards wealth and capital. His heart is manifestly towards the mill-owners ; his lips occasionally for the operatives.' [1] Whatever the scruples of provincial Tories, the Conservative party sought to ensure its future by an alliance with the industrial interest.

Ignored in Parliament the Tory Factory Reformer

[1] Hodder, vol. i. p. 408 (1842).

sought his allies outside. Thus the Tory contribution
to the Ten Hours movement was unofficial. When the
Tory combined it was not in the lobbies of St. Stephen's
but on the platform of public meetings. What is of
more significance, he combined with Dissenters, Chartists
and even Liberals. Outside of Parliament he was no
longer tied by the bonds of party discipline. Away from
the thraldom of party, Tory social zeal found ready
response among all classes. In the country at large there
existed an enthusiasm for the 'Condition-of-England'
question which never received adequate expression in
Parliament. For once Tory opinion discovered itself on
the popular side.

The universal appeal of Factory Reform was the subject
of much misgiving on the part of contemporary partisans
of the strict school of *laissez-faire*, who were dumbfounded
to find themselves in a minority. Holyoake, a veteran
advocate of Free Thought and No-Nonsense, wrote indignantly of the curious conglomeration of supposedly
conflicting interests identified with Factory Reform.
Eighteen years before the incident which Holyoake related had taken place Oastler's Fixby Compact, ' a leveller
of power,' [1] had given much offence to the orthodox
of Manchester and Leeds. And now, so late as 1850,
Holyoake was mortified to see the Earl of March, Lord
John Manners, Thomas Fielden, Ferrand and Stephens
seated together on the platform of a factory meeting.[2]
Here indeed was Tory Radicalism in its most portentous
form. Members of Operative Conservative Societies,
Co-operators who followed the Radical Mallalieu, Tory

[1] Alfred, vol. i. p. 124.
[2] Holyoake (G. J.), *Life of Joseph Rayner Stephens*, p. 98.

County gentlemen, and skilled industrial operatives found themselves in complete agreement on the remedy needed for social distress. The popularity of the ' Ashleyites ' provoked the resentment of the orthodox. Miss Martineau, genuinely alarmed by the outrage upon her narrow, utilitarian morality, was too concerned even to be fair.[1]

In their fervour for righting social wrongs Die-hard Tories of Peel's Right Wing inherited all the pious enthusiasm of the ' Saints ' who had gone before. The social outlook of the ' Saints '—a homely evangelical faith interpreted in terms of Christian charity—was neglectful of the claims of theory. The ' Saints ' had no interest in praising or condemning any particular economic or political opinion ; their simple, social views were easily accommodated within the tenets of political economy. Scarcely a single Evangelical held profound first principles which drove him irresistibly towards the destruction of the industrial system. The ' Saints ' saw that the industrial system had come to stay, and they acquiesced.

Because they entertained no general principles on the relative merits of rival economic systems, they have been taunted with a total lack of principle at all. The social outlook of the Humanitarians has been inseparably associated with a gross and callous fatalism, which is often reprobated but seldom explained.[2] It is true that

---

[1] *The History of England during the Thirty Years' Peace* (ed. 1850), vol. ii. pp. 540-550.

[2] Cf. Hammond (J. L. and B.), *The Town Labourer, 1760-1830*, new edition (1925), ch. xi., for an account of the social implications of the Evangelical Revival. Paley has received strictures out of all proportion to his faults, cf. Raven (C. E.), *Christian Socialism, 1848-1854* (1920), p. 8. Here it is stated that Paley was ' selected by the panic-

the personnel of the Evangelical movement, no less than Evangelical morality, provided many opportunities for criticism. Factory meetings were often held in Dissenting chapels, and a godly bias was given to the campaign. The movement held a special attraction for those curious human types which had previously supported Anti-Slavery—fanatics, monomaniacs, enthusiasts, pious Evangelical females—whose terrible earnestness appalled the sense of proportion of philistine Whigs and Tories. The sisters Hannah and Martha More are hardly attractive characters to the present age. Nevertheless, in their day, though London faintly scoffed, the mass of middle-class Englishmen were on the side of these quaint, earnest ladies.

Although the 'Saints' had no head for philosophy, they held decided views on questions of practical morals. The body of Low-Church opinion, and not Church only but Chapel opinion of all shades, while continuing to contemplate the miseries of the present world and the glories of the world hereafter, was none the less ranged wholeheartedly on the side of Factory Reform. The Factory movement provided a practical form of activity for a warm-hearted, effusive public. Ashley, in taking up the Cause, was not ploughing the lonely furrow he imagined. And because Factory Reformers concentrated rather on practical wrongs than upon theoretical injustices, they were able to crown their labours with a legislative triumph.

stricken aristocracy to proclaim on their behalf " that truly excellent religion which exhorts to contentment and submission to the higher powers." ' The author endows the aristocracy with a corporate will which he has not proved to exist.

THE ' CONDITION-OF-ENGLAND ' QUESTION

The time has gone when a case could be proved by the dogmatic assertion that public opinion during the first half of the nineteenth century was governed by the Intellectuals of the time. The Factory question was but one of the many questions in which the enlightened found themselves ignored. They raged but were unheeded. That same warm-hearted, almost blatant, sentimentality which in our own time drives the British public to subscribe to all manner of impossible causes, in spite of our philosophers, was as active then as it is to-day. And it was this sentimentality and social sympathy which inspired our countrymen, while all the time they were trying hard to convince themselves that they were strictly impartial and strictly utilitarian. The British public is not, nor has it ever been, impartial wherever social wrongs are concerned. Morality had arrived at its zenith of sensitiveness when a Whig Duke could bring himself to act as Chairman at a meeting of London wet nurses ' to consider the propriety of discouraging the consumption of Godfrey's Cordial and Daffy's Elixir until the opium question shall be arranged with Christian-like justice to the Chinese,' [1] when the exclusive *Gentleman's Magazine* could dilate with unaffected grief upon the late Miss Hannah More's charitable bequests in aid of distressed Clergymen's daughters.[2] Not even the most reactionary of Tories was able to resist the new glamour of the public meeting ; Newcastle appeared with Kenyon on the Protestant platform of Exeter Hall.

It is not difficult to ridicule the fulsome sentimentality with which Englishmen of those times—for all the

[1] *Morning Herald*, June 24, 1840.
[2] Vol. 103, p. 372, October 1833.

affected stoicism of their Intellectuals—were in the habit of investing the great social questions of the time. But when all its foolishness has been considered, the fact remains that it was this wave of sentimentalism pervading all classes which saved England from the horrors of a class war. Continental writers, confronted by a paradox in the almost simultaneous victory of the school of Bright and the school of Ashley, have taken refuge in the conclusion that the Ashleyites were Socialists in their desire to extend the sway of the Legislature over the conditions of industrial labour.[1]

The mistake is excusable. But it was not for the first time that a philanthropic, half-reactionary, movement has made appeal to the humanity of the State because it feared the inhumanity of the Government.

(B) The Poor Law

The controversy over the Poor Law Amendment Act of 1834 ended in a complete fiasco. Scarcely a year after the Act had come into force a fury of wild resentment burst with dramatic violence upon the country. The storm raged for seven years and then died down as swiftly as it arose. Public interest was drawn off on other questions, and the tornado of these seven years subsided in an anti-climax of exaggerated calm.

In this curious movement of revolt against an Act of Parliament the Tory party played a subsidiary, but none the less important part. No other clash of political and social opinions during the century emphasized with

[1] Cf. Redlich, vol. i. p. 136.

greater clarity the essential difference between Tory sentiment and Conservative policy. The necessities of Parliamentary tactics more than once drew Peel from the narrow way of Tory rectitude. Faced with the problem of adjusting a reactionary following to suit the changing circumstances of the day, the leader can have had little time to indulge in waging sentimental warfare on behalf of distressed minorities. The Tory opposition to the Poor Law of 1834 was a lost cause from the beginning.

The position of Peelite Conservatism in that year was precarious in the extreme. Only the year before the Reformed House of Commons had received the shattered, nerve-racked remnant of what was once Pitt's proud legion. George Canning and Reform between them had rent the party asunder, and the rent was not yet mended. Reform itself came too soon and too precipitately to force all the jarring elements of Toryism to work heartily together. By 1834 the party was still resting from the last battle ; it was too weak for another.

Besides, it was Peel's deliberate policy to avoid a head-on conflict with the Whig Government. And to the annoyance of his more eager friends he maintained that attitude until he was strong enough to strike back effectively.

Peel had to ask himself, finally, whether it were really worth while to make the Poor Law a party question. The New Poor Law could at least be hardly worse than the old. On all personal grounds he was driven towards the principles of the Bill. Peel was haunted by the ugly dilemma that, had his party opposed Poor Law in 1834, they would have courted defeat ; while had they done so in 1837-38, when the national distress might have made opposition popular, they would have been taunted with opportunism and inconsistency.

The motives which influenced the Parliamentary Conservative party as a whole to support, or at least to acquiesce in the Act, are pretty clear. It is always difficult in public, as in private, life to oppose a measure dialectically impregnable. The dialectical triumph of 1832 had warned Tories of the fate of those who resist 'the spirit of the age.' The New Poor Law was defensible from all points of view ; the old Law was manifestly unsound. The new Law, permeated with the principles of reason and economy, could be opposed only by the muddled of mind. Behind Peel were therefore ranged the Intelligentsia of the Conservative party.

At the time of the passing of the Bill Parliamentary opposition was negligible. Here and there an isolated Tory or Radical would make an impassioned or casual protest, and sit down. That was all. The group which carried out a semblance of regular opposition was small and, in divisions upon the Bill, rarely exceeded fifty members.

The attitude of this Parliamentary opposition is, however, worthy of notice. Radical and Tory combine against the tendency to centralize the Poor Law administration. The Attwood family, divided by the barriers of party, were united in opposition of the Bill ; William, by a gesture of selflessness managed for once to speak in opposition without dragging in the family currency schemes.[1] Muntz, a monomaniac in currency problems,

[1] *Hansard,* lvi. 441, February 8, 1841. Poor Law Amendment Bill, 2R.

could not thus resist.[1] Sir Francis Burdett thought that
the Poor Law Commissioners could not possibly have
an adequate knowledge of local requirements and that
centralization would prove disastrous.[2] Disraeli mourned
the revolution in local government which the Act would
precipitate.[3] The Radical Wakley, in a Tory speech
delivered amid derision from the Ministerial side, told
the House that the great landed aristocracy, who thought
proper to desert their posts, were the natural leaders of
the poor.[4]

During the debates of 1834, early in the controversy,
Cobbett, with only a few months of life still remaining
in front of him, fought the Bill with heart and soul.
The House, he said, was about to do a terrible thing.
They were about to dissolve the bonds of society ; they
were going to break faith with the working man . . .
it was said in Scripture . . . and Cobbett resorted to the
Bible as the poor man's last defence.[5]

Parliamentary resistance in 1838 and 1841 spent itself
in fruitless divisions. After Cobbett's death the sting
was taken out of the Opposition. In the Lords the
Bishop of Exeter was the only champion of the Poor
Law Opposition who could stand the racket of a brush
with Roden or Brougham. Phillpotts' Anti-Poor Law
friends, Stanhope and Buckingham, found themselves
lashed unmercifully by the Scot.

Definitely organized opposition did not arise until the
Act was two years old and its effects were making them-

---

[1] *Hansard,* lvi. 404, February 8, 1841. Poor Law Amendment
Bill, 2R.
[2] *Ibid.,* lvi. 166.   [3] *Ibid.,* lvi. 375.   [4] *Ibid.,* lvi. 382.
[5] *Ibid.,* xxiv. 1052, July 1, 1834.

selves felt in the country. But the formation of an opposition headquarters in the shape of a National Anti-Poor Law Society by a group of Tories in the capital was long preceded by agitation in the country. The first signs of trouble appeared during the winter of 1834-35, when the Home Secretary received widespread appeals from Justices for drafts of metropolitan police and even for the military, in view of possible disturbances in the coming General Election.[1] Anxious letters to Whitehall indicated that Sussex, Kent and Bedfordshire were the chief centres of disaffection. Turbulent meetings of agricultural labourers were reported at Rye and Uckfield.[2] And if the affairs of violence which occurred at Hebden Bridge or Wolverhampton were merely fracas between rival gangs of election roughs,[3] the meetings in Kent and Sussex concerned the sterner question of bread.[4]

A year later, when the New Poor Law, from being an academic question for legislators, became a practical question for hungry workmen, rural opposition soon broke out. The first signs of trouble appeared during the spring and summer of 1836. In June an eccentric Cambridgeshire parson, the Rev. F. H. Maberly, went the round of East Anglia, rousing the labourers and causing alarm not only in the Episcopal palace of Norwich but in Parliament. Maberly had harangued the labourers at Royden, a restless place in which dis-

---

[1] Home Office Papers, 41. 12, *passim.*
[2] Home Office Papers, 41. 12, Correspondence, December-January, 1834-35.
[3] *Ibid.,* Lord John Russell to Lieut.-Col. Wemyss, May 15, 1835. Lord John Russell to Hill (H.), May 29, 1835.
[4] *Ibid.,* Lord John Russell to Foster (J. F.), May 16, 1835.

turbances over wages had already occurred, and the Home Secretary had sent him a peremptory warning that further disturbance would render him liable to arrest.[1] Letters were exchanged between Lord John Russell and the Bishop of Norwich, under whom Maberly held a title. The Bishop was greatly perturbed, and, when in the following year Stanhope presented a petition to the Lords purporting to have come from the agricultural labourers of Cambridgeshire, he joined with the Duke of Richmond in a particularly rancorous attack upon Stanhope's good faith.[2]

Elsewhere country clergymen were showing some signs of leading a mild opposition. While Maberly (Oastler's 'Curate of the Poor Man's Church ') was rousing strife in the Eastern Counties, the Rev. H. Luxmore held meetings in North Devon, though he does not appear to have taken an active part in the movement until 1841,[3] when an Eton master, the Rev. W. G. Cookesley, whose influence did much to mould the college studies of Young England youths, both spoke and wrote against the Act.[4] The sententious John Wythern Baxter, in a list of 'blessed exceptions,' prints a roll of clerical opponents of the New Poor Law; [5] eighteen names appear under that of Henry, Bishop of Exeter. It is to be noticed that in Baxter's list the greater number of the Anti-Poor Law clergy are country parsons from the agricultural South and East. The Rev. G. S. Bull was

---

[1] *Ibid.*, Lord John Russell to Maberly, June 17, 1836.
[2] *Hansard*, xxxviii. 1914, July 15, 1837.
[3] *Times*, March 11, 1841.
[4] *Morning Herald*, January 19, 1841. Monypenny (W. F.), *Life of Benjamin Disraeli, Earl of Beaconsfield*, vol. i. p. 202.
[5] *The Book of the Bastilles* (1841), p. 93.

one of the few clergymen from the industrial areas. The parson of Bolton-le-Moors, whom Baxter does not mention, was another.

As can be seen, there was a profound religious motive underlying much of the opposition of the Act of 1834.[1] There were religious leaders of the school of Dr. Chalmers who adopted an impartial and judicial attitude. Chalmers disliked the provisions of the Poor Law, though he saw no inherent evils in the appointment of Poor Law Commissioners. In a plan which he conceived in 1824 for a reform of the existing Poor Law administration in England he had suggested Parliamentary Commissioners with very limited executive powers.[2] How far Chalmers' proposals were removed from the spirit of the times may be seen in his contention that parochial visitings ought to become a part of our social system and the principal preventative against pauperism.[3] Small wonder that a Scottish Reforming mob smashed Chalmers' windows in 1832. Oastler used to declare that, had the Church of England been faithful to her mission, the New Poor Law could not have been passed ; while the stern Evangelical spirit in Parson Bull of Brierley called up Hosea to testify against the Bill.

Agitation in the industrial districts followed in the winter of 1836. Feargus O'Connor had arrived in Leeds in the preceding August, and the *Northern Star* was pouring forth its fiery denunciations of Commissioners. All through 1837 and 1838 Anti-Poor Law meetings were

[1] Hovell (M.), *History of the Chartist Movement* (1925), p. 85.
[2] *Tracts on Pauperism. On the Parliamentary Means for the Abolition of Poverty in England* (1824).
[3] Select Works. Preface to vol. xiv., *The Christian Policy of a Nation.*

held in the large cities and towns of the North and Midlands. The Commissioners found that their orders were openly flouted by Mayors and Boards of Guardians.[1] Assistant-Commissioner Power reported from Bradford that local constables sided with the mob in offering him personal violence.[2]

After rural opposition had been smouldering for some time, a Central Anti-Poor Law Association was formed in London. This body had Lord Stanhope for its first President.[3] By February 1837 the Secretary of the South Lancashire Association was in correspondence with Stanhope and the London body.[4] In July of the same year Oastler presented Stanhope with an address from the Anti-Poor Law delegates of Yorkshire. In February 1838 Stanhope urged Baxter to establish an Anti-Poor Law Association in Hereford.[5] Meanwhile Oastler had come to town to address meetings and to advise and help generally with the machinery of the movement.[6] The Opposition, aided by powerful press support,[7] grew rapidly throughout 1837 and 1838. Vast crowds began to collect under the sombre Brown Flag of Opposition.

Stanhope put tremendous enthusiasm into the work, and, although his headstrong vigour occasionally brought

[1] Ministry of Health Records: Minute Books, vols. viii. (1836)–x. (1837).

[2] Parl. Papers (1837–1838), xxxviii.

[3] I have to record my obligations to the present Earl Stanhope, who kindly examined the correspondence of the fourth earl—unfortunately in vain—for evidence bearing upon the Central Anti-Poor Law Association.

[4] Baxter, p. 430. R. J. Richardson of Salford was the local secretary.

[5] Stanhope to Baxter, February 14, 1838. Baxter, p. v.

[6] Letter to the *Times*, July 11, 1837.

[7] For a list of the Anti-Poor Law newspapers, see Baxter, p. 57.

him into awkward situations, these did not damp his ardour in the least. He never lost an opportunity of publicly attacking the Poor Law on every available occasion. He was openly rebuked by Lord Wynford for introducing contentious Poor Law matter at a Central Agricultural meeting.[1]

The character of the local Anti-Poor Law Associations differed from county to county. The Metropolitan Association was composed, it would appear, almost equally of bourgeois and skilled-labour elements, though the high officials were peers and gentlemen. The South-Lancashire branch was of the same social constituency. There were the Fieldens, Oastler, Stephens, O'Connor, Matthew Fletcher ('an apothecary of no respectability,' reported one of the Home Secretary's Lancashire correspondents), Hodgetts an Overseer, Eliza Dixon, a female operative, and Seed, a violent Manchester manufacturer.[2] The Nottingham Poor Law opponents had Roworth the Mayor and the neighbouring gentry at their head.[3] The Nottingham Board of Guardians, elected in 1841, refused to recognize an already-completed Union. One of the Bradford Anti-Poor Law leaders, who worked with John Fielden in the early days of opposition, was M. Thompson, a 'Tory Magistrate.'

Since the Tory explanation of the social distress resembled that of the Radicals in so many particulars, it will at this point be convenient to examine the Radical point of view.

---

[1] *Times,* June 18, 1836.
[2] Home Office Papers, 40. 40.
[3] Napier (W.), *Life of General Sir Charles James Napier* (1857), vol. ii. pp. 93, 111.

THE 'CONDITION-OF-ENGLAND' QUESTION

Cobbett blamed the aristocracy for the evil condition of the poor and railed much at the *parvenu* Tory noblemen —Pitt's men, he called them—for their neglect of the labourer's social condition. Oastler in his usual fiery way called the New Poor Law the result of a bargain between the landlords and the factory masters. The Capitalists came in for much of the blame.[1] O'Connor, who was hotly for the movement in 1838, was violently against it in 1841. The new Intellectuals, whose Radicalism had nothing akin to that of Cobbett and Oastler, had their own views upon the cause of distress. According to this school the people wanted, above all, education. ' The 43rd of Elizabeth has been amended—some say deteriorated—Christmas beef and Sacra Privata, with the periodical produce of Charity balls and mendicity societies, are still doled out to them ; but education, and a patient, anxious investigation into their real state and claims, such as our times and dangers call for, has been talked of and written of, but not carried out : for the Government and the priesthood are squabbling for the initiative, and the people meanwhile are destroyed for lack of knowledge.' [2]

It was not an uncommon practice among Whig and Liberal partisans to attribute Anti-Poor Law unrest to Tory inspiration. ' The Tories have been tampering with the labouring classes in the manufacturing districts,' wrote a Whig critic of one of J. R. Stephens' speeches at Manchester.[3] And there were plausible reasons for suspicion. When it was observed that tumultuous meet-

---

[1] *Times*, February 23, 1837. Meeting at the Freemasons' Tavern.
[2] *The Claims of the People. A Letter to the Aristocracy and the Priesthood* (1840)
[3] *Morning Chronicle*, January 10, 1837.

ings of northern operatives gave public thanks to the *Northern Star* and the *London Times*, and hailed their proprietors as twin protectors of the oppressed, political opponents could scarcely refrain from drawing conclusions.[1] The truth was that a tacit understanding already existed between Radical and Tory Poor Law opponents, but not the kind of connection that was commonly suspected. In 1832 Cobbett had denounced Walter's newspaper as 'the bloody, bloody old *Times*.'[2] Had he lived till 1837 he would have had the pleasure of finding Walter in complete agreement with his ideas on the Poor Law.

If the Anti-Poor Law agitation was not directly inspired by the Tory party, as Whig pamphleteers insisted, it was at least inspired by Tory sentiment. Stephens, though a Radical in oratory, was a Conservative in politics.[3] Throughout 1837 he and Oastler were working hand in glove with Stanhope, assisting the distribution of Anti-Poor Law broadsheets and helping with press propaganda.[4] Of the two Oastler seems to have been in closer communication with the Central Association, probably for the reason that he was then a responsible local representative.[5] Stanhope corresponded regularly with both. John Walter made the Poor Law question the principal issue in his Berkshire and Nottingham election campaigns. He whom Cobbett had held up before the Berkshire electors as a tyrant, 'supported by that un-

---

[1] *Manchester Guardian*, February 7, 1838.
[2] *Rural Rides*, p. 638.
[3] Holyoake (G. J.), *Life of Joseph Rayner Stephens* (1881), p. 11.
[4] Stanhope to Stephens, May 11, 1837 (*ibid.*, p. 93).
[5] Stanhope to Oastler (*Times*, May 9, 1837).

principled political prattler, Jepthah Marsh,'[1] now led Cobbett's old adherents to the poll, pledging his loyalty to Cobbett's opinions on the New Poor Law. It was Oastler and his Manchester friends who subsequently met Walter and presented him with a requisition ' signed by influential electors of the Tory and Chartist parties,' requesting him to become a candidate.[2]

In January and February 1838 the *Northern Star* contained notices of Tory and Radical Anti-Poor Law meetings taking place side by side. Operative Conservative societies spent the year listening to denunciations of the Commissioners.

Oastler and Stephens at this time took great pains to assert their Toryism. Both disclaimed any part in the People's Charter. Oastler justified his attitude by appealing to the necessities of the hour. At a Huddersfield meeting held in 1837 a man in the crowd, seeing Oastler seated beside Feargus O'Connor, shouted derisively, 'A Tory and a Radical ! ' Oastler thus baited turned upon the heckler and lashed him sorely, adding, ' It is perfectly true that there is a wide difference in our abstract principles between Mr. O'Connor and myself ; but our ultimate object is the same.' ' They know me perfectly,' he continued, facing his audience of operatives, ' they know that I am out-and-out ultra Tory.'[3]

It is pertinent at this point to ask why, if the Anti-Poor Law opposition was permeated with Toryism, it failed to rally the Parliamentary party to the support of its policy.

---

[1] *Rural Rides,* p. 638.   [2] Alfred, vol. ii. p. 166, note.
[3] Oastler (R.), *Damnation ! Eternal Damnation to the Fiend-Begotten,* ' *Coarser Food,*' *New Poor Law* (1837).

The obvious answer is that the Anti-Poor Law opposition had no policy at all which the Parliamentary party could support had it so desired. Even had Stanhope and his friends provided the Tory party with a practicable alternative to the New Poor Law administration, the result would still have been doubtful. What would have happened? Would the Anti-Peelite forces within the Conservative party have come into their own and forced their will upon the political world of the time? Would the party of Young England have provided the old Intransigents with a programme and a faith? Would Cobden and the rising commercial class, instead of finding themselves the triumphant party in 1846, have discovered instead that they were being beaten from the field by a resuscitated Country Party armed with a policy of social reform and high Protection, and basing its power upon the landed interests? No one can tell. It is true that several of the leading spirits of the Tory interest who, six years before, had been execrated by the mob, were in 1838 acclaimed by the people as the champions of the popular cause. Old Lord Eldon became a popular hero; while in his last years he thought himself forgotten by all parties—a complete nobody—his name was on the lips of thousands as ' that good Lord Eldon.' [1] This, however, is certain. Toryism, having failed to unite on three successive questions—Catholic Emancipation, Reform, and the Poor Law—was not given another opportunity.

There were other causes for the weakness of the Tory Poor Law policy. A fundamental unsoundness in the

[1] Roberts (S.), *Truth : or the Fall of Babylon the Great, being an address to the Ratepayers of the Kingdom* (1845).

methods of the Tory leaders ensured their ultimate defeat.

It is vaguely possible, if Tory opposition outside Parliament had been placed on firmer ground, that even Peel and the managers of the Conservative Poor Law policy might have been moved by the pressure of forces from without. But the Parliamentary party was not prepared for a general assault upon the Whig ministry, hence opposition to the Poor Law, despairing of help from Parliament, had necessarily to recruit its strength in the constituencies.

Forced back upon the country for its support the leaders of the Anti-Poor Law opposition were driven to make use of expedients which seriously weakened their appeal to the public. Agitation was still regarded by the more decorous people of the age as a questionable weapon of party politics. Agitation carried on outside the walls of Parliament, with a view to coercing or influencing the Lords and Commons inside, was, by universal Tory opinion, contemplated with feelings of repugnance. There were Tories who openly gave vent to their contempt of those demagogic electoral methods which characterized Canning's whirlwind Liverpool campaigns. Throughout the first half of a century still overshadowed by the spectre of the Bastille, agitation was deemed improper to any but the extreme Left Wing of public life. It is not without significance that the Tory Democrat is a political phenomenon unknown before the time of Lord Randolph Churchill. Richard Oastler, never a Democrat, was compelled to bear the stigma of being called a Chartist, because he scrupled not to declare his Yorkshire indignation to the common people.

This sentiment was not confined only to eccentric Tories who never heard of Political Unions ; it was a feeling common to the *bourgeoisie* of England. By Londoners the evil memory of popular agitation was kept alive mainly by the bitter recollection of houses looted and broken glass ; and whether the leader of a particular phase of agitation were a Lord George Gordon, or a Wilkes or even a Wesley, the ugly fact was in no way disguised that fomenting the ignorant masses by loud and dramatic speeches was hardly calculated to engender social peace. The same attitude of mind which fostered a suspicion of politicians like Hunt and Attwood who promised too much, fostered also a suspicion of speechmaking in general. After the oratorical frenzy of 1831 and 1832 people grew wary of men who sought to initiate social reforms by holding mass meetings of the working classes.

Hence there is nothing incongruous in the circumstance that, although Tory feeling provided a strong motive of action for the Anti-Poor Law opposition, Anti-Poor Law agitation itself was branded as disreputable by many who adhered to the Tory party. Judged by their methods the agitators were conscientiously believed to be advocating the right cause in an altogether wrong way. For all his enthusiasm in fighting the Commissioners Stanhope offended many by his indiscretions. Anti-Poor Law opposition was his obsession, and he aired his views on the most inappropriate occasions. This highly combative tendency brought him into frequent collision with fellow Peers in the House of Lords ; often he suffered a dialectical drubbing from Brougham or Roden. The Bishop of Exeter, not less combative and more hardened

to attack, lashed the Whig ministry until Melbourne in
desperation and somewhat spitefully compared him by
implication with ' those worst of demagogues, who,
through the agency of the press or public meetings,
were trying to excite public opinion against the operation of that law.' [1] This feeling, shared by many friends
of the movement, that the official opposition to the New
Poor Law was disreputable, became intensified when it
was discovered that the movement had attracted a considerable number of those cranks and fanatics who so
often batten upon public excitement.

In the face of these difficulties the more sober portion of the opposition could do little. The growing
extremism of the Anti-Poor Law rank and file disgusted
the rural Tories. The fact was, the orthodox Tory of
the time, whether he was a member of Parliament or
not, was caught in a dilemma. If he agitated against
the Poor Law Amendment Act, he was ridiculed in
Parliament as a fighter against the light, an incendiary, a
clodpoll ; if he supported the Act, he was denounced
outside of Parliament as a tyrant. All that weighed in
the scale on the side of authority—Reason, Church, and
State—all were forces which demanded loyalty to the
law. Only a few Tories could face that.

There can be little question that the decision of the
Tory Parliamentary group to sacrifice the Anti-Poor
Law opposition as the price of Conservative party unity
removed the last barrier to the conversion of Anti-Poor
Law sentiment into open political Chartism.

At what particular point of time the Left Wing of the
Anti-Poor Law Opposition became Chartist it would be

[1] *Hansard*, xxxviii. 1146, June 1, 1837.

difficult to say. Up till 1838 a Tory-Radical union supporting an energetic Tory-Radical Parliamentary party might still have been within the bounds of possibility. Oastler and Stephens were still vehemently denying before the discontented masses of the northern counties that either was for the Charter. For the present Anti-Poor Law meetings throughout the country, though turbulent,[1] could scarcely be considered dangerous. Here and there, as in East Anglia, there had been a tendency since 1836 for these meetings to tail off into Radical demonstrations. But the Norfolk correspondent who reported this also told the Home Secretary that even there the local magistrates were over-apprehensive of danger.[2] All that can profitably be said is that, during 1838, the more desperate sections of the Opposition enlarged their programme to include a more Radical policy. The Left Wing leaders, frustrated in their attempts to bring a Parliament representative of the *bourgeoisie* to heed the cry of distress, began to cast about for a substitute for the Houses which had betrayed their interests. 'If the Legislature,' said Oastler, scenting trouble, 'has discovered that the affairs of the nation are so desperately intricate that they cannot by their wisdom secure either life or property, then the only rational constitutional plan is to call a *National Convention*, and not to deliver us over to three Commissioners.'[3] If Parliament would not redress their wrongs, they must change Parliament.

[1] Stanhope to Stephens, May 11, 1837 (in Holyoake, *op. cit.*, p. 93). Stanhope complains of a tendency to introduce irrelevant matter into petitions sent to him.
[2] Barclay (J. P.) to Home Secretary, December 25, 1838. (Home Office Papers, 40. 40.)
[3] *Damnation ! . . . to the . . . Poor Law* (1837).

THE 'CONDITION-OF-ENGLAND' QUESTION

(C) SOCIAL UNREST

It was not until the Anti-Poor Law agitation of 1837 became active Chartism in 1838 that national attention was first drawn to the social condition of Engand.

From a discussion of poverty the theme of social unrest follows logically as effect follows cause. The tremendous changes which had come over the industrial arrangements of the country had their consequence in a change in the structure of English society. The concentration of factories and mills had produced round the chief coalfields a vast mass of half-organized and wholly undisciplined workers. While England was deep in Reform and Corporation Bills or speculating upon the future of Melbourne and Peel, a proletarian society had come silently into being. And when the urgency of the industrial problem forced itself upon the attention of the Government, statesmen found themselves confronted by a social phenomenon wholly outside the limits of their experience, an urgent problem clamouring for solution.

A fatal ineptitude clogged the imagination of public men. Some, labouring to hide their ignorance, affected an attitude of perky cocksuredness, talking largely of the want of Useful Knowledge and Political Economy among the restive masses. Some, with Cobbett, sought an explanation in the breakdown of the Apprentice Laws, the decay of the craft spirit, and the dissolution of the guilds of skilled labourers. Others blamed the contraction of the currency.[1] Everybody fumbled for the explanation which could not be found.

[1] The burthen of the Tory opposition to the Bank Act of 1844.

The clergy, born and bred under a parochial system which was giving way under their eyes, found the spectre of class war already at their doors. ' Is it true,' asked a Tory Archdeacon, baffled for a solution, ' that there is a great and widening separation between man and man ? Thus the bonds which of old held high and low of English society together are melting away.' And the Archdeacon went on to talk of the poison ' which creeps on to the trading classes, to the shopkeeping classes, and thence even to the rural districts.' ¹ It was the poison of social war. Parson Bull saw a vicious circle of discontent. ' The poor and distressed among us are attributing their calamities to the wealthy—to the multiplication of the Leviathan steam power of the nineteenth century—to the burdens of the State, and their unequal distribution. . . . The rich are recriminating upon the poor labourers, and telling them that their own indolence and profligacy rendered these innovations necessary which have in so many cases superseded human agency ; and thus the burden is shifted from shoulder to shoulder, but amid all these contentions God is forgotten.' ² Newman, turning aside for one moment from contemplating the City of God to survey the secular kingdom of Peel and Brougham, quickly convinced himself that society was rotten, and returned in disgust to his Theology.³

Others put the blame upon specific classes. George Condy, a northern lawyer and a friend of Oastler's,

---

¹ Wilberforce (R. I.), *A Primary Charge to the Clergy of the Archdeaconry of the East Riding* (1841).
² *The Oppressors of the Poor : and the Poor their own Oppressors. A Sermon, etc.* (1839), p. 13.
³ Newman to Bowden (J. W.), March 13, 1831. (*Letters and Correspondence of John Henry Newman* (1891), vol. i. p. 237.)

wrote of the money-grabbing fever lately come over the nation, ' a monstrous, a portentous greediness of gain, which it seeks at the cost of the hunger and sufferings of the industrious classes.' [1] The clergy, especially the Tractarians, received their share of censure for their supposed indifference to the distressed. What are the poor, wrote one of their accusers, compared with Puseyism, Mr. Ward or black or white gowns ? [2] The manufacturers, feeling the attack upon themselves, retorted that the Protectionist squire and parson stood between the labourer and cheap bread. Remove the tax on bread, and social unrest would disappear. Alison, with even less discrimination, railed at every gentleman of Lanarkshire from the duke down to the bonnet laird for resisting every effort he had made to get a rural police established before the trouble began. [3] He seems to have been obsessed by a nightmare of Glasgow in the grip of a revolutionary Commune, and parallels the apathy of the local Tories with the selfish disinclination of the French *noblesse* to pay taxes.

To understand the Tory attitude towards the problem of social unrest it is imperative to recognize that this unrest had two aspects. There was unrest in the agricultural counties and unrest in the industrial districts, each confronting the Tory legislator with a separate problem for his attention. Language suitable for describing the grievances of the rural labourer is inapplicable in assessing the wrongs of the industrial operative. These two aspects of social unrest demand separate treatment, even

---

[1] Condy to Oastler (1833). (In Alfred, vol. ii. p. 53.)
[2] Roberts (S.), *Truth : or the Fall of Babylon, etc.* (1845), p. 45.
[3] *Autobiography*, vol. i. p. 350.

though the ultimate cause of both be the same. More muddled thinking has arisen from their confusion than from most of those historical heresies of the last century which social historians have bequeathed to us.

Elucidation of rural discontent, the first aspect of the double-edged social problem to be considered here, has been much hindered by the tendency manifested by some schools of thought to import terms borrowed from the vocabulary of industrial unrest. It has been the fashion to portray rural England of the early nineteenth century as the battleground of conflicting interests. On one side are placed the landowners and country gentry as a whole—the rural governing class, jealous of their rights and ready to oppose tooth and nail each successive liberty claimed by the labourers as their right. On the other side are posted an army of landless peasants, cowed but potentially hostile, illiterate, restive, ever groaning under the weight of agrarian tyranny and ready at the first opportunity that offered to throw off the yoke of the oppressor. Lord Abinger, a recent convert to reaction, scarcely a Tory, confided to Samuel Bamford the cheerless opinion : ' There will always be, under all governments, two great divisions of mankind ; the one which lives by its own labour, without property, the other which lives by the labour of others, which it employs by means of property. The society is more or less wealthy as the last class preponderates over the first.' [1] This was the preposterous consequence of the theorizing of a narrow mind. If Abinger's is taken to

[1] Abinger to Samuel Bamford, April 13, 1843 ; Bamford (S.), *Passages in the Life of a Radical* (ed. 1859), p. 432.

be normal Tory doctrine, it will not be difficult to construct a theory of class war.

Such a doctrine is in perpetual conflict with the patent facts and circumstances of the time. To make of the landed gentry a single, disciplined caste, as some by implication tend to do, is to imagine the non-existent. Similarly to regard the peasantry as desperate proletarians (even though they were dispossessed from the soil) defeats altogether the ends of historical research.

It is by applying to rural labourers the same methods of investigation which are applied to industrial operatives that the cardinal error is invited. Assumptions, true enough of the industrial areas, are simply irrelevant if applied without discrimination to the land. For the purposes of investigation into the point of view of the agricultural labourer in the thirties and forties, the methods of industrial research cannot be applied.

For one reason the rural areas, as we have already noticed, preserve a homogeneity of thought impossible in industrial society in which men are in the habit of thinking along different lines. In the socially self-centred and economically almost self-sufficient country life there was altogether lacking the groundwork of those disorders which, during these fourteen years, characterized industrial civilization.

It was not that all classes in the country (least of all the labouring class) were satisfied with their worldly lot ; far from it. The labourer, especially south of the Trent and Mersey, was on the whole miserably rewarded for his services. He was housed wretchedly and generally underfed. His chances of self-improvement were almost nil. And yet in spite of all this he did not rise against his landlord and his tenant employer. He was not as a class enthusiastically drawn towards either Luddism or Reform. Chartist delegates found that they made less than no headway among the rural population. An army of professional lecturers trained in dialectic, and sent into the country by the Anti-Corn Law League, for the most part encountered nothing but half-hostile apathy among the agricultural workers.

To talk of the 'aspirations' of the rural labouring class during this period is beside the point, for the simple reason that this class did not possess a corporate consciousness at all in the sense of a 'class aspiration.' Country labourers were not much given to political aspirations. They cared little for any of the political questions which at that time were agitating the masses of Manchester, Birmingham or Glasgow.

An explanation suggested by some is that the agricultural labourer was too brutish in his ignorance, too cowed by tyranny, too 'kept down,' to engage in political speculation.

But there is another side of the question. To assume a desire for political thought or political activity is tantamount to mutilating history to fit controversial political theory. Because the rural districts in the interval between Luddism and Free Trade failed to produce a Lovett or a Doherty, it is not to be inferred as a sign of political unregeneracy. After all there is the risk latent in an argument of this sort that an equally reasonable theory might be advanced suggesting that the absence of Lovetts and Dohertys might have left the world a happier place to live in. One must be prepared to hear denials that a passion for violence and reform necessarily make for social happiness, especially in country places.

The agricultural labourer was not inclined to violent thought or action. Asked whether the average agricultural worker was in the habit of calculating problems of prices and values, a Wiltshire farmer in his evidence before the Select Committee on Agriculture (1833) replied, ' They do not calculate.' [1] Their general hostility to revolutionary action is revealed in their half-hearted attitude towards the disturbances of 1830-31.

A Radical, imbued with a lively horror of serfdom, might draw sinister conclusions from this. Reformers blamed the landed classes for rendering the labourer helpless to defend himself. ' The great disease of the English Social system is constant interference with the labouring people. A shoe cannot be mended for a child in a village, or a new pair of stockings purchased, except through the complicated instrumentality of overseers and magistrates. The people have in this way been taught that everything ought to be done for them.' [2] ' The degree of slavery,' wrote a reverend pamphleteer, ' may vary with the nature of the law, the custom of the country, the force of public opinion, or the character of the master ; but the principle is the same, whenever the labourers have not the free power of selling their own labour.' [3]

There has never occurred in England anything approaching an agrarian class war. In the complicated

[1] Report on the Present State of Agriculture and persons employed in the same, 1833, v., Q. 8381.

[2] *Morning Chronicle*, November 23, 1830.

[3] Brereton (C. D.), *The Subordinate Magistracy and the Parish System considered, etc.* (1827).

agricultural economy subsisting during the first half of the nineteenth century any alignment of classes into two hostile armies was historically impossible. There were insufficient materials for a social war. Hunger alone will not make a revolution, and hunger in 1830 was inarticulate. Distress must be universal before the danger point is reached, as the theorists of social revolution insist. And what is more, even desperately hungry men require leaders and the elements of organization.

Throughout the winters of 1830 and 1831 rioting was by no means as universal as rural distress, nor was distress the only cause of discontent. Rightly or wrongly there were contemporaries who held that hunger was only one of the motives which caused farmhouses to be pillaged and ricks to be burnt. A witness before the Select Committee of 1833 reported that the Wiltshire labourers were fed, clothed and furnished, and in every way better than he had ever known. He thought that in his own district (Marlborough) the able-bodied men in the villages were mostly employed.[1] In addition the Wiltshire labourer was fortunate in his perquisites ; he got, beside his pay, beer and generally a cottage rent free.[2] And yet the Kennet valley, where the witness lived, was nightly lit by the blazing stacks of hay and straw in the bleak winter of 1830-31.[3]

Another witness believed that the labourers implicated in the recent disturbances were influenced by politics rather than distress.[4] Reform had made them restive. A third complained that there was not nearly the same good feeling between the farmers and their labourers

[1] 1833, v., Q. 10,973.   [2] *Ibid.*, Q. 10,968.
[3] *Times*, December 1830, *passim*.   [4] 1833, v., Qs. 1033-34.

THE ' CONDITION-OF-ENGLAND ' QUESTION

as before the fires. The labourers were not so willing
to work, their character had deteriorated.[1]

It is not suggested that political restiveness was the
sole cause of unrest. A Cumberland landlord was quite
certain that in his county over-population and consequent
high rentals had resulted in a decided worsening of the
labourers' condition.[2] The trouble everywhere was that
where there was enough work to go round, there was no
distress ; where not, workers were in a bad way. A dozen
witnesses made it clear that only the fear'of fires—bluntly,
intimidation—kept wages up to their panic level. And
wages were down again in 1833.

Thus, while discounting the natural desire of the landed
classes to rebut the accusation that distress was due to
their neglect, it is clear that contemporaries found the
problem of active revolt puzzling, to say the least. Tory
members in Parliament and Tory witnesses before Select
Committees were not altogether wrong in suggesting
political agitation as an influence making for discontent.

Much colour is given to this view by the fact that fires
and riots occurred according to no rational plan. Disturbances occurred where distress was least as well as in
areas of extreme depression.[3] Bad outbreaks of fire
occurred in Kent ; and yet an expert who knew both
Kent and Midlothian declared that Kentish labourers
enjoyed considerably more luxuries than their Midlothian
fellows.[4] Witnesses were generally agreed that the inspiration to revolt came from political rather than from
economic sources.

[1] *Ibid.*, Qs. 2223-24.   [2] *Ibid.*, Qs. 6617 foll.
[3] *Ibid.*, Qs. 1033-34.   [4] *Ibid.*, Q. 3294.

TORYISM AND THE PEOPLE

Throughout the winter of 1830 the horrid spectre of
Captain Swing moved over the southern countryside.
Who was Swing ? He was supposed to be an incendiary
from ' abroad,' one of a band of disreputable characters,
tramps and others of the road, perhaps a revolutionary
agitator from London. The naivety of the rumours widely current among the
educated public proves that agricultural riots were not
an everyday feature of English rural life. People had
not become sophisticated by them. It was strongly suspected at the time that the greater number of the fires
in the Vale of Pewsey had been the work of two men,
both ' foreigners,' and certainly not agricultural labourers.
' One is about forty years of age,' ran a wild rumour,
' rides a long-legged, light carcassed sorrel-coloured horse
—what is vulgarly called a blood horse—with a switch
tail ; wears knee-caps or overalls ; sometimes has a drab
great coat ; generally seen riding fast through villages
or towns, with something different from a common
riding stick. . . . It is supposed that the thing which is
carried in the hand is not a walking-stick, but some un-
lawful weapon or gun.' [1]   As for the reputed ringleader
of revolt, nobody believed that Swing was a labourer.
There was another rumour, somewhat disturbing to
good Protestant susceptibilities, that the Captain had
been found with sheaves of Evangelical and Millennial
literature in his gig.[2]

If Lord Ellenborough's word is to be trusted, Peel
himself seriously thought that the fires in many cases
were perpetrated for stockjobbing purposes by agents

[1] *Taunton Courier*, November 29, 1830.
[2] *Morning Chronicle*, December 20, 1830.

212

sent from London.[1] Others hinted darkly that tenant
farmers were at the bottom of it, giving the men beer
and urging them to excess.[2] The most impossible stories
gained the widest currency. The mystery in which the
disturbances were enveloped gave rise to the universal
belief that the riot had a political origin.[3]

The agitation for the Reform Bill, which convulsed the
populations of London, Birmingham, and the provincial
centres, was not unfelt in the rural districts. Observers
were begining to notice that dark characters were passing
through the country districts, fomenting the people. The
labourer, unused to the language of Reform, gave his
sullen attention ; his uneducated mind dwelt upon the
novelties of these orators.

Yet all civil disturbances are not the invariable result of
serious causes. There must have been cases of unpopular
landlords or tenants who had their ricks burnt down by
the frothy youth of the neighbouring villages. Some
bad fires in Wiltshire were said to have been started by
village boys piqued by being caught red-handed stealing
poultry.[4]

Only by taking into consideration the fact that Luddism
was commonly thought to be a subversive political movement can the repressive attitude taken up by the Tory
party be adequately judged. A century before the fires
of 1830 the possibility of a rural class war would have
been laughed out of court. The landed classes, Whig

---

[1] Law (E.), (Lord Ellenborough), *A Political Diary, 1828-1830* (1881):
entry under November 14, 1830.

[2] *Morning Chronicle*, December 14, 1830.

[3] Cf. Buckingham and Chandos (Duke of), *Memoirs of the Courts and
Cabinets of William IV. and Victoria* (1861), vol. i. p. 113.

[4] 1833, v., Q. 979.

and Tory, still thought in terms of an agrarian society which by 1830 was passing away. For one who holds as a basic principle that society is a hierarchy of classes, ranks and privileges, to imagine a class war other than as a destroying demon is impossible. Whig and Tory repressed with the harshest rigour because they saw in the revolt of the ' industrious classes ' the destruction of society. And since the *Jacquerie* remained a ghastly portent within living memory they can scarcely be blamed for their point of view.

No sooner had Peel emerged from the General Election of 1837 than the ' Condition-of-England ' question was thrust before the notice of the Conservative leaders. The Tory group within the party was now to come face to face with one of the storms which rocked Toryism to its foundations.

Chartism is usually regarded as the component of two distinct elements, the one revolutionary, and the other reactionary, in character. Chartist leaders, according to their sympathies, have been classified as adherents of one or other school. Thus O'Brien and William Carpenter find themselves differentiated from Oastler, Stephens, and Attwood, the first group placing its hope of social amelioration in the future, the second seeking to bring back the social perfections of the past.

Both groups were in a sense Utopian. The social-revolutionary Chartists were engrossed in contemplating a hypothetical future ; the Tory Chartists sought their inspiration in a non-existent, if golden, past. Both were romantics, both idealists ; and if the Utopianism of the Left Wing is to be raised to the dignity of a political theory, then there is no reason why a similar honour should not be paid to the retrospective imaginings of the Right.

Were exception taken to the division of the Chartist movement into two groups, it would be on the grounds of omission. There were shades of Chartist opinion which are not readily accommodated within this artificial, if plausible, duality. For there was a third group within the Chartist ranks. Such was the school of Sturges and the Complete Suffrage party. These formed a Liberal-Chartist element within the Chartist movement. They were in fact Left-Wing Reformers—Continentals would be justified in calling them Meliorists, Progressists —who stood nearest the orthodox Liberalism of the day. They were equally far removed from Revolutionary and from Tory Chartism.

Over the Liberal contribution to the Chartist movement there need be no delay. The ideas associated with the slogans of Universal suffrage, Progress and Reform governed the policy of the moderate Chartists. The sponsors of the Charter may have advocated or desired a degree of progress and reform far in excess of that desired by their slower Liberal cousins on their right flank, their views on education and self-improvement may have been less exclusively middle-class than Macaulay or Hume would have approved. But these differences do not make them revolutionaries. No one could call the clauses of the People's Charter either revolutionary or Tory.

The Democratic Socialist of the present day, who prefers to trace the descent of his political ideas from the moderate elements of the Chartist movement, may do so without feelings of historical impropriety. Even those among the Chartists who most detested the Russells and the Broughams yet exhibited in their ideas the dominant Liberal principles of the time. Lovett and his colleagues of the London Working Men's Association were revolutionaries only in the sense that they attacked the capitalist system at their meetings. Their remedies for existing social evils were the reverse of revolutionary. Theirs were the orthodox and popular salves for the distress which bore so heavily upon the labouring classes. They advocated steady, progressive reform by means of education and moral enlightenment. They breathed the authentic air of philosophic Liberalism, and in their attitude towards popular education they differed little from Brougham or Bowring.

From the mild precepts of the moderate Chartists the Social Revolutionary party turned in disgust. And here was the fatal weakness of the Revolutionaries : like the Tory Chartists they had no constructive policy worthy of the name. There was another weakness equally fatal. Both Revolutionary and Tory Chartism were the direct product of industrial conditions. There was no intellectual apparatus to give direction to their policy. They had no Bentham to provide their theoretical background, and no Karl Marx to furnish them with the imposing sanction of history. Bentham they could not read ; *Das Kapital*, even had it then been written, they would not have understood. The scope of their appeal was limited to the needs of a hungry industrial proletariat, their revolutionary vocabulary was local, provincial ; it was inapplicable to the needs of any class but their own.

Their principles were not even applied to the whole of the proletariat. Throughout the period of Chartist agitation there were vast bodies of operatives, drawn mainly from the ranks of skilled labour, whose interests seem to have been almost fully absorbed in Friendly Society and Trade Union activity. It was among the residue, the unskilled masses, that the more violent teaching found the readiest response. It was, in fact, this very narrowness of the basis of Revolutionary Chartism which was the prime cause of the complete failure to win over the rural areas to the Chartist cause.

A common belief among landlords and tenants led them to suspect that much of the discontent among agricultural labourers was due to the presence of vagrants and mysterious itinerant agitators. Farmers still remembered the devastation which followed in the wake of Captain Swing. Some had painful recollections of broken thresh-ing machines and haystacks gutted by fire. Others, not without misgiving, called to mind Cobbett's inquisitorial visitations and his uncanny capacity for exposing rural abuses. During the Dorchester trials a well-meaning magistrate, a Mr. Woolaston, visiting George Loveless in prison, cautioned him against being deceived by idle fellows who were going about the country.[1] In the following year the Home Secretary requested a Man-chester correspondent to find out whether any com-munications were passing between the Manchester Union and the labourers in the southern counties.[2] There is reason to suppose that this fear was widely held in the country districts.

In 1839 Chartist missionaries were preaching the

[1] Loveless (G.), *The Victims of Whiggery, etc.* (1837), p. 9.
[2] Lord John Russell to Foster (J. F.), May 16, 1835. (Home Office Papers, 41. 12.)

language of the social revolution to the agricultural labourers of the south and west. These apostles appear to have made the local industrial workmen—Cornish miners and Wiltshire weavers—the first object of their mission. To their meetings came also, it seems, bodies of farm labourers, interested in the novelty, if not convinced. Local dignitaries took the Chartists seriously. Richard Moyle, Mayor of Penzance, writes anxiously to the Home Secretary for advice. The Tory Mayor cannot stomach the class-war doctrines of the missionaries. He prides himself that his was a part of Her Majesty's Dominions ' in which there is no clashing of interests between the agriculturist and the manufacturer—in which the labouring classes are in constant employment, where absolute poverty is not known—where loyalty is proverbial, and contentment almost universal. But all this admirable order of things is threatened to be overturned and Society disjointed by a party of itinerant politicians—who style themselves *Chartists* and do profess to be Missionary Delegates from the National Convention.' [1] The Mayor concludes by asking the Home Secretary what to do about it.

This is an illustration of the impression made by the Chartist doctrines upon a local Tory dignitary of the West.

General Napier, quartered during this time at the storm-centre of unrest, gives the impression that the Chartists were a vast, undisciplined mob, without leaders and without organization, impotent from their failure to combine.[2] The cause of the unrest ? Napier puts the

[1] Richard Moyle to Lord John Russell, March 14, 1839. (Home Office Papers, 40. 41.)
[2] *Life*, vol. ii. p. 5.

blame on the rulers of the age ; ' the Whigs and Tories are the real authors of these troubles by their national debt, corn laws, and new poor law.' Chartist orators were at that moment saying exactly the same. Napier had strong views upon the subject of the magistracy of the northern districts. ' The magistrates are divided into Whigs, Tories and personal enmities ; and every mother's son of them ready to go any length for his sect and creed. The town magistrates are Liberal for fear of the populace ; the country bucks are too old, and too far-gone Tories to have hopes of gaining popularity now by being radical ; so they labour to get troops near their own homes. *Funk* is the order of the day, and there is some excuse, for the people seem furious enough.' [1] But even the sympathetic, super-sensitive General longed for spies.[2] Four years later, when Peel's Conservative party had come into power, its leaders considered South Lancashire still too upset by Chartism and the League to undergo the rigours of a by-election.[3]

The fury which impelled the mobs of Lancashire and Yorkshire to burn and violate was not always the fury of revolution. It was more often the resentment of desperate men who believed themselves to have been cheated of something they once possessed. Contemporaries found it difficult to understand the innate Toryism of an industrial mob. So the name Tory

[1] *Ibid.*, vol. ii. p. 8. (Napier to his brother William, April 9, 1839.)
[2] *Ibid.*, vol. ii. p. 28. (Journal, April 23, 1839.)
[3] Lord F. Egerton to C. Arbuthnot, October 1841. (Peel Papers, Addit. MSS. 40,484.) Writing of the ' state of feeling in this fearful vicinity,' Egerton adds, ' for my part, in living in it at all, I always feel as if I were toasting muffins at a volcano.'

Chartism came into existence to connote a social force which nobody could explain.

This curious movement, Tory Chartism, half revolutionary, half reactionary, may now be viewed in its true perspective. By those who lived at the time the term Tory Chartist was used as a part of the general stock-in-trade of political abuse. It was so loosely used that it is difficult to assign to it any particular meaning at all. Oastler was called a Tory Chartist because he advocated Protection from Chartist platforms. Walter was assuredly a Tory Chartist because he voted Conservative yet preached resistance to the New Poor Law. The term was stretched to cover that pathetic little band of mild monomaniacs : Urquhart, Charles Attwood and the anti-Palmerstonians whom the *Quarterly Review* somewhat unnecessarily calls 'impertinent obscurities of Newcastle and Carlisle—gnats on the chariot-wheels of Europe.' [1]

O'Connor and the Left Wing further misused the term. In a letter dealing with the approaching West Riding Election of 1841 O'Connor urges his working-class readers to have nothing to do with Tory Chartists. 'You have a good many Tory Chartists—Urquhart, Charles Attwood and all the Cobbettites are Tory Chartists, every one of them.' [2] Only the month before O'Connor was frantically singing the praise of the Tory Chartist leaders—'Ye have a noble choice, men of Huddersfield ; an absent or a present friend—your good old King Oastler, or Pitkeithly, both sworn foes

---

[1] Vol. xi., December 1840.
[2] *Northern Star*, July 3, 1841. It is amusing to find in this issue a graceful reference to Disraeli's election contest at Shrewsbury.

of Whiggery.' Nottingham must see that John Walter is victorious, ' Out ! Out ! with the bloody Whigs ! . . . Nottingham, glorious Nottingham, must again return Walter, *not as a Tory*, but as an enemy of the Whigs.'[1] Thus raved O'Connor, whom the Whig newspapers dubbed the most dangerous Tory Chartist of them all.

O'Connor attacked any one who questioned his complete sovereignty over the Chartists of the North. ' Fudge. Snap your fingers at such humbugs,'[2] is the phrase by which he dismisses the Yorkshire Tory remnant of the Anti-Poor Law Opposition. George White was howled down at a meeting of Birmingham Chartists by Anti-Corn Law hecklers who bawled to him that he was a Tory. Next evening White squared with his audience by reviling Toryism at the top of his voice—a veiled tribute to the mailed-fist of O'Connor, and to the intellectual latitude permitted to the true servants of the People !

Had Sir Richard Vyvyan placed himself at the head of the Chartist movement and Newdegate become editor of the *Northern Star*, the Tory-Chartist connection could not have been more intimate. However revolutionary the speeches of Vincent and O'Brien on their missionary journeys, or the speeches of O'Connor in the Convention, the more responsible of the Tory-Chartist representatives delivered themselves of uncompromising Tory sentiments. Thomas Attwood, introducing the National Petition to the House of Commons in 1839, spoke only of restoring lost privileges, and of regaining the rightful

[1] *Ibid.*, June 12, 1841.
[2] *Ibid.*, July 3, 1841.

property of the industrious classes.[1] Cooper's Leicester operatives asked nothing more than the repeal of the New Poor Law and a tax on property.[2] In the hollows of the Welsh hills the Toryism of Rebecca and her Children was made manifest. By day the discontented Welshmen denounced the Reform Bill and the New Poor Law, and foretold the ruin of all farmers if the Corn Laws were repealed ; by night they burned the workhouses, the Whig Bastilles.

Stephens, who had little of the Revolutionary in him except his words, broke with the National Convention when that body talked of establishing a national holiday, a general strike, of the working classes.[3] He was as firmly opposed to general strikes as he was to democratic chapels. Oastler, who cannot rightly be termed a Chartist at all, contended that the Charter did not originate with the working people, but had been foisted upon them from above, by the Radicals who affected to guide and educate the movement.[4] His point was that the leaders of all parties had allowed themselves to drift away from the working classes. Statesmen who professed to be leaders of the people were ignorant of the social condition of the masses.[5] And who was to be the saviour of the working classes ? Peel ? No, for

[1] *Hansard*, xlviii. 222 foll., June 14, 1839, and xlix. 220 foll., July 12, 1839.

[2] Operatives of Leicester to Lord John Russell, December 25, 1838. (Home Office Papers, 40. 40.)

[3] Sermon at Stalybridge, July 21, 1839. (*Times*, July 27, 1839.) Stephens has been called an ' apostle of terrorism ' for telling the rich to make their will [Beer (M.), *A History of British Socialism*, vol. ii. (1920) p. 41]—a conclusion justified only on a literal interpretation of Stephens' somewhat rhapsodic language.

[4] Fleet Papers, vol. i., No. 12.   [5] *Ibid.*, No. 31.

Peel had abandoned his Toryism for the commercial Conservatism of the Manchester Cotton Lords.[1] Or was Richard Cobden, with the rising power of the League at his back, to give the promised lead? Emphatically no, for the League was of the middle class, the new society, which was now known to be indifferent to the social condition of the working people. 'The *Leaguers*,' wrote Oastler, ' have cunningly contrived to divide these classes, the aristocracy and the working people, that they may the more easily conquer them both. *My object is, and it always has been,* to unite them.'[2] The Aristocracy? No, for the natural leaders of the people had forsaken their duty and had gone away in search of gold. Even Young England, upon which Oastler beamed approvingly, was powerless to help the workers. Young Englanders were sincere but they were too academic in their discussions. 'Old England,' he prophesied, ' will outlive "Young England," unless the latter step into the old lady's empty slippers and take care of her neglected children, as well as make fine speeches and quote the classics.'[3]

As Toryism differed in essence from the Liberalism of the time, so it stood miles apart from the principle of the Social Revolution. Although Marx borrowed this period of English social history to furnish an example of the transition of the Capitalist State, the apostles of

---

[1] *Ibid.*, vol. ii., Nos. 10 and 22. 'The die is cast,' he writes when he hears of Peel's fiscal proposals of 1842, 'the mask is thrown away— the Whiggery of Conservatism is now arrogantly displayed in sight of the deceived and ignorant people of England. . . . Did you mark the assassin-like approach of Graham ? ' (No. 22.)

[2] *Ibid.*, vol. ii., No. 46.

[3] *Ibid.*, vol. iii., No. 45, November 4, 1843.

Revolutionary Communism were never important in England during the first half of the century. In an industrial society permeated with Tory sentiments there was little opportunity for the development of the spirit of class-consciousness, which, in Marxian theory, inevitably precedes the Social Revolution. Even the intellectual accompaniment of class war, the Social Revolutionary vocabulary, was hardly known in England ; and there is the additional consideration, that the most violent of English Social Revolutionaries were those who made speeches, not those who manned the barricades.

Few indeed of the Chartists can properly be termed Social Revolutionaries in a serious sense. Most of them had but vague ideas about the revolution and no ideas at all about governing the country when the revolution was over. Vincent of the London Working Men's Association spoke a heady language on his missionary tours as a delegate of the Convention. ' The tocsin shall sound,' he told the labourers of Trowbridge ; ' the trumpet shall flourish, and the bonfires shall be lighted on the tops of the hills. They would meet with torches every night before they meant to make the strike, but the signals would be the bonfires on the hills. It was no good for them to begin at Birmingham at one time, at Glasgow at another, at Lancashire at another, . . . they must make a grand strike altogether and the bonfires on the hills would be the signal.' [1] Vincent was the bearer of the crude gospel of Syndicalism. His were stirring phrases, valiant on the platform, useless as incitements to revolt.

[1] From the sworn evidence of a witness, John Clark, a local magistrate, to Lord John Russell, December 13, 1838. (Home Office Papers, 40. 40.)

For all the eloquence of the Chartist missionaries, their gospel made but slight impression upon the rural countryside. The agricultural labourer might listen attentively to Oastler, Hunt or Cobbett, men born and bred on the land. It was a more difficult matter for the labourer to understand the language of the Chartist 'foreigners,' however captivating their creed might be. Since the days of Captain Swing town agitators were not welcome in the country parts. The Chartist missionaries were safe enough in Trowbridge, where there was a colony of weavers to receive them; but in Devizes, where there was no industrial population to speak of, they were mobbed (as Wesley was mobbed before them) and sent out of town. The doctrines of Chartism were never adapted to the requirements of the agricultural labourer.

With Revolutionary Chartism the essential principles of Toryism had but one solitary element in common— neither had the slightest belief in the Meliorism, the Liberal Democratic ideas of the Reformers. In all else Revolutionary Chartism and Toryism stood poles apart.

It was inevitable that both worked rather outside than within the walls of Parliament. Politics of the day were the virtual monopoly of the men of the Centre; the official political struggle was between Peel and Melbourne or Peel and Russell. Sometimes Peel would win, sometimes Melbourne or Russell. Toryism on the Right and Chartism on the Left never had a predominant influence in Parliament between 1832 and 1846. Both were inarticulate in Parliament because both were confronted by political groups who sponsored the fashionable and dominant ideas of the time.

This does not mean that there were any ties which held Toryism and Chartism together in the provinces. In the first place there was the somewhat paradoxical difference that, while Revolutionary Chartism more or less acquiesced in industrial civilization, Tory Chartism emphatically did not. Disguise, as Vincent might, the ends of his political creed, the fact remained that the formula which others invented and which he and his friends adopted, ' the whole produce of labour,' in no way excluded industrialism, factories and slums. Whenever the Social Revolutionaries within the Chartist movement made appeals to the masses they invariably made appeals to the social instincts of their audiences. They appealed almost wholly to the materialistic aspirations of the people and held out to them material prosperity as the reward of revolutionary action. They would abolish the master manufacturer, the capitalist, or, with diminished insistence, the landlord, and the magistrate. They would render to the workmen the whole produce of his labour. Neither in England nor on the Continent was there much talk among the Social Revolutionaries of abolishing the machinery of the industrial system.

Tory Chartism went further, for in this sense the Tory Chartists were the more radical. Tory Chartism, according to the utterances of its leaders, would advance beyond the mere alleviation of the condition of the people. It would bring back those social conditions under which it believed all classes in society enjoyed prosperity. It would go behind the Industrial Revolution as an excrescence upon a once-happy countryside of the pre-industrial Golden Age. The Toryism of Oastler and Stephens led them towards Rousseau and Natural Law.

Besides, the appeal which the Tory Chartists made to the masses of industrial workers was less materialistic than that of their Left-Wing associates. Tory Chartists appealed direct to God and to the past—to tradition. And the story of the Chartist movement will reveal the fact that the idea of a Golden Age occupies a place equally important in the speculations of political theory with that of the class war of Engels and Marx, though few would commit themselves to decide which of the two points of view were the more historical.

The Toryism, then, of the Reactionary Chartists was the direct antithesis of the Revolutionary Chartism of Vincent and his friends. The Tory or feudal view of society as a hierarchy of protectors and protected, a vision very much alive in the minds of the leaders of the reactionary group, excluded everything of proletarian politics. English Socialism and Continental Utopianism were equally foreign to its point of view. The entire outlook of the Social Revolutionaries, their premises, their conclusions, their very language, were unintelligible to them. Revolutionary Chartism took its stand on what it conceived to be the mutual hostility of classes ; Tory Chartism with equal emphasis maintained that, where classes were living in mutual hostility, ordered society could not exist at all.

Moreover, it was not only on political and social grounds that there lay so impassable a gulf between Tory and Revolutionary Chartism. The antithesis was even greater when it came to religion. Those of the working classes who followed Oastler and Stephens and Bull followed men imbued with a strong sense of authority in spiritual no less than in temporal matters. In this light we can appreciate the hostile attitude which the Tory-Chartist leaders adopted towards the movement of which Robert Owen was sponsor.

It is a simple matter of history that the Tory group within the Parliamentary Conservative party produced no effective plan for grappling with the 'Condition-of-England' question. There is some truth in the reflection of Lord Morley's, that the sum of Tory social effort, through the agency of Parliament, ends after fourteen years in the childish bathos of Young England.

Yet the implied stricture is founded on a misinterpretation of the character of Toryism. There was actually no concerted Tory effort in Parliament to relieve social distress and to prevent its recurrence. There was, in fact, no concerted Parliamentary effort at all. The problem of national distress among the working classes was too patently an innovation for legislative certitude or united political action. Reason prompted the Tory member of Parliament towards the removal of feudal and economical barriers which tended to hinder the laws of competition. Sentiment called him to support the Ten Hours Bill, which not so much hindered competition as it removed its sting. Resentment and blind panic drove him to abolish the Poor Law, condemn the Political Economists, and restrict machinery.

The discontented masses, when hard times brought less wages and less food, turned feverishly from the contemplation of a sordid present to the vision of a golden past. They shunned the Broughams and Places and Lovetts, and turned to the Cobbetts and Oastlers and Ferrands. Only after the disinherited masses had forgotten their origin, and the third and fourth generation of them had become mentally, as well as economically, proletarian, did they turn vaguely in their thousands towards the remedy of revolutionary social change. When the Golden Age was too far distant to recall, the feeling got abroad that their only hope of ending the existing régime lay in smashing it.

There is a reason for the power of Tory Chartism over the industrial masses during periods of unrest or distress. Though English Socialism was an English product, the revolutionary ingredient came from abroad. Marxian theory owed much to the intellectual influences of the Continent. Toryism, on the other hand, owed little influence to outside sources. Whatever the influence of Paris upon Benbow and Carlile, it would be simply foolish to add that Wellington or Peel learnt from Metternich how to play the tyrant.

The two views differed radically in their social implications. The language of the class war is couched in terms of industrial struggle ; the proletarian vocabulary is meaningless if applied haphazard to agrarian discontent. Marxians went farther and acquiesced in the accomplished facts of industrialism ; Tories of the strictest school never did. Perhaps it was that Tories refused to acquiesce in a social condition which they did not understand ; for though industrialism may have brought ready money to many a needy landowner, it did not bring a surrender to all the implications which industrialism brought in its train. Tories approached the social question with doubt and dismay ; Revolutionary Socialists applied their remedy with confidence and energy.

Regarded from another angle the Social Revolutionary

idea enshrined in the *Communist Manifesto* loses somewhat of its crusading glamour. Of the two points of view under examination Toryism is the farther removed from the bourgeois conception of Democracy—that grand objective towards which the instructed generation of Mill and Gladstone were marching with unquestioning faith. The men who created Tory legislation during the fourteen years which followed the Great Reform Act rejected the Democratic view; Communists, on the other hand, continued to pay it lip service. It is a curious commentary upon the evolution of political and social theories that the friends of Marx and Engels, who set out deliberately to root out those bourgeois, Liberal, capitalistic institutions which oppressed the workers, should have ended by embodying in their creed the entire intellectual structure, half politics, half metaphysics, of the régime which they purposed to destroy.

CHAPTER VI

SOCIAL CONSEQUENCES OF
THE FALL OF RURAL TORYISM

THIS concluding chapter is an attempt to estimate the extent to which the political elimination of the Landed Interest modified the relation between the Tory party and the working classes. The fall of Peel's Great Conservative Party marks one of the crucial periods of English history, for it was at this time that the old feeling of corporate unity, which had sustained the Landed Interest through so many dark days, departed for ever, and the historic Country Party finally disappeared from public life.

Up to 1846 the strength of the Parliamentary Tory party was based upon the land. This fact must be held constantly in view or the Tory social attitude is unintelligible. During the years covered by this review the term 'Industrial Toryism' was without meaning. There was no Industrial Tory party or Industrial Tory group with an outlook or a policy of its own.

Of all the assaults delivered against the Tory party those directed against the Tory strongholds in the towns were the least effective. The old close corporations did little to assist the cause of political Toryism, and their transformation under the Act of 1836 detracted nothing from the real strength or prestige of the party. It was when the powerful forces of the manufacturing interest, acting through the medium of the Anti-Corn Law League, turned to attack the Tories in their provincial fastness, that Toryism began to give way. On the land the Tory party fought its last fight, and on the land it was beaten. Before the blows of the League had their final effect, agricultural England gave every appearance of economic independence and political self-sufficiency. Protective duties had of course been partly, though only partly, responsible for what economic independence there was. But the homogeneity of the Landed Interest was not dependent upon legislation for its maintenance. Even during years of bad harvests and agricultural depression the economic structure, and indeed the point of view, of rural England remained uncompromisingly insular.

The relation of each part of the socio-agricultural hierarchy to the other was regulated by this self-same autonomy. The hierarchy with its three gradations of landlord, tenant and labourer comprised the Landed Interest, and the dividing lines between the three classes within it were fairly clearly drawn.

Though the Landed Interest possessed every appearance of a social and economic unity, it never became an effective political force, unified under a single directive head. Even under the stress of the menace to its political existence at the hands of the Anti-Corn Law League it lacked the power of effective combination. Not all the efforts of the Agricultural Protection Societies in 1844 nor of Disraeli and Bentinck in 1846 succeeded in rallying the shattered remnants of the Country Party.

Successive Governments had left the Landed Interest very much to itself. Even after 1832 the rural magistracy found itself little troubled by the demands of the Central authorities. What interference there was from Whitehall galled most when it was in connection with the administration of the Poor Law. On the other hand, the agricultural interest asked few favours of the Government, once protective duties had been conceded. Nobody seems to have considered the necessity of having a member of the Cabinet especially devoted to the cause of agriculture. ' In your House of clerks and " powder monkeys " you have ministers of war, of colonies and of trade, but no minister of agriculture,' wrote Feargus O'Connor oracularly, as though he were imparting a prophetic message to the landed classes.

Long before the lecturers of the Anti-Corn Law League began to penetrate the country districts the usual homogeneity of England was passing away. There were already at work certain forces militating against the local supremacy and exclusiveness of the Landed Interest.

Some time towards the end of Melbourne's administration the Landed Interest became half aware that it was isolated. One or two of its leaders attempted to found an association to protect the rural interests, but there was as yet no enthusiasm to unite. Political Economists still comforted their readers by drawing attention to the common interests of agriculture and industry, how that the prosperity of the one was bound up with the prosperity of the other. Poulett Thomson reiterated the optimistic platitudes which Huskisson had made in 1822.

There were influences which tended to impinge upon the landed hegemony, influences entirely beyond the landlord's control. The construction of railways brought armies of comparatively well-paid labour gangs into the quietest parts of the country. These gangs drew off the farmer's best men and demoralized whole villages. In the railway company promoter the landlord met his match, generally his superior. Railway companies were thrusting their lines through the countryside, indifferent alike to local susceptibilities and to a sense of beauty.[1] Company lawyers would come down and browbeat small landholders into yielding up their land.[2] The tradesmen who crowded railway compensation juries, knowing nothing of the technicalities of surveying or assessment, increased the possibilities of injustice.[3]

Occasionally there would be a local civil war between the anti-railway landowner and his pro-railway neighbours. A party of tradesmen in Stamford got up a violent agitation against the Marquess of Exeter. The fight was taken before the public, and rude verse and strong language were freely used.[4]

The railways were introduced on commercial grounds ; there was no philanthropy in it, and the glamour of cash down generally prevailed. The London and Birmingham company found little opposition in acquiring land by purchase on that line. Often there was a rush to sell land as there was to buy railway stock. 'The passion for gain, now thoroughly awakened,' wrote Alison of the Railway Mania of 1846, 'seized upon all classes, pervaded both sexes, swept away all understandings.' Oastler (one suspects with Mr. Hudson in view) commented unfavourably upon the new elements which the

---

[1] Report on Railways, 1845, x., Q. 106.
[2] *Ibid.*, Qs. 372, 374, 407.   [3] *Ibid.*, Q. 403.
[4] Report on election petitions, Stamford, 1847-48, xiv., Qs. 2987 foll.

Railway Mania was introducing into the Tory party. But by the time the influence of the railways had made itself fully felt in the country districts, a far more deadly enemy had arrived.

The Toryism of the country interests stood far off from the intellectual tendencies of the time. Provincial Tories, who before had shied at Political Reform, now ran foul of Free Trade. They saw the world around them obsessed by a raging passion for Progress and Reform; they were not convinced. Doubtful of the future they clung the more desperately to the established institutions in Church and State. The Landed Interest was of all these institutions the most fundamental.

The scepticism of Tories weighed heavily against them. They were to suffer the penalty which all incur who fight in desperate rearguard actions against what is loosely termed the spirit of the age. The Tory country gentlemen and the provincial parson were the butt of the gibes of Cockney wit. The rural Tory was either a petty tyrant or an egregious fool. His indifference to Reforming enthusiasm made him an object of relentless and spiteful raillery which he had already undergone when he ventured to speak his mind about Canning or about the Society for the Diffusion of Useful Knowledge.

It was not, however, until the days of the Anti-Corn Law League that the full force of intellectual obloquy fell upon the unregenerate Tory, who added to his offence by being also a Protectionist. For this type of Tory there was positively no hope whatever. To be a Tory was bad enough, but to fly in the face of the principle of Free Trade, which was proved infallibly to be logical and reasonable, and which the whole world was shortly to adopt, was to fight against the light itself. It was with reason that rural Tories were called ' clodpolls ' and ' hawbucks ' by the Anti-Corn Law lecturers.

The year 1841 marked the opening of the struggle between the Protectionist and Free Trade parties. The League appeared to be undertaking an impossible task. The census of 1831 revealed the fact that 28 per cent. of all the families of England were able to be classed as forming the Agricultural Interest. And the numerical power of that interest declined slowly, for in 1851 the census returns showed that there were still nearly 50 per cent. of the English population living in rural districts and therefore largely devoted to agriculture.[1]

League propaganda began to make itself felt in the larger towns as early as 1841. Before the year was out operations were begun in a still wider field. The Protectionist landlords were to be baited on their own estates, and the League turned towards the country. A primary condition of success was the development of public interest. Popular enthusiasm must be roused. If the League could only reproduce on behalf of the abolition of the Corn Law something of the interest which accompanied the Reform struggle—which in fact created the Reform struggle—this first condition of success would be made.[2]

[1] Figures quoted from Clapham (J. H.), *An Economic History of Modern Britain : The Early Railway Age, 1820-1850* (1926), pp. 66, 67. It is of interest to notice, however, that a Parliamentary opponent of the Corn Law of 1815 urged as his principal argument that Great Britain was geographically a commercial country, and that a Corn Law was a retrograde attempt to change the natural character of the country. (Philips (G.), *Hansard*, February 17, 1815.)

[2] Surtees (R. S.), *Hillingdon Hall* (1844), ch. v. ' In short,' says Mr. Jorrocks of the League's activities, 'this is not a good genuine

Secondly, popular enthusiasm must be directed towards a single goal.[1] In this the League judged the English public with great foresight. The framers of the People's Charter, when they drew up their Six Points, neglected an important rule in catering for the public. Men like to follow one public question at a time ; they seldom follow more. While Reform was the cry, the factory children and the negroes were forgotten ; while Abolition of Slavery was the all-absorbing question, there was no time to think of Reform. The directors of the Anti-Corn Law League made sure that, when the Repeal of the Corn Laws had once become the popular cry, Repeal should have no rival.

Thirdly, a moral and a social pretext must be provided for the public. Repeal was to possess a great social value, and passages from Althorp's budget speech of 1831 were rescued from oblivion to prove that the grand object of Free Trade was the relief of the lower classes.[2] The League was the poor man's friend, though Muntz, in the course of a controversy with the *Corn Law Circular* in 1840, pointed out that, if it was unholy to raise the price of bread to the poor man, it was equally unholy to reduce wages so that the poor man could not buy his bread.[3]

There was some attempt made by the League during 1842 and 1843 to alienate the masses who adhered to the

'ome-brewed grievance, frothin' up at the bung-'ole of discontent, but a sort of seakaley, hothouse, forced thing.'

[1] ' To produce a great public movement, a cry must be *simple and single*—complication or multiplicity are alike fatal to any general excitement.' (*Ibid.*, vol. vi. p. 323.)

[2] Morley (J.), *The Life of Richard Cobden*, vol. i. p. 169.

[3] Muntz (G. F.), *Letters upon Corn and Currency* (1841), p. 9.

People's Charter, though in spite of seemingly unnecessary alarm on the part of scandalized Tories, the League was not prepared to swing very far to the Left.[1]

The League, after the manner of an experienced propagandist, set about telling the people that the Corn Law question involved no complicated issues. It was a simple question between a patriotic, enlightened public and a selfish, sectional interest. There was a habitual tendency on the part of speakers and writers in favour of Free Trade to assume that public opinion was identified with their cause. When Cardwell from his seat in the House of Commons claimed somewhat superciliously that there was a growing sentiment in favour of Free Trade, the Tory *Morning Post* retorted that there was about as much public sentiment existing in favour of Dr. Solomon's Cordial Balm of Gilead.[2]

The religious appeal of the League was developed and extended and the Almighty was made to render yeoman service as a Free Trader. From the *Wesleyan Chronicle*[3] come warnings of the imminence of the next election, when all those who would not sin against God and despise their own birthright are invited to have a fling at the monopolists. In a broadsheet published by the League in 1846, the story of Noah's Ark (with accompanying illustration) is recommended to the notice of militant Nonconformity:[4] 'If Noah had shut him-

---

[1] Alison (A.), *History of Europe*, vol. vii. p. 87. Alison noticed the emphasis with which monopolies were denounced in the Chartist Petition of 1843, and concluded that there were grounds for suspecting a Chartist-League alliance. The murder of Peel's private secretary in the same year strengthened his conviction in the matter.

[2] *Morning Post*, February 28, 1846.

[3] April 1844, *passim*.   [4] In Place Coll., vol. x.

self up in his ark, and let his family eat nothing but what could be grown upon his decks, he would soon have had an outcry against population, and an Emigration Committee ; and Shem, Ham and Japheth would have been " distressed manufacturers " '—a naive confession of Muntz's contention that the professed object of repeal was to enable the merchant to compete with the foreigner ; ' And how,' asked Muntz, ' can he do that, unless by a reduction of wages ? ' [1]

Dissenting ministers were found in plenty among the warmest supporters of the League. They introduced into the Free Trade movement a ranting, crusading spirit which had tremendous effect upon their working-class congregations.[2] The League, not without reason, taunted the clergy of the Establishment with favouring the other side ; Bishop Phillpotts, ' Saint Henry ' of Exeter, came in for much condemnation on this score.[3] He was one of thirteen bishops of the poor man's church who voted against untaxing the poor man's loaf. Samuel Roberts, the vehement Welsh preacher, who saw God working for Free Trade, complained that in his father's time the essays for the Eisteddfod ran no chance of a prize unless they advocated Protection. Poor John Roberts' essay was rejected by ' Protectionist priest-judges, low-souled conservators of antiquated systems of restriction.' [4]

To the lesser instruments of propaganda the League

---

[1] *Corn Law Circular*, October 8, 1840.
[2] General Napier noticed this as early as 1840, though he attributed unworthy motives to their zeal. (To Colonel W. Napier (1841, undated). *Life*, vol. i. p. 153.)
[3] The *Free Trader*, March 5, 1842.
[4] *Farmer Careful, etc.* (1881), p. 35.

gave equal attention. Free Trade songs and Anti-Corn Law poetry were printed on single sheets and distributed among the poor classes. The doggerel of Ebenezer Elliott served to strengthen the belief of the faithful that their cause was not without ethical purpose. Free Trade literature was always cheap, and always accessible. While Protectionist societies were laboriously vending heavy treatises at a shilling apiece — a price prohibitive to potential working-class readers—the League was pouring forth vast quantities of penny, halfpenny, and free tracts, of tasteful format, calculated to appeal to working men.

The provincial Anti-Corn Law societies, though they seem to have been supported almost exclusively by the shopkeeping and general lower middle classes, were assiduous in their work of spreading propaganda everywhere. The balance-sheet of the Mitcham Anti-Corn Law Association for the year ending March 31, 1842, yields interesting information on the nature of its activities. Of £35, 11s. 2d. expended by the Association during the year no less than £30, 10s. was expended on Anti-Corn Law literature. Thus the Association was primarily propagandist. Expenditure under other heads was insignificant, ranging from a 'delegate's expenses to a general meeting in Manchester, £1,' to 'flags, 1s.'[1]

Lastly, there were the professional lecturers sent by the League into almost every quarter. These itinerant agitators were business men in every sense of the word. They were paid to agitate ; it was their mission to do their work effectively and, irrespective of the merits of their case, to convince the tenants and labourers who attended their rural meetings.

[1] In Place Coll., vol. vii.

CONSEQUENCES OF FALL OF RURAL TORYISM

Unfortunately there is little means of ascertaining the nature of the reception which the lecturers were given in the country parts.[1] It is doubly uncertain to what degree they impressed the agricultural labourers to whom they addressed their pleas. Their attitude towards Protectionist landlords whom they encountered was scarcely conciliatory. They transgressed without scruple the old-established tradition among political parties of asking the landlords' permission to canvas the tenants and labourers within their domains. A Protectionist pamphleteer draws a half-amusing, half-tragic picture of a Free-Trade meeting in an imaginary village and of the reception which the various village characters accord to the lecturer, ' a smooth-tongued fellow, that hires himself out at so much a week to go about the country and agitate, as they call it.' [2]

The Protectionists in their chagrin brought forward exaggerated charges against the lecturers of the League. With the memory of ' Swing ' and burning ricks to reinforce their rancour landlords and tenants could not be expected to receive these new agitators in a spirit of peace. They recognized the enmity with which they were regarded by the interests behind the League. Not unreasonably Protectionist members made free play with accusations of sedition and incendiarism. Small wonder that the treatment which the lecturers received at the hands of their rural opponents drove them to return to their Manchester headquarters with stories of universal agrarian revolt, of West Country labourers ' as ready for

---

[1] Prentice (A.), *History of the Anti-Corn Law League* (1853): a sincere though biassed authority.
[2] *Old England's Commerce* (1843).

pikes and pistols as the most excitable people in the factory towns.'[1]

If a reason were sought to explain the unqualified success of the League in its struggle against the Tory Protectionist interests outside the walls of Parliament, an answer might be found in the aptitude with which its leaders appealed to the reason and the passions of the middle classes. That class was the most susceptible to emotional appeals and, after four years of hard campaigning, the economic theory of Free Trade was indelibly branded in the minds of the middle-class electorate and transformed by bourgeois sentimentalism into a dogma of almost religious significance.

The agricultural labourers did not share this enthusiasm nor did the efforts of the League suffice to give the impression that the Free Trade question vitally interested the country labouring classes. Toryism, with all its glaring political defects, seems to have retained the affection of the bulk of the labourers in the southern countries. Leaguers prided themselves on the fact that theirs was primarily a middle-class cause fought with middle-class weapons. 'You never heard me cant about the superior claims of the working classes,' said Cobden disdainfully in the House of Commons, 'to arbitrate on this great question.'[2] Whatever the purpose of the lecturers in the industrial centres and in the provincial towns, their object in the country districts was not so much to win the agricultural labourer to the doctrines of Free Trade as to drive a wedge into the unity of the Landed Interest. The picture so often presented to the readers of Anti-

---

[1] Morley (J.), *The Life of Richard Cobden*, vol. i. p. 156.
[2] *Hansard*, lxxxiv. 281, February 27, 1846.

Corn Law literature of an awakened peasantry struggling for freedom against a selfish aristocracy [1] is in the nature of a myth.

It is admittedly impossible to arrive at a just estimate of the headway made by the League in converting the agricultural labourers. The statistics quoted by contemporary partisans are strongly suspect.[2] Here and there are indications that the lecturers met with considerable working-class opposition. In the industrial districts they ran foul not only of Chartists but of the organized Trade Unions. The Committee of delegates from ' the several Metropolitan trades ' saw fit to petition Parliament on behalf of the operatives engaged in the various manufactures of London against tariff reduction, on the ground that they could not compete with untaxed and cheaply-fed mechanics on the Continent.[3] The wretched hand-loom weavers periodically petitioned Parliament against Free Trade. On the whole it appears that the lecturers were safe enough so long as they kept to the larger country towns and places like Rye or Banbury, where a warm welcome was generally given to a Radical. Cobden had a mixed reception at Taunton during his tour in the spring of 1843.[4] On occasion there happened a rough-and-tumble meeting such as that held at Christchurch on New Year's Eve of 1845, when Tory labourers flooded

[1] See Green (F. E.), *A History of the English Agricultural Labourer, 1870-1920* (1920), for a dramatization of this theme from the Socialist point of view.

[2] Prentice (*op. cit.*, vol. ii., *passim*) records many village meetings but without particulars. He is so frankly a partisan that he is unlikely to have recorded set-backs received by the lecturers.

[3] Copy of Petition in Place Coll., vol. viii.

[4] Prentice, *op. cit.*, vol. ii. p. 70.

an Anti-Corn Law meeting and carried a Protectionist resolution by three to one.

Faced by the fact that the League was attempting to eliminate the Landed Interest as a political force by severing the bonds which held its parts together, provincial Protectionists began to think of resistance.

Before resistance could be thought of there must be created the rudiments of an organization by means of which Protectionists might force their claims upon the public. It is necessary to remember that, at the height of the League campaign in the country districts, the Landed Interest had no corporate political unity at all. It was wholly without political organization. Socially and economically landlords, tenants and labourers formed a definite interest; politically they were helpless. They possessed no political centre of gravity, no central association, no machinery for united action. The circumstances in which Protectionists found themselves were so entirely novel that they knew not how to resist the enemy.[1] The transformation of an unorganized Landed Interest into an organized Protectionist party was a feat equalled only by the establishment of the League.

The magnitude of the work is made clear when it is realized that the Protectionist organizers had no machinery upon which they could build a political party. They had no basis upon which to work. Existing societies and associations were of no use to them. They could not take over bodily the framework of the new Agricultural Societies and turn these into political

[1] Speech of Thompson (H. S.) (Report of the Proceedings of the . . . Yorkshire Protective Society (1844)).

associations. Agricultural Societies were not founded as a medium for political action. And apart from their non-party composition, there already existed a strong bias against them. They were unpopular with a numerous body of tenants throughout the country. It was a common grievance that the Societies had fallen into the hands of a group of scientific amateurs and farmer-chemists, young gentlemen who took up farming for a hobby, who in the prevailing scramble for land ' rush like the frequenters of a Theatre under attraction or alarm and crush and cripple their neighbours and themselves by a reckless and uncalculating zeal.' [1] To these Societies, grumbled the same tenant, came the ' Ricardo race of politicians '—theorists unacquainted with the soil.[2] A third complains that, instead of grappling with the question of security for the tenant and labourer, they frittered away their funds in granting premiums for pigs preposterously and uselessly fat.[3] Besides, to seize the Societies from the Free Trade minority would have been a disastrous piece of political violence.

Neither could the Protectionists make use of the system of Conservative Associations already formed in every county. Not only were the relations between the Landed Interest and the party leaders equivocal and indefinite, but the very fabric of these associations was unsuitable. Peel had neglected—perhaps by design—to create a Central Union of provincial Conservative Associations, and without headquarters the Protectionists were impotent. One

---

[1] Hall (G. W.), *The Connection, etc.*, part ii. p. 43.
[2] Hall (G. W.), *Letter to Viscount Milton, etc.* (1832), p. 43.
[3] *A Few Words to the Agriculturist of England on Tenancy and Occupation.* By a Tenant Farmer (1845).

may imagine the disastrous consequence which would have followed from the confiscation of the Conservative party machine by a body already half hostile to the Conservative leader. Nevertheless the attitude of many county Conservative Associations left no doubt of the trend of rural Tory feeling. At the seventh anniversary dinner of the Buckinghamshire Conservative Association, Grenville Pigot and Sir Thomas Freemantle, representing the Government, were badly heckled during their defence of Peel's policy.[1]

It was evident, too, that the burden of organizing and maintaining resistance to the League was bound to fall to the Tory wing of the Conservative party. ' There was no essential bond,' wrote Morley, ' between the maintenance of agricultural protection and the Conservative policy . . . although however the Conservative party was not necessarily bound up with protection, the Tory party were committed to it by all the ties of personal interest.' [2] Personal interest combined with a dozen other factors determined the Tory position, and although prominent Whigs from many quarters added their strength to the Protectionist cause, the heart of the battle was sustained by the Tory rank and file.

It would be difficult to ascertain the exact date on which the Agricultural Interest began to take active steps to resist the attacks from without. The mutiny which occurred in the ranks of the Conservative party in 1842, the year of Peel's political zenith, was regarded by Disraeli as a portent. Peelite Conservatism depended for its life upon the support of the Landed Interest; once

---

[1] *Morning Post*, January 24, 1844.
[2] Morley, *op. cit.*, vol. i. p. 167.

that interest broke away from its political allegiance, the days of the Great Conservative Party were numbered.

In July 1842 Sir Richard Vyvyan, a Cornish member and a Tory, who had lain low ever since the hurly-burly days of Corporation Reform, published his bitter attack against the soulless dictatorship of the Prime Minister and the party chiefs. He complained that independent members were willy-nilly compelled to vote for the New Corn Law, the Income Tax, the Tariff; and that Peel's Tariff policy was an attack upon the wages of the Cornish tin miner.[1] Two other agricultural members, Lord Ossulston and Blackstone, joined him in revolt. Disraeli noticed the portent and bided his time.

Throughout 1842 the country districts had been quiet enough, and Conservative political activity seems to have limited itself mainly to half a dozen Protectionist speeches at annual gatherings of Conservative Operative Societies.

The year 1843 opened amid growing scenes of discontent in the agricultural counties. Protectionist districts were being baited by the lecturers of the League. It was during this year that the urgent necessity of organizing the Landed Interest into an effective unit dawned upon local Protectionist leaders.

A strange obscurity surrounds the origin of the organized Protectionist defence. Prentice states that a ' Central Agricultural Society ' was founded on February 26, 1839, at a meeting in Willis's Rooms.[2] But Prentice is in error. The *Times* report makes it clear that this was not an inaugural meeting. A society was already actively or latently in existence. It should be noticed

[1] *A Letter from Sir Richard Vyvyan, etc.*, p. 4.
[2] Prentice, *op. cit.*, vol. i. p. 116 (*Times*, February 27, 1839).

that Cayley, together with a body of Old Whigs, had already by their attendance openly identified themselves with what was already the Tory-Protectionist cause. This early society fell to pieces. Peel's fiscal and commercial policy enunciated in 1842 paralysed any independent activity on the part of his supporters of the Country group. They knew not whether to follow the Minister or disown him; they were restrained from disowning him by the knowledge that they had no effective leader to put in his place. Confusion and disappointment, they themselves record, struck them dumb and prevented their organizing resistance.[1]

Early in the new year of 1843 the Protectionists at last began to realize that they must organize or their cause must perish. There was as yet no sign of any general mutiny or collective hostility to the party leaders. Tories in the constituencies seem at this time to have considered that district organization was sufficient for the requirements of Protectionist defence. Not until many months after the county associations had been established was a National Union so much as contemplated. The London Central Society came as an afterthought. An Essex *Association for the Protection of British Agriculture* was formed almost entirely, it was said, on the initiative of the local tenantry, in March or April 1843.[2] Sussex and Lincolnshire followed close. In June the Berkshire Protectionists had their county society in being.[3] By harvest the movement had spread to

---

[1] Speech of Lord Beaumont (*Morning Post*, February 4, 1845). At York a year before he complained that for years the agents of the League had been disseminating free literature among the country people in Yorkshire, and the Protectionists had made no reply.

[2] *Morning Post*, January 11, 1844.   [3] *Ibid.*, January 11, 1844.

Kent.[1] Yorkshire established its association early in the following year.[2]

As a document drafted by Tories from a county previously loyal to Peel, the rules of the Berkshire society reveal a significant change in the Tory point of view.[3] Tories were beginning to realize what they never realized before : that unless they buried their prejudices against counter-organization and counter-propaganda, they would be quickly annihilated as a serious political force in the country.

The framers of the rules frankly admit the success of the League, and tribute is paid to the power of its wealth and the oratory of its lecturers, to its influence with the press, and to its admirable organization. Opposition on the part of the Landed Interest was therefore a matter of life and death. Then follows the significant paragraphs: ' The only way to render this opposition effectual is by associating for mutual defence. The experience of the last few years has shown that individual efforts, however valuable, avail nothing against the pertinacious demands of organized bodies influencing public opinion, and unopposed by those who differ from them.'

'Governments—however well-intentioned, and Parliamentary representatives—however zealous and faithful, will frequently require to have their hands strengthened by the powerful and influential support of the country. Such support cannot be given, except by the agency of

---

[1] *Ibid.*, January 12, 1844.

[2] Report of the Proceedings of the . . . Yorkshire Protective Society (1844).

[3] Rules and Regulations of the Berkshire Association for the Protection of British Agriculture and other Branches of Native Industry (1844).

an association, and without it we must not expect them always to resist the pressing demands of our enemies. In other words, we must rely more on our own exertions, and less on the unsupported efforts of our friends in Parliament.' [1]

The official party leaders would have been well advised to take the message of these rules seriously to heart. They imply a great change of mind on the part of a county association overwhelmingly Tory in complexion. Two distinct propositions were put forward, one of them of considerable interest to Peel and the party chiefs. First, that the Berkshire Protectionists were beginning to realize that the Parliamentary Conservative party was not supporting their interests as well as it might ; secondly, that if the Conservative party chose to cut adrift from its Tory moorings, the Tory party would look to itself. ' Governments—however well-intentioned, and Parliamentary representatives—however zealous and faithful . . .' The sentiments behind these words sounded the death-knell of the Peelite Conservative machine.

Growing discontent with the policy of the Government was accompanied by the conviction of the desperate need for organization. With a ring of county associations already formed, the next step to be taken was the establishment of a Protectionist headquarters in London. On February 19, 1844, a Central Society was called into being ' by a greater unity of purpose and economy of means, to give better effect to the objects of the Associations lately formed in the country.' A Committee composed

[1] Rules and Regulations of the Berkshire Association for the Protection of British Agriculture and other Branches of Native Industry (1844). Rule 3.

half of landowners, half of tenant farmers, was formed with Richmond and Buckingham at its head. Within a few days Cayley issued a manifesto containing the framework of a National Protectionist policy. The authority of Adam Smith is cited in support of the country interests, and there is a disavowal of any intention on the part of the Society to interfere in Parliamentary elections.[1]

With the completion of the Protectionist defences against the attacks of the League, the position occupied by the rural labouring classes in the battle-order may be discerned more clearly. Here a fundamental difference is to be observed between the policy of the League and that of the organized Landed Interest. While the League made every attempt to enlist the support of the rural labourers, the Protectionist party made scarcely any attempt at counter-propaganda.

Nevertheless arguments drawn from the economy of rural labour occupied a prominent place in the Protectionist apology. It was held that the Corn Laws protected the labourers from competition with the labour of foreign countries. This theme, in a score of different forms, buttressed the central Protectionist argument. Some speakers emphasized the pacific character of the English labourer. Lord Feversham at York maintained that tenants and cottagers deserved well of Parliament. ' They have never embarked in schemes of wild agitation, by setting up one interest of the country against another interest—setting class against class.'[2]   A Conservative

[1] Cayley (E. S.), *Reasons for the Formation of the Agricultural Protection Society, addressed to the Industrious Classes of the United Kingdom.* (Published by the Society, 1844.)

[2] Report of the Proceedings of the . . . Yorkshire Protective Society (1844).

Government ought not therefore to expose them to danger. Others contended that Free Trade would throw much of the land out of cultivation, and drive the agricultural labourer to live upon the bounty of others. Stafford O'Brien thought that the labourer was better off in former times ' when influence, when the care of the poor, were more completely in the hands of the Landed Interest and of agriculture than they were at present—in other words, before money-ocracy had become so very powerful.' [1]

While the Protectionists make no endeavour to mobilize the labourers into a gigantic popular movement against the League, there is evidence enough to show that the creation of such a movement was at least possible. Newspaper notices of various workmen's meetings reveal the existence of considerable Protectionist sentiment during the years of the controversy. But there was a universal aversion to such a course. Proposals for sending Protectionist lecturers to Manchester for the purpose of rallying the Tory and ' Ten Hour ' working men against the manufacturers and the League met with no support. [2]

The spirit of discontent, brewing throughout 1844 among the Landed Interest, broke into open revolt as the year drew to an end. The *Morning Post* identified itself even more closely with the Country Party, and began to lash Protectionist members into reluctant activity, taunting them for their silence in the face of Cobden's dialectical onslaughts. [3] The difficulty was to

---

[1] *Morning Post*, February 4, 1845.
[2] The proposal was made by R. P. Milnes of Frystone at the inaugural Protectionist meeting at York (Report, etc., *op. cit.*). Lord George Bentinck urged farmers to proclaim their principles in boroughs and cities. (Speech at Lyme Regis, August 5, 1846.)
[3] *Morning Post*, December 1844.

make the country gentlemen aware that they were engaged in a fight for their existence; their belief in Peel's friendliness was incredible, and their faith was their ruin.

At Knaresborough, Ferrand, a popular member with the local labourers, opened the attack against Peel and the party leaders.[1] Knightley, Miles, and Palmer were stirring up revolt in their constituencies. All the old arguments connecting Free Trade with a starving peasantry were reiterated with appropriate variations. Knightley condemned the new ' agricultural chemists ' —the Manchester men who were buying up farms and turning farmers of the old sort off the land.[2] Throughout the following year the amateur capitalist-farmer got his due of calumny from Protectionist speakers.

Rumours of Peel's defection were already common property; Protectionists grimly admitted that they entertained no illusions as to the fate of Protection at the hands of the electors. ' Then will our landowners discover whether the Minister to whom they, at the cost of character and of property, have adhered, will adhere to them—or place himself openly at the head of the congenial spirits who, in the Manchester Chamber of Commerce, regulate the industrial relations of England.' [3]

It was reasonable that the Ministerialists should return the ill-feeling. Colonel Wyndham rebuked the gentlemen of the Central Society for their excessive partisanship. ' Assembled in conclave in Bond Street,' he complained, ' they issued their mandates to the minor societies in the country, my Lord Duke all the time

[1] *Ibid.*, December 7, 1844. [2] *Ibid.*, December 1, 1844.
[3] *Ibid.*

pulling the strings behind the scenes ; and these minor societies, under the influence of these mandates, persecuted the representatives of the people.' [1]   Peel, who was not accustomed to bandy words with those who served him, maintained party discipline in full rigour. The Government newspapers opened a vigorous campaign against the malcontents.   Knightley spoke bitterly of the virulent attacks by certain Conservative organs against his conduct in Parliament.[2]   The Somerset Protectionists had made the same complaint in the preceding December.[3]   Acting within his rights, Peel seems finally to have forbidden members of his Government to attend Protectionist meetings.[4]

The opening months of 1845 brought Conservative civil war into the constituencies.   It now became dangerous to support the Government at an agricultural meeting ; those who dared suffered for their temerity. While in the year before it was still held improper to condemn the party leaders at a Protectionist meeting—a local Tory's denunciations were publicly disclaimed at a Buckinghamshire gathering [5]—in 1845 condemnation was the general rule.   Chichester Protectionists celebrated Christmas by burning copies of the *Times* outside the Corn Exchange.[6]

On January 23, 1846, Peel made his great speech explanatory of his conversion to Free Trade.   ' He would not withhold the homage due to the progress of reason

---

[1] *Hansard*, lxxviii. 1183, March 19, 1845.
[2] Speech at Northampton (*Morning Post*, January 23, 1845).
[3] *Morning Post*, December 4, 1844.
[4] *Ibid.*, December 18, 1845.
[5] *Ibid.*, January 24, 1844.
[6] *Ibid.*, January 1, 1846.

and truth by denying that his opinions on the subject of Protection had undergone a change.' With his own hands Peel destroyed the mighty fabric which he had created, and the Great Conservative Party, the work of fourteen years of patient building, was rent in twain.

After the disaster the Protectionist leaders attempted to save the Landed Interest from the wreckage and to create a Parliamentary Protectionist party.

It was too late. When the long debates on the Corn Importation Bill at last drew to an end, it seemed that an era of English history ended with them. Despair settled down upon the Protectionist ranks and there seemed little left to fight for. Ferrand saw the salvation of the agricultural Tory party in a daring bid for the support of organized labour, a policy of opposition to the Maynooth grant, alteration of the New Poor Law, support for the Ten Hours Bill, and altogether a vigorous counter-offensive against the Manchester interest.[1] Disraeli, with hollow optimism, talked of rallying the Country Party. But it was not the Country Party that emerged from the ruin of 1846 but a party which drifted within two years into impotent little groups, separated on questions which to-day surprise us by their insignificance. It was a pathetic bathos which moved Bentinck to confide to the editor of the *Morning Post* that 'the Jew question has virtually broken up the Protectionist party.'[2]

. . . .

I have laboured at some length to describe the suc-

[1] *Times*, January 30, 1846.
[2] Bentinck to C. E. Michele, 1848 (undated), in Lucas (R.), *Lord Glenesk and the Morning Post* (1910), p. 31.

cessive stages by which the Landed Interest approached its final decline and fall. This I have done designedly, because I sought to show the Protectionist attitude towards the rural labouring classes during each phase of the struggle.

I intended primarily to prove that neither the Landed Interest in general, nor the Protectionist Societies in particular, ever regarded the economic and social condition of the labourers as an isolated question. The interests of the labourers were considered as one with the interests of the whole rural hierarchy. In waging a defensive campaign against the League the Protectionists fought, not for the benefit of any one class within the hierarchy, but for the hierarchy itself. This was not altruism. The Protectionist view, that they were all— landlord, tenant and. labourer—part of one single and independent interest, may have been inaccurate in fact and in policy, but it was at least what they believed. Their insistence on the essential unity of the Landed Interest formed part of their feudal, organic view of society.

Secondly, I sought to show that the Landed Interest, even in the hour of danger, refrained from making capital out of a public appeal to the labourers. The wealth and local prestige of the great Protectionist land-owners might have been devoted to the organization of a violent popular movement directed against the League and the manufacturing interests. Superficial reasons might be adduced to support the possibility. That the Landed Interest did not go to this length is witness to a deep-seated disapproval of popular movements or mass excitement of any kind.

The presumption is that the bare idea of initiating such a movement did not seriously occur to the Protectionist leaders. Unlike the trained business men who stood behind the League, landlords and tenants had no out-standing ability for organization, and their complete ignorance of the methods of popular propaganda has been already demonstrated. The proposal to repay the Leaguers in their own coin by sending Protectionist lecturers to agitate among the industrial operatives was suggested but not adopted. It was as yet no part of legitimate Tory tactics to ' dish the Whigs.'

There remains to consider the influence of the landed defeat upon the labour policy of the Conservative party. We now know that the repeal of the Corn Laws obscured a change less spectacular but more profound. The extent of the disaster is not to be measured in terms of material losses in the General Election which followed the resignation of the Conservative Ministry. An analysis of the number of seats lost and won in the election of 1847 shows that the defeat was not of men but of morale. The Landed Interest had lost confidence in itself and in the soundness of its historic prejudices. Henceforward the reality of power and the control of the national affairs passed to the manufacturing interests and to classes uninspired by contact with the soil. Their views were now to mould the labour legislation of successive Governments, Liberal and Conservative, and their standards of social justice to regulate the relations of class with class.

CONCLUSION

THERE was nothing altruistic in the relation between the Tory party and the people during the period covered by this survey. The doom of Toryism was pre-determined by the iron force of impersonal circumstances. The course of its development and the tragedy of its decline were incidents far beyond the power of any statesmen, however creative, to alter or delay.

Toryism was in direct antithesis to all the political ideas of the Victorian age. The Tory party was neither intellectual nor bourgeois nor, of course, Victorian in its point of view. Unlike the systems of Marx and of the Christian Socialists, Toryism possessed no theoretical basis and no metaphysical apparatus. It was neither rich in great leaders at its head nor strong in discipline in its body. It held no attractive appeal for a generation which took its politics from Gladstone and its economics from Mill. It had no exact counterpart in Right-Wing movements at home or abroad. Burke left no Charles Stuart or Charles Maurras to endow it with the glory of a Royalist crusade. Toryism lacked both the romantic glamour of the Jacobite cause and the wayward brilliance of *L'Action française*. The very limitations of Toryism half explain its power.

Chief among the causes which influenced the Tory connection with labour problems was the fact that the Tory party was not an independent political entity with

CONCLUSION

an organization of its own. Between 1832 and 1846
it was a group within a party, sharing the Parliamentary
fortunes, and the political machinery, of the larger party.
Because the Tory group never fully acquiesced in its
position within the Conservative party, and because of
its rooted prejudice against Peel's political machine, Tory
Parliamentary activity in the work of labour legislation
was therefore circumscribed and stultified.

Ultimately the Tory attitude to the great working-
class problems of the day was little affected by the trend
of Parliamentary politics. Toryism outside Parliament
represented a body of opinion, a political, economic and
social view of society. This Tory view originated in
the conditions of pre-industrial England. Tories were
accustomed to approach the problems of the working
classes from the standpoint of men nurtured in a feudal
and paternal economy.

The preconceptions which influenced their attitude
towards every section of public and domestic affairs they
carried into their relations with the political activities of
the working people. In conformity with their political
ideas they distrusted the movement for Parliamentary
reform, and opposed all proposals for extending the
franchise irrespective of rank and function in the State.
Their failure to adapt their opinions to the changes in
the class relationships which accompanied the Industrial
Revolution, and to admit the principle of labour combination as a necessary element of industrial society,
coloured their attitude to the whole problem of the
rights and duties of organized labour within the social
structure.

In the early stages of industrial change Tory abhorrence

259

of the new alignment of classes broke out under the form of opposition to the growth of capitalism, and to the unregulated introduction of machinery. Later, when it became apparent that industrial society had come to stay, Tory acquiescence was grudgingly and fitfully given, but the incompatibility of Tory principles with the new industrialism became manifest in a Tory alliance with the working classes to mitigate its evils by using the authority of the State to regulate the power of the manufacturing interest.

The Tory attitude towards the problem of social unrest and social revolution was governed by the mutual hostility between the paternal Tory conception of society and the atmosphere of class war. Tory ideas could not be brought into harmony with proletarian conditions. The same reasons which rendered Tory principles inconsistent with the politics of the social revolution rendered them equally inconsistent with the social and economic consequences of industrialism. And when the future of class relationships came to be controlled on the one hand by the unstable conditions of a highly-developed capitalism, and on the other by the stark crudity of the class struggle, there was no longer any room for that narrow, personal, organic if muddle-headed economy which was the basis of Tory labour ideas.

BIBLIOGRAPHY

I.—MANUSCRIPT SOURCES

British Museum :
Additional Manuscripts. The Correspondence of Sir Robert Peel, chiefly MSS. 40,309; 40,404; 40,415; 40,424; 40,455; 40,484; 40,486.

Public Record Office :
Home Office Papers, 40. 26 (Distress, 1830); 40. 30 (Distress, 1832); 40. 40 (Disturbance, 1838); 40. 14, 43 (Disturbance (Provincial), 1839); 41. 12 (Disturbance to 1837, transcripts).

Ministry of Health Papers. Poor Law Commissioners for England and Wales; Minute Books, Vol. VIII. (1836) foll.

II.—PRINTED SOURCES

(a) PARLIAMENTARY PAPERS

Report on artisans and machinery.	1824 V.
Report on the laws respecting friendly societies.	1825 IV.
Report on the regulation of the labour of children in mills and factories of the United Kingdom.	1831-32 XV.
Report on the present state of agriculture and persons employed in the same.	1833 V.
Report on election petitions : Liverpool.	1833 X.
Report on bribery at elections.	1835 VIII.

Report on Orange Institutions in Great Britain
and the Colonies.   1835 XVII.
Report on the state of agriculture.   1836 VIII.
Report from the poor law commissioners.   1837 LI.
Two reports on combinations of workmen.   1837-38 VIII.
Report on election petitions : Cambridge,
Ludlow.   1840 IX.
Six reports on the act for the regulation of
mills and factories.   1840 X.
Report from the poor law commissioners
on the continuance of the poor law commission.   1840 XVII.
Report on election petitions : Lewes, Reading.   1842 V.
Report on the payment of wages in goods.   1842 IX.
Report on railway labourers.   1846 XIII.
Report on election petitions : Stamford.   1847-48 XIV.

Parliamentary Proceedings, etc.

Hansard : Parliamentary debates.

(*b*) NEWSPAPERS AND PERIODICALS

Blackwood's Edinburgh Magazine.
The Bolton Chronicle.
The Christian Socialist. A Journal of Association (1850-51).
The Church of England Quarterly Review.
The Anti-Corn Law Circular.
The Edinburgh Review.
The Free Trader.
The Halifax and Huddersfield Express.
The Halifax Guardian.
The Leeds Intelligencer.
The Leeds Mercury.
The Liverpool Standard.
The Manchester Guardian.

BIBLIOGRAPHY

The Morning Chronicle.
The Morning Herald.
The Morning Post.
The Norfolk Chronicle.
The Northern Star.
The Oddfellows' Magazine ; New series, Vols. I.-XII.
The Place Collection (chiefly of newspaper cuttings) in the British Museum.
Politics for the People (1848).
Punch, or the London Charivari (1841 foll.).
The Quarterly Review.
The Reading Mercury.
The Sheffield Courant.
The Sheffield Mercury.
The Taunton Courier.
The Times.

(c) CONTEMPORARY BOOKS AND PAMPHLETS

An Earnest Appeal to the Aristocracy, Middle, and Operative Classes. London, 1840.

Anglo Catholicus (Pseud.) (Lord John Manners ?) What are English Roman Catholics to do ? The question considered in a letter to Lord E. Howard. London, 1841.

Baines (E.), Jun. The Social, Educational, and Religious State of the Manufacturing Districts. London, 1843.

Bankes (G.). Speeches of George Bankes, Esq., M.P., at the Late Agricultural Meetings of Sturminster and Blandford. London, 1846.

Baxter (G. R.W.). Book of the Bastilles. London, 1841.

Bernard (J. B.). Appeal to Conservatives on the Imminent Danger to which the Nation is exposed from the Democratic Propensities of the House of Commons. London, 1835.

TORYISM AND THE PEOPLE

Brereton (C. D.). The Subordinate Magiſtracy and the Parish Syſtem considered, etc. Norwich, 1827.

Budworth (P. J.). The Proſpeſts and Policy of a Tory Adminiſtration. London, 1838.

Bull (G. S.). The Gospel of Chriſt recommended to Coal Miners. A sermon, etc. Bradford, 1834.

The Oppressors of the Poor ; and the Poor their own Oppressors. A sermon, etc. Bradford, 1839.

Cayley (E. S.). Reasons for the Formation of the Agricultural Proteſtion Society, addressed to the Induſtrious Classes of the United Kingdom. Published by the Society. London, 1844.

Central Society of Education. Papers. London, 1837-39.

Chalmers (T.). Seleſt Works. Vols. VI., IX., X., XII., XIV.-XVI., XIX., XX. Glasgow, 1836-42.

Claims of the People, The. A Letter to the Ariſtocracy and the Prieſthood. London, 1840.

Cobbett (W). Cobbett's Political Regiſter, Vols. LXIX.-LXXXV. London, 1830-34.

Cobbett's Legacy to Labourers. London, 1834.

Rural Rides. New edition, with notes by James Paul Cobbett. London, 1853.

Coleridge (S. T.). On the Conſtitution of Church and State. London, 1830.

Conservatives and Deſtruſtives ; or Mob Force Considered and Illuſtrated. London, 1832.

Conservative Reform ; or a Further Development of the Principles and Policy of the Peel Adminiſtration ; in a Letter to a Conservative Whig. London, 1835.

Conservative Whig. Three Letters addressed to the Rt. Hon· Lord Viscount Melbourne and the Rt. Hon. Sir Robert Peel, Bart., on the Present State of Parties, urging the Necessity of Union. By a Conservative Whig. London, 1835.

Cookesley (W. G.). An Address delivered at the Town Hall,

BIBLIOGRAPHY

Windsor, at the opening of the Windsor and Eton Literary and Scientific Institution. Eton, 1836.

Copland (W.). A letter to the Rev. C. D. Brereton, in reply to his ' Observations on the Administration of the Poor Laws in the Agricultural Districts.' Norwich, 1824.

Croker (J. W.). The Croker Papers. The Correspondence and Diaries of the Right Honourable John Wilson Croker, etc. Edited by Louis J. Jennings. Vols. ii., iii. London, 1884.

Denison (E.). Bishop of Salisbury. A Charge delivered to the Clergy of the Diocese of Salisbury. London, 1846.

Disraeli (B.). Coningsby. London, 1844.

Sybil. London, 1845.

Lord George Bentinck. A Political Biography. London, 1851.

Duncombe (E.). The Justice and Centralization, or the Parson and the Constitution. London, 1840.

Engels (F.). The Condition of the Working Class in England in 1844. (1845). Translated 1892. Reprinted. London, 1920.

Fielden (J.). The Curse of the Factory System. London, 1836.

Gaskell (P.). The Manufacturing Population of England : its Moral, Social and Physical Conditions, etc. London, 1833.

Artisans and Machinery, etc. London, 1836.

Gregory (W.). Mr. Gregory's Letter-Box, 1813-1830. Edited by Lady Gregory. London, 1898.

Greville (C. C. F.). The Greville Memoirs. (i) A Journal of the Reigns of King George IV. and King William IV. Edited by Henry Reeve. Vol. iii. London, 1874.

(ii) A Journal of the Reign of Queen Victoria, from 1837 to 1852. Vols. i., ii. London, 1885.

Hall (G. W.). Letter to Viscount Milton, etc. London, 1832.

The Connection between Landlord and Tenant and Labourer

in the Cultivation of the British Soil ; their Rights, their Duties, and their Interests. London, 1841.

Kingsley (C.). Yeast. A Problem. London, 1851.

Lewis (G. W.). The Conservative Principle considered in reference to the Present State of the Country. London, 1842.

Loveless (G.). The Victims of Whiggery, being a statement of the Persecutions experienced by the Dorchester Labourers. London, 1837.

The Church Shown Up, in a letter to the Rev. Henry Walker, Vicar of Haslebury, Bryant, Dorsetshire. London, 1838.

Macqueen (T. P.). The State of the Nation at the Close of 1830. London, 1831.

Manning (H. E.). A Charge delivered at the ordinary visitation of the Archdeaconry of Chichester. London, 1846.

Muntz (G. F.). Letters upon Corn and Currency. Birmingham, 1841.

Newcastle-under-Lyme (Duke of). An Address to all Classes and Conditions of Englishmen. London, 1832.

Thoughts on Times Past tested by Subsequent Events. London, 1837.

Newman (J. H.). Pseud. ' Catholicus.' Letters on an Address delivered by Sir Robert Peel, Bart., M.P., on the Establishment of a Reading Room at Tamworth. London, 1841.

Oastler (R.). A Few Words to the Friends and Enemies of Trade Unions. 1833.

A Letter to those Sleek, Pious, Holy and Devout Dissenters, etc. Bradford, 1834.

The Huddersfield Dissenters, Stark-staring mad ! ! ! Leeds, 1835.

Yorkshire Slavery. The ' Devil-to-Do ' among the Dissenters of Huddersfield. Leeds, 1835.

BIBLIOGRAPHY

Damnation ! Eternal Damnation to the Fiend-Begotten, ' Coarser Food,' New Poor Law. Leeds, 1837.

West Riding Nomination Riot. A Letter to Viscount Morpeth. London, 1837.

Address. No. I. : To the People of England [single sheet]. 1838 ?

The Fleet Papers. London, 1841-42.

Paul (W.). A History of the Origin and Progress of Operative Conservative Societies. By William Paul, Secretary to the Leeds Operative Conservative Society, the first instituted. Leeds, 1839.

Peel (R.). Sir Robert Peel. From his Private Correspondence. Edited by Charles Stuart Parker. Vols. II., III. London, 1899.

Phillpotts (H.). Bishop of Exeter. A Charge delivered to the Clergy of the Diocese of Exeter. London, 1845.

Praed (W. M.). The Political Poems of Winthrop Mackworth Praed. Edited with notes by Sir George Young. London, 1888.

Roberts (S.) of Sheffield. Truth ; or the Fall of Babylon, being an Address to the Ratepayers of the Kingdom, etc. Sheffield, 1845.

Rogers (J.). The Establishment of Conservative Associations considered. London, 1835.

Report of the proceedings of the Landowners, Farmers and others resident in the County of York, interested in the Welfare of British Agriculture, for the establishment of the Yorkshire Protective Society. London, 1844.

Rules and Regulations of the Berkshire Association for the Protection of British Agriculture and other branches of Native Industry. Reading, 1844.

Slaney (R. A.). A Plea to Power and Parliament for the Working Classes. London, 1847.

Stanley (E. G. G. S.), Earl of Derby. A Letter to the Rt.

Hon. Lord Stanley, by the younger brother of a dis-
satisfied Country Gentleman. London, 1836.
The Morality of Public Men. A Letter to the Rt. Hon. the
Earl of Derby. London, 1852.
Surtees (R. S.). Hillingdon Hall; or The Cockney Squire;
a Tale of Country Life. London, 1844. '
Tales of the Brummagem Toryhood. No. 1. Birmingham,
1836.
Thorp (R.). Practical Conservatism : its Nature and Uses.
London, 1840.
Toryism. Thoughts on the State and Prospects of Toryism.
By R. S. S. London, 1837.
Vyvyan (R.). A Letter from Sir Richard Vyvyan, Bart.,
M.P., to his Constituents upon the Commercial and
Financial Policy of Sir Robert Peel's Administration.
London, 1842.
Walsh (J.). Popular Opinions on Parliamentary Reform
considered. London, 1842.
Wilberforce (R. I.). A Letter to the Most Noble Marquis of
Lansdowne on the Establishment of a Board of National
Education. London, 1839.
A Primary Charge to the Clergy of the Archdeaconry
of the East Riding. York, 1841.

(*d*) SECONDARY SOURCES

Airlie (M.) Countess of. Lady Palmerston and her Times.
Vol. II. London, 1922.
Alfred, pseud. (Samuel Kydd). History of the Factory Move-
ment, 1802-1847. London, 1857.
Alison (A.). Essays, Political, Historical and Miscellaneous.
Edinburgh, 1850.
History of Europe, 1815-1852. Edinburgh, 1853-59.
Some Account of my Life. Edited by Lady Alison,
Edinburgh, 1883.

BIBLIOGRAPHY

Baernreither (J. M.). English Associations of Working Men. Translated by Alice Taylor. With Preface by J. M. Ludlow. London, 1899.

Bamford (S.). Passages in the Life of a Radical. New Edition. London, 1859.

Beer (M.). A History of British Socialism. London, 1919-20.

Bready (A.). William Huskisson and Liberal Reform. Oxford, 1928.

Buckingham and Chandos (Duke of). Memoirs of the Courts and Cabinets of William IV. and Victoria, from original family documents. London, 1861.

Buckley (J. K.). Joseph Parkes of Birmingham. London, 1926.

Caird (J.). English Agriculture in 1850-1851. London, 1852.

Clapham (J. H.). An Economic History of Modern Britain. The Early Railway Age, 1820-1850. Cambridge, 1926.

Cromer (Earl of). Disraeli. London, 1912.

Dicey (A. V.). Lectures on the Relation between Law and Public Opinion in England during the Nineteenth Century. London, 1905.

Dictionary of National Biography. Edited by Leslie Stephen and Sydney Lee. London, 1885, etc.

Dobbs (A. E.). Education and Social Movements, 1700-1850. London, 1919.

Faulkner (H. U.). Chartism and the Churches. A Study in Democracy. Columbia University Studies in History, etc. Vol. 73, No. 3. New York, 1916.

Gamage (R. G.). History of the Chartist Movement. Newcastle, 1894.

Greg (R. H.). The Factory Question Considered, etc. London, 1837.

Gregory (B.). Sidelights on the Conflicts of Methodism. London, 1898.

Haile (M.) and Bonney (E.). Life and Letters of John
Lingard, 1771-1851. London, 1911.

Halévy (E.). Histoire du peuple anglais au XIXᵉ siècle. III.
De la crise du Reform Bill à l'avènement de Sir Robert
Peel (1830-1841). Paris, 1923.

Herries (E.). Memoirs of the Public Life of the Right Hon.
John Charles Herries. London, 1880.

Hodder (E.). The Life and Work of the Seventh Earl of
Shaftesbury. Vols. I., II. London, 1886.

Holyoake (G. J.). The History of Co-operation. London,
1875-76.

The Life of Joseph Rayner Stephens. London, 1881.

Hovell (M.). The Chartist Movement. Manchester, 1925.

Hutt (W. H.). The Factory System of the Early Nineteenth
Century. *Economica*, No. 17, March 1926. London,
1926.

Kebbel (T. E.). History of Toryism : from the Accession
of Mr. Pitt in 1783 to the death of Lord Beaconsfield in
1881. London, 1886.

Latimer (J.). Annals of Bristol. Eighteenth-Century :
Bristol. Nineteenth-Century : Bristol, 1887.

Law (E.). Lord Ellenborough. A Political Diary, 1828-
1830. Edited by Lord Colchester. London, 1881.

Lowell (A. L.). The Government of England. London,
1908.

Lucas (R.). Lord Glenesk and the Morning Post. London,
1910.

Ludlow (J. M.) and Jones (L. L.). Progress of the Working
Classes, 1832-1867. London, 1867.

Mackay (T.). History of the English Poor Law, 1834-
1898. London, 1904.

Manners, Lord John. Lord John Manners. A Political and
Literary Sketch comprising some account of the Young
England Party and the Passing of the Factory Acts. By a
Non-Elector. London, 1872.

BIBLIOGRAPHY

Martineau (H.). History of England during the Thirty Years' Peace. London, 1849-50.

Menger (A.) The Right to the Whole Produce of Labour. Translated by M. E. Turner, with an Introduction and Bibliography by H. S. Foxwell. London, 1898.

Moffrey (R. W.). A Century of Oddfellowship. Manchester, 1910.

Morley (J.). The Life of Richard Cobden. London, 1881.

Monypenny (W. F.). The Life of Benjamin Disraeli, Earl of Beaconsfield, Vols. I., II. London, 1910, etc.

Napier (W.). The Life of General Sir Charles James Napier. London, 1857.

Ostrogorski (M.). Democracy and the Organization of Political Parties. Translated. London, 1902.

Penty (A. J.). Protection and the Social Problem. London, 1926.

Prentice (A.). History of the Anti-Corn Law League. London, 1853.

Rae (W. F.). Political Clubs and Party Organization. Nineteenth Century. Vol. 15, May 1878. London, 1878.

Ramsay (A. A. W.). Sir Robert Peel. London, 1928.

Raven (C. E.). Christian Socialism. London, 1920.

Redlich (J.). Local Government in England. Edited with additions by Francis W. Hurst. London, 1903.

Robinson (G.). David Urquhart. Oxford, 1920.

Scott (J.). Earl of Eldon. The Public and Private Life of Lord Chancellor Eldon, with selections from his Correspondence. By Horace Twiss, Esq. Vol. III. London, 1844.

Seymour (C.). Electoral Reform in England and Wales. New Haven, 1915.

Smith (T. S.). A Letter to the Metropolitan Sanitary Commissioners. London, 1848.

Local Self Government. London, 1851.

Thomas (J. A.). The House of Commons, 1832-1867. A Functional Analysis. *Economica*, No. 13. March 1925.

Timbs (J.). Club Life in London. Vol. 1. London, 1866.

Toynbee (A.). The Industrial Revolution of the Eighteenth Century in England. London, 1908.

Victoria History of the Counties of England, The. London, 1901.

Wakefield (C. M.). The Life of Thomas Attwood. Privately printed. London, 1885.

Wallas (G.). The Life of Francis Place, 1771-1854. London, 1898.

Webb (S. and B.). The History of Trade Unionism. With Bibliography. London, 1898.

Revised edition. London, 1920.

English Local Government from the Revolution to the Municipal Corporations Act: The Parish and the County. 1 Vol. London, 1906.

The Manor and the Borough. 2 Vols. London, 1908.

Whibley (C.). Lord John Manners and his Friends. Edinburgh, etc., 1925.

INDEX

S

INDEX

275